INTERNATIONAL ENERGY AGENCY

ENERGY POLICIES
of Poland

1994 SURVEY

OECD
OCDE

INTERNATIONAL ENERGY AGENCY
2, RUE ANDRÉ-PASCAL, 75775 PARIS CEDEX 16, FRANCE

The International Energy Agency (IEA) is an autonomous body which was established in November 1974 within the framework of the Organisation for Economic Co-operation and Development (OECD) to implement an international energy programme.

It carries out a comprehensive programme of energy co-operation among twenty-three* of the OECD's twenty-five Member countries. The basic aims of the IEA include:

i) co-operation among IEA participating countries to reduce excessive dependence on oil through energy conservation, development of alternative energy sources and energy research and development;

ii) an information system on the international oil market as well as consultation with oil companies;

iii) co-operation with oil producing and other oil consuming countries with a view to developing a stable international energy trade as well as the rational management and use of world energy resources in the interest of all countries;

iv) a plan to prepare participating countries against the risk of a major disruption of oil supplies and to share available oil in the event of an emergency.

* IEA participating countries are: Australia, Austria, Belgium, Canada, Denmark, Finland, France, Germany, Greece, Ireland, Italy, Japan, Luxembourg, the Netherlands, New Zealand, Norway (by special agreement), Portugal, Spain, Sweden, Switzerland, Turkey, the United Kingdom, the United States. The Commission of the European Communities takes part in the work of the IEA.

ORGANISATION FOR ECONOMIC CO-OPERATION
AND DEVELOPMENT

Pursuant to Article 1 of the Convention signed in Paris on 14th December 1960, and which came into force on 30th September 1961, the Organisation for Economic Co-operation and Development (OECD) shall promote policies designed:

— to achieve the highest sustainable economic growth and employment and a rising standard of living in Member countries, while maintaining financial stability, and thus to contribute to the development of the world economy;

— to contribute to sound economic expansion in Member as well as non-member countries in the process of economic development; and

— to contribute to the expansion of world trade on a multilateral, non-discriminatory basis in accordance with international obligations.

The original Member countries of the OECD are Austria, Belgium, Canada, Denmark, France, Germany, Greece, Iceland, Ireland, Italy, Luxembourg, the Netherlands, Norway, Portugal, Spain, Sweden, Switzerland, Turkey, the United Kingdom and the United States. The following countries became Members subsequently through accession at the dates indicated hereafter: Japan (28th April 1964), Finland (28th January 1969), Australia (7th June 1971), New Zealand (29th May 1973) and Mexico (18th May 1994). The Commission of the European Communities takes part in the work of the OECD (Article 13 of the OECD Convention).

TABLE OF CONTENT

LIST OF TABLES

LIST OF FIGURES

FOREWORD

Poland's experiences with economic reform are at the centre of the debate on the shock therapy approach to the task of turning the economies of central and eastern Europe and the former Soviet Union into market economies. The bird's-eye perspective on macroeconomic developments needs to be supplemented by sector and industry studies.

This survey, which builds on the IEA's Energy Policies of Poland – 1990 Survey, deals with the implications for the energy sector of reform policies formulated and implemented since 1990. It sheds light on, among other things, the changes that have taken place in energy sector legislation and regulation, energy pricing, energy industry organisation and Poland's security of energy supply. It also discusses recent and expected energy demand developments and provides information on Poland's environmental problems, many of which are related to energy production and use.

The Polish authorities have taken difficult steps under adverse circumstances to prepare the energy sector for the requirements of a market economy. However, the survey points out that much remains to be done, especially in the areas of pricing, restructuring and privatisation.

This survey has been undertaken in close co-operation with the Polish Ministry of Industry and Trade. The IEA wishes to express its gratitude to the Ministry and to the other state organisations and companies that provided information to the survey team and discussed approaches to their tasks with team members.

Robert Priddle

Executive Director

INTRODUCTION

This survey has a dual purpose. It is intended to support the Polish Government in its formulation and implementation of market oriented energy policies. It is also aimed at providing interested parties in IEA Member countries with topical information on Poland's energy situation. It goes into considerable detail on Poland's energy resources, production, trade and security of supply, energy pricing and industry regulation, energy supply costs and the financial state of companies, organisational and ownership issues, energy end-use efficiency matters and the links between Poland's energy situation and its formidable environmental problems.

Compared to the IEA's Energy Policies of Poland – 1990 Survey, the present report testifies through its highlighting of new issues and challenges, as well as through its reporting on progress, to the remarkable changes the energy sector has undergone. However, it also notes that real energy price adjustments have slowed, that energy industry restructuring plans have met with resistance from employees and that little has happened in the area of privatisation. The survey repeatedly urges the Government to press on with reform and move further and faster than planned, rather than allow the implementation of plans to be delayed.

Chapter 1 of the survey – which is based on fact-finding missions undertaken in June and December 1994 – states the main issues and summarises the IEA's main recommendations. Chapter 2 provides a fuller summary of the report. In Chapter 3, the macroeconomic and political context of the post-1990 energy sector developments is sketched. This chapter also deals briefly with reform in the area of research and development. Chapter 4 provides energy balances and a discussion of the state of Poland's energy statistics. Chapter 5 is about energy end-use efficiency issues.

Chapters 6-9 deal with the coal, electricity/district heating, gas and oil industries. These chapters are structured in roughly the same way, describing the institutions making up the industries and – where relevant – existing and planned regulatory arrangements, outlining demand and supply developments, touching on environmental issues, analysing price and cost developments and discussing restructuring and privatisation plans. Chapter 10 comments on the outlook for new energy sources such as solar and wind energy, and Chapter 11 goes into detail on Poland's environmental situation, on policies to deal with the problems and on available financial and other resources.

The members of the survey team were:

Guy Caruso
Team Leader, Director of the Office for Non-Member Countries, IEA

Ottar Skagen
Country Desk Officer and Project Co-ordinator, Non-Member Countries Division for Europe, Middle East and Africa, IEA

Christian Duvigneau
The World Bank, Poland

Malcolm Keay
Energy Diversification Division, IEA

Nigel Lucas
Imperial College, University of London, United Kingdom

Robert Ovart
Energy Diversification Division, IEA

David Rubin
Energy Conservation and Efficiency Division, IEA

Paul Sankey
Energy Statistics Division, IEA

Erik Sørensen
ECON Energy, France

The following institutions were visited:
Ministry of Industry and Trade
Ministry of Environmental Protection, Natural Resources and Forestry
Ministry of Finance
Ministry of Foreign Economic Relations
Ministry of Physical Planning and Construction
Ministry of Privatisation

Bank for Environmental Protection
Central Planning Office
Energy Conservation Foundation
Energy Information Centre
Energy Restructuring Group
Institute of Power Engineering
National Agency for Energy Conservation
National Fund for Environmental Protection and Water Management
Polish Foundation for Energy Efficiency
State Committee for Scientific Research

Ciech, oil and chemicals trading
CPN, oil product wholesaling and retailing
Europol Gaz, gas transmission pipeline building and operation
Katowice Holding Company, coal production
Krakow-Leg CHP plant, electricity and heat production
PERN, crude oil and refined product pipeline transportation
Petrochemia Plock, oil refining
Polish Oil and Gas Company, gas supply, oil production
Polish Power Grid Company, electricity dispatching and transmission
State Hard Coal Agency, coal industry monitoring and advising
Weglokoks, coal exports
Weglozbyt, domestic coal sales

Polish Academy of Sciences, Mineral and Energy Economy Research Centre
Polish Chamber of Liquid Fuels, organisation of private oil product wholesalers and retailers
Progress and Business Foundation, consulting services
Upper Silesian Chamber of Mines, organisation of mining companies

European Union Representative Office
British Gas (Poland), natural gas exploration
Honeywell (Poland), equipment supplies
Neste Oil (Poland), oil product imports, wholesaling and retailing
Statoil (Poland), oil product imports, wholesaling and retailing

CHAPTER 1

MAIN ISSUES, SUMMARY OF RECOMMENDATIONS

OVERVIEW

Poland's current energy situation is characterised by:

- a total primary energy supply (TPES) that was 28 per cent lower in 1993 than in 1987, but that bottomed out in 1992 and appears to be on the rise again;

- energy use per capita that since 1990 has been below the average for OECD Europe, though the energy consumption to GDP ratio is two to three times higher than the average for OECD Europe;

- heavy reliance on domestically produced coal not only for electricity generation but also for heat generation in industry, agriculture and residential and commercial buildings;

- energy prices that on the whole remain under various forms of government control and are below economic costs;

- sufficient electricity generation capacity to cover Poland's power needs for several years to come, but with a high share of ageing and inefficient plant;

- a near total dependence on imported oil, and a high and increasing dependence on imported natural gas;

- a relatively flexible oil import supply system, with facilities for switching between Russian and non-Russian supplies;

- an inflexible gas import supply system, with only one significant foreign supplier – Russia – and high cost barriers to diversification;

- hard coal exports that fell steeply in the early 1990s but appear to have stabilised, retaining their importance from a balance of trade perspective, though they are outweighed by oil and gas imports – Poland is now a net energy importer;

- inadequate strategic stocks of crude oil and refined products;

- overstaffing and relatively low productivity throughout the energy sector;

- severe environmental problems related to the low energy efficiency, the dominance of coal in TPES and a lack of pollution abatement equipment for certain pollutants, especially SO_2.

These imbalances, strains and levels of dependence impose difficult trade-offs and hard choices on Poland's energy policy makers. Certain aspects of Poland's current socio-economic situation – high unemployment, high inflation, a lack of funds for investment in both the private and the public sector and a lingering lack of consensus on how fast to proceed with

15

economic reform – make the task even less enviable. On each issue the Government has to weigh short term against long term concerns and manoeuvre between the imperatives of economic rationality and the demands of managers, workers, farmers, the unemployed and the international community. Many of these groups have spokespersons within the Government, and all are endowed with channels through which they can raise sympathy for their causes and put pressure on decision makers.

Nevertheless, Poland's energy policies have evolved considerably over the last four to five years. The country's energy legislation is being revised to reflect the transition from a centrally planned to a market based economy and the priorities of the post-1989 democratically elected governments. New organisational forms are being developed to secure effective implementation of the new policies and laws.

A new, comprehensive energy law is scheduled to be submitted to the Sejm (Parliament) in early 1995. The latest version of the draft law is under (presumably) final review by an inter-ministerial committee reporting to the Council of Ministers. This law will, among other things:

- allocate responsibilities to ministries and other government bodies at central, regional and local level;

- establish a framework for the licensing of energy companies;

- regulate companies' access to Poland's electricity grid and gas, oil and heat pipeline networks;

- provide guidelines for the setting of prices and tariffs;

- provide guidelines for deciding on energy efficiency standards;

- provide for the establishment of an energy sector regulatory authority.

The drafting of the energy law has taken a long time mainly because of disagreement on policies within the Government. Some oppose limiting political intervention in energy pricing to industries with elements of natural monopoly, and many officials are ambivalent about establishing an independent regulatory authority, as discussed below under "The need for a regulatory regime". Even though the submission of the law to the Sejm was seen as imminent, at the time of writing (end 1994) considerable uncertainty remained about the gist of the text the Sejm would receive. There is also fear among the Government's liberal advisers that market oriented principles in the law may be watered down as secondary legislation is developed.

According to Article 1 of the latest available draft of the new energy law (dated November 1994), the Government's main targets in the energy field are to:

- secure Poland's supply of energy and fuels;

- achieve efficiency in the production and use of energy and fuels;

- develop competitive conditions in the energy industries;

- protect customers' interests;

- minimise costs.

These targets can be attained in a number of ways. Figure 1.1 shows some of the measures, or types of measures, that may be enacted. IEA Member countries' experience indicates that broadly based policy packages combining demand and supply side measures have a better chance of success than single policy strategies.

THE NEED FOR FURTHER ADJUSTMENT IN PRICES AND PRICING POLICY

The Government's energy pricing policy choices will probably have a greater impact on Poland's security of energy supply, energy consumption structure and habits, and environmental situation than will any of its other policy choices. Polish energy companies' incomes and financial strength will depend on how prices develop. Foreign energy companies will evaluate possible projects in Poland in the light of the outlook for prices, among other things. Regarding the demand side, economists and western policy makers have come to favour economic incentives such as end-user price increases over "command and control" measures to encourage energy savings.

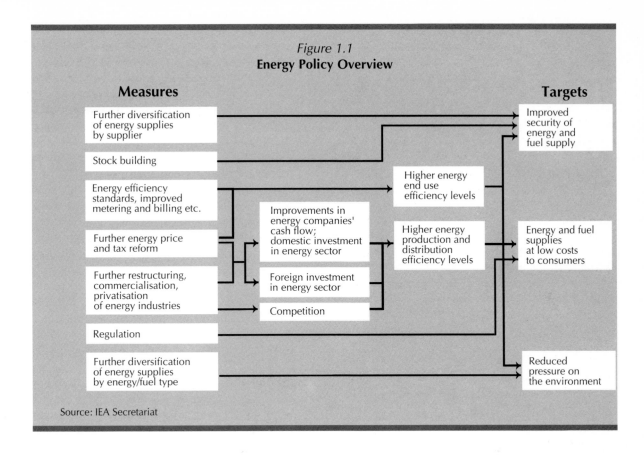

Figure 1.1
Energy Policy Overview

Source: IEA Secretariat

The Polish energy and fuel price structure is considerably less distorted now than before the transition to a market economy started. Domestic coal prices have increased rapidly since 1990 and now cover recorded – if not necessarily true – production costs. Households, which used to pay less than industry for electricity, heat and gas, now pay more. Direct state subsidisation has been phased out for all energy industries except district heating.

However, a fair amount of indirect subsidisation and cross-subsidisation remains. And energy prices, as noted above, are still by and large subject to government control and below economic levels. Most prices jumped in real terms in 1990, but only electricity, heat and gas prices to households continued to outpace the consumer price index in the following years. Coal prices to industry rose above their 1990 level in 1993, but motorists and industrial fuel users paid less – in some cases significantly less – for oil products, gas and electricity in the latter year than in the former. Polish authorities have apparently either underestimated inflation when deciding on energy and fuel price adjustments, or felt constrained in their ability to align prices with economic costs.

While agreeing that energy prices remain too low, Polish officials often argue that since Polish households already spend a much higher share of their real disposable income on energy and fuels than the average OECD household, Poland must be given time to accomplish the alignment of prices with costs. The Government's current strategy with respect to the remaining controlled prices is to adjust and eventually liberalise them rather slowly, taking the social costs of the transition process and the competitiveness of Polish industry into consideration.

Granted, large segments of the Polish population have suffered severe hardships as a consequence of the economic transformation, further energy price increases will increase the pressure on living standards and the Government cannot very well ignore the short term social impact of its decisions. However, the Government should continually examine and re-examine the trade-offs between its diverse concerns and its methods of supporting those in need of support, striving to move as fast as it can under the circumstances. Ultimately energy has to be paid for somehow, and until each consumer group is asked to cover the full costs of its supplies, somebody else must foot the bill, with skewed incentives and dislocation effects rippling through the economy as inevitable results.

The draft energy law stipulates that energy and fuel prices and tariffs should reflect, among other things:

- energy enterprises' justified working costs, capital costs and development costs including environmental protection costs;

- consumers' interests in reasonable prices.

The law leaves it to the ministries in charge of the various energy industries and to the Ministry of Finance to interpret the concepts of "justified costs" and "reasonable prices".

Looking at individual fuels, domestic coal prices are now within the range of import and export parity prices for coal of similar qualities, and appear at first sight reasonable. However, their stability is far from guaranteed. To the extent that the Polish coal industry underrecords costs, prices should be higher. However, in a more open market, they might be lower.

The Government should consider stabilising coal prices by encouraging long term contracts for a substantial but declining share of the supply of coal to power stations, with the remainder of sales to Polish customers subject to competition.

With respect to the network based fuels, however, prices, which are set by the Ministry of Finance, should definitely be raised further in real terms. Electricity prices in 1993 were 40-50 per cent below economic costs. The Ministry intends to bring them up to economic levels over a period of five to six years by allowing them to increase periodically at a rate of 1.5 times the expected inflation rate during the forthcoming period. This multiplier may be too small to deliver the desired results, however, and there remains a risk that electricity pricing will continue to be subordinated to general economic and policy considerations. Gas prices are estimated at between 50 per cent (for households) and 80 per cent (for industry) of supply costs. They cover operating costs for the Polish Oil and Gas Company (POGC), but do not generate funds for replacement of capital or system expansion. This situation is untenable in light of the Government's ambitious programme to expand gas use. Heat prices are closer to cost-covering levels, but gaps remain.

The Government should decide on a programme of real electricity price increases that will align prices with their economic levels within a few years. Low income households may be compensated for electricity bill increases directly through cash payments. The Government should ensure that the momentum of its gas price reforms is maintained and consider revising its plan to increase prices by some 30 per cent during 1994-97; defining a period at the end of which prices should cover all costs would be more appropriate. Regarding heat prices, the aim should be to abolish all public price subsidies. The Government should also provide for increased penetration of heat meters and heat flow controls, and replace the most widespread tariff system – which fails to stimulate consumers to economise on their heat use – with billing according to actual heat consumption.

Regarding oil products, fuel oil and some other product prices reflect supply and demand, but the Ministry of Finance sets maximum prices for gasoline and diesel fuel.

For as long as this policy is upheld, the Ministry may be well advised to standardise the price setting procedure further, clarify to the public the underlying principles, concerns and trade-offs and shorten the intervals between adjustments.

THE NEED FOR FURTHER RESTRUCTURING AND PRIVATISATION

All Polish energy and fuel industries are undergoing a difficult transformation. They need to be turned from monolithic, lethargic, more or less inefficient state organisations, wedded to a culture inherited from the communist age, into flexible, efficient and accountable systems of companies ready to compete with each other and with foreign businesses.

The restructuring and privatisation of the energy sector has proceeded rather slowly because of opposition from trade unions and other quarters. Some consolidation of firms into holding companies has taken place with the objective of strengthening the industries' ability to fund themselves without destroying the potential for competition. Some state owned enterprises have been transformed into state owned joint stock companies (i.e. corporatised or commercialised). So far only some ancillary functions have been privatised. Commercialisation implies curtailing workers' influence on decisions to the benefit of managers and customers, and privatisation will take that process further. The unions, fearing for their members' jobs, are sceptical, and most companies will indeed have to shed workers to become competitive. However, in a longer term perspective there are no workable alternatives to rationalisation. Moreover, in the longer term, the envisaged restructuring processes and ownership changes may bring more job creation than the workers now expect.

Most of Poland's 70 **coal** mines have been grouped into six coal companies and one holding company, which now operate as Treasury owned joint stock companies. Although the industry has shed nearly one-quarter of its peak workforce, further rationalisation seems inevitable. Yet, the present mine closure and restructuring programme does not provide strong incentives to miners, company managers or the Government to push ahead.

Forced to choose between a structure that would facilitate financial consolidation of the industry and one that would create effective competition – and thus incentives to cut costs – in the industry, the Government seems to have opted for the former. This is understandable, but it should be considered an intermediate option; competition should be encouraged with increasing vigour as restructuring progresses. The Government should furthermore analyse the economics of mine closure carefully and consider all possible ways to speed the streamlining of the industry.

The **electricity** industry now comprises three layers of companies, dedicated to generation, transmission and distribution. Within each layer, companies are or will be organised as financially independent joint stock companies. The future organisation of the industry has been hotly debated within the industry itself as well as in government circles, and as of end-1994 questions still awaited settlement. Discussions have focused on the pros and cons of merging the existing generation and

distribution companies into holding companies and gradually introducing competition among generators, giving uneconomic entities time to adapt.

As the industry will have to undertake massive plant replacement and pollution abatement investments in the years to come, and as companies and individual investors will require stable legal and institutional frameworks to make those investments, the Government should speed up its decision on the future of the electricity industry.

The **district heating** industry consists of nearly 500 companies created from about 50 bigger enterprises through a reorganisation at municipal level. Some of the new companies may not be financially viable.

At this stage, the Government should take care that the companies are licensed according to a model used nationwide. The Government should furthermore require the budgets and accounts of companies owned by municipalities to be kept separate from other local activities. As the industry appears to suffer from having to report to, and take orders from, a variety of public authorities at central, regional and municipal level, the Government should work out a clear division of responsibilities among those bodies.

In the **gas** industry, POGC has sole responsibility for exploration and production (for both gas and oil) as well as gas imports, transmission, storage and distribution. There is broad agreement that this structure is suboptimal; POGC is too large and unwieldy and embraces too many different types of activity. The Government has adopted a plan for transforming POGC into separate, independent companies for exploration, drilling, production, transmission and distribution in stages. However, the implementation of the plan has hardly begun, and the Government apparently continues to ponder alternative approaches maintaining the unity of POGC.

Many aspects of the Government's gas industry plan are commendable, and the Government is strongly advised not to backtrack on its original intentions, but rather elaborate on them, e.g. by accelerating the spinning off and eventual privatising of POGC's upstream activities. There are

suggestions in the plan of a continued blurring of the roles of government and state company. The Government needs to establish a clear distinction between its role in deciding on an energy policy framework and the commercial operation of companies, including state owned companies, within this framework.

Successive Polish governments have tried to reach agreement on a restructuring and commercialisation/privatisation plan for the oil industry. The authorities see a need for rapid modernisation of the oil industry in general and the refinery subsector in particular. They can hardly accomplish this without letting foreign capital into the industry. However, they also want to retain direct influence over the industry and secure as much as possible of its revenue for the state. These concerns are seen as inconsistent with allowing foreigners to hold significant shares in the companies that form the core of the industry. Efforts on the part of these companies to position themselves for the future have also complicated the search for an acceptable plan.

The Government should decide on a restructuring and privatisation plan, and start implementing it, as quickly as possible. At present, sensible investments are delayed as companies wait for a clarification of the future rules of the game, and resources may be wasted as companies aiming for vertical integration may duplicate each others' efforts.

THE NEED FOR A REGULATORY REGIME

Electricity, heat and gas transmission and distribution are considered examples of natural national or regional monopolies. To ensure that improvements in efficiency of supply benefit consumers instead of leading to unreasonably high profits for a few companies, these industries should be regulated. Structural and ownership changes are envisaged for the network based energy industries and it would make sense to establish a regulatory regime at the same time.

At present there is no independent body carrying out this function. Prices are set by the Ministry of Finance in a process of balancing the industries' needs against the necessity of holding inflation

down, the Government's social concerns and various special interests. This situation easily leads to decisions inconsistent with sound energy economics.

The draft energy law sets up a potentially effective framework for regulation. It contains principles for price setting and provides for unbundling of accounts and establishing an independent Energy Regulatory Authority (ERA). Wording in the draft law, however, indicates an unwillingness to make the ERA truly independent and powerful, and tasks allocated to the ministries appear to overlap both with ERA functions and with tasks that should be performed by the industries themselves.

A regulatory body needs to be seen to be independent and have sufficient authority and legal power to make and enforce its own decisions. The Government should give careful consideration to this need. If it does not, there is a danger of the ERA becoming just an unnecessary extra layer of bureaucracy, of continued government interference in the commercial operations of the industries and of prejudice to the possibility of attracting foreign capital in the form of investments or loans.

SECURITY OF ENERGY SUPPLY CONSIDERATIONS

Large reserves of coal and lignite offer an important degree of security of energy supply. Poland's coal mining is concentrated in a few regions with serious structural unemployment problems, however, and although the reduction of the coal industry workforce has proceeded relatively smoothly, the miners have on occasions used, or threatened to use, their industrial power to protect their jobs and wages. The authorities' interest in energy and fuel diversification appears rooted in security of supply concerns as well as in energy efficiency and environmental issues.

The post-1989 Polish governments have accomplished an impressive diversification of the country's oil imports. Before the Council for Mutual Economic Assistance (CMEA) broke up, Poland depended on Russia for nearly all its crude oil and refined product supplies. In 1993 the country obtained a little over half of its crude supplies and most of its product supplies outside of Russia. Moreover, the infrastructure is in place to allow Poland to get all its oil from countries other than Russia should the need arise.

In a wider sense, however, Poland's security of oil supply is not adequate: its crude oil and refined product stocks are far below what is considered prudent among IEA Member countries. The exact level of stocks is considered classified information; however, the Government seems to consider a level corresponding to 30 days of net imports a reasonable target for 2000.

The Government is urged to set a more ambitious goal for oil stocks, and to work out a plan including a deadline for arriving at an acceptable level of stocks.

Poland continues to rely on Russia for nearly all of its imported gas. POGC is studying other supply arrangements, but as all the alternatives are more expensive than Russian gas, there is no guarantee that any of them will materialise in the foreseeable future. Meanwhile the load factor of demand looks set to deteriorate.

The Government should take a variety of steps to increase the flexibility of Poland's gas supply system. It should consider adjusting its acreage release and taxation policies with a view to attracting more foreign investment in the gas industry, it should ensure that the gas industry is able to build more underground storage capacity and it should consider introducing flexibility in purchase contracts and incentives for interruptible contracts. All options should be assessed and compared to establish the least cost mix.

CHALLENGES AND OPPORTUNITIES ON THE DEMAND SIDE

The efficiency of energy use could be improved in all sectors of the Polish economy. Poland has a lot of heavy, energy-intensive industry. Factories use old equipment representing outmoded technology and bearing witness to years of poor maintenance. Management practices continue to reflect distorted prices and a lack of incentives to economise on inputs. The residential/commercial sector, relying mainly on district heating and small, local coal-fired boilers for heat, is characterised by low levels of insulation, a lack of metering of heat consumption, billing systems that give no incentive to cut down on heat consumption – and a lack of ways for households to adjust consumption even if the motivation existed.

The problem of low energy end-use efficiency levels may be attacked in a number of ways.

Any strategy must involve bringing energy and fuel prices to end-users up to cost covering levels. The IEA countries' experiences indicate that no measure, or group of measures, will deliver the desired results if not underpinned by price incentives. In addition, consumers must be able to respond to such incentives, implying that price, tariff and billing system reform should be accompanied by steps to equip all dwellings and businesses with metering and control systems.

Energy efficiency standards and labelling systems for cars, appliances and other equipment are well established measures in IEA countries, and should be considered for inclusion in the Polish Government's energy efficiency policy package.

Energy efficiency in heavy industry might be raised most effectively through co-operation between the Government and subsectors or individual companies. The Government could finance audits to make companies aware of the nature and extent of their problems and help them establish their priorities. It could also offer advice on what to do and how to measure results.

With respect to the residential/commercial sector, the Government should consider offering financial support to enable owners to invest in the energy efficiency of their buildings or apartments. It could target loans for district heating to achieve improvements in end-use efficiency in addition to reduced heat losses in production and distribution. It could enlist the expertise of the electricity distribution companies by encouraging or requiring them to plan and operate their systems on the basis of least cost principles,

i.e. to consider demand-side as well as supply-side possibilities.

On an institutional level, the Government should consider strengthening, and allocating the necessary resources to, the newly formed National Energy Agency to enable it to develop credible energy efficiency improvement programs and catch decision makers' attention.

PROTECTING THE ENVIRONMENT

Poland's mass of heavy industry, inefficient ways of using energy, fuel consumption structure and lack of pollution abatement equipment have led to enormous environmental problems. Air pollution levels are much higher than in OECD countries. Water pollution, stemming partly from the coal industry's dumping of saline water into rivers and from refineries' emissions of insufficiently treated water, has caused major problems for downstream water users. Solid waste disposal from coal mines and power plants gives rise to contaminated run-off and harmful dust.

Emissions of most pollutants have declined over the past five to six years. In the beginning, this was mainly because of industrial contraction due to declines in domestic and foreign demand for Polish goods. More recently, structural change, fuel substitution and investment in equipment to reduce emissions have played important parts. As the economy continues picking up, vigorous efforts on the side of the Government to further structural change, energy efficiency improvement and pollution abatement will be necessary to prevent emissions from picking up too.

The need for investments in pollution abatement equipment and other environmental facilities has been estimated at US$ 12-13 billion by 2000, but during this period funds will be very scarce.

Decision makers on all levels will have to set environmental priorities. Although everybody realises this, a thorough cost-benefit analysis of all suggested policies and measures has not yet been undertaken. The Government should initiate such an analysis as quickly as possible.

Poland's emission problems are linked to its energy inefficiency problems and lack of pollution abatement facilities. The polluter pays principle is in force, but energy companies need cash to fund environmentally motivated investments.

Further energy price reform should receive high priority for environmental as well as economic reasons. Emission fees and fines are well established in Poland; however, the system of taxes should be refined, tax levels should be raised – or at least not be allowed to fall – in real terms and the authorities should grant fewer waivers. Arrangements for and techniques of emission trading should be studied carefully and their legal status clarified.

The Government should also strive to keep its industry restructuring and privatisation policies and its energy and fuel substitution plans on track. Reducing the burning of coal – especially the use of small, inefficient coal-fired burners – by a few percentage points would cut air pollution levels significantly.

Poland has set very ambitious ambient air quality standards covering a long list of substances. In some cases they are stricter than European Union standards. Few emitters will be able to meet the deadlines for compliance, however, and monitoring facilities are in place in only a few regions and for only a few substances. The standards thus could easily become paper regulations.

The Government should modify its air quality targets with a view to making them more realistic. Companies then should be made to conform to the revised standards and phase-in schedules.

Closer co-operation on environmental issues is needed between central government, the voivodships (provinces), local government and industry. Furthermore, Poland's environmental policy making institutions and implementation agencies need to be strengthened on all levels, including the company level.

CHAPTER 2

SUMMARY OF SURVEY

ECONOMIC REFORMS

The post-1989 Polish governments have come a long way in their efforts to stabilise the economy and create a foundation for sustainable economic growth. GDP, which dropped by almost 12 per cent in 1990, increased by 5 per cent in 1994. The recovery has become progressively more widespread. Exports increased by nearly one-fourth in 1994, resulting in smaller than expected trade and current account deficits. Consumer price inflation, which reached 550 per cent in 1990, was about 32 per cent in 1994. Current trends are, on balance, encouraging.

The social costs of the transformation, however, have been considerable. Unemployment is estimated at 16.7 per cent. The authorities are under heavy pressure to increase spending.

Some structural changes were fairly easily implemented. Most prices, and the bulk of Poland's foreign trade, were liberalised in early 1990. The ability to acquire and dispose of property, and freedom of entry into most activities, were institutionalised at the same time. These changes have led to explosive growth in the number of private companies, which now account for more than half of GDP and almost 60 per cent of total employment.

However, it has proved more difficult than expected to complete the process of price and trade liberalisation, and above all to turn state owned enterprises into privately owned companies. Many state enterprises – including some core energy enterprises – have been commercialised, i.e. transformed to Treasury owned joint stock companies, with the intention of selling part of the shares to private interests; only a few have actually been transferred to the private sector.

The post-1989 Polish Governments' industry policies have included consolidating large numbers of firms into a small number of holding companies to achieve a pooling of financial resources. Although many industries need such action, this policy is not without risks. Holding companies may be used to transfer the burden of keeping weak firms alive from the state to the stronger firms in the groups, and a loss of efficiency and dynamism can result.

ENERGY DEMAND

Poland's TPES fell by 19 per cent from 1989 to 1993, mainly in line with steep declines in economic activity following the introduction of economic reforms. Residential consumers have cut down on their coal use because of a combination of income declines and coal price increases. Structural change and energy efficiency improvements have only recently started to affect energy consumption patterns.

23

The shares of individual forms of energy in TPES have changed moderately since reform policies were introduced. Coal's share was 77 per cent in 1993 as in 1989. The share of oil increased from 13.3 per cent to 14.3 per cent while that of gas rose from 8 per cent to 8.4 per cent. There are many reasons to assume that structural change and substitution will gradually adjust the structure of Poland's TPES towards that of OECD Europe's energy supplies. For the foreseeable future, however, the Polish economy will remain coal intensive.

Energy use in industry fell by more than 30 per cent from 1989 to 1993, and its share in total final consumption (TFC) declined from 37 per cent to about 33 per cent. Industry will probably continue to lose ground to other sectors. The transport sector's share in TFC increased from about 11 per cent in 1989 to 13 per cent in 1993 and will probably continue to grow.

In a policy paper submitted in late 1992 and again, in revised form, in late 1993, the Ministry of Industry and Trade (MoIT) presents two TPES scenarios. A high growth case has primary energy supplies in 2010 exceeding their 1990 level by 46 per cent, implying average annual growth in 1991-2010 of a little less than 2 per cent. A low growth case combines circumstances that provide for a 23 per cent increase in TPES from 1990 to 2010, or about 1 per cent a year. Starting from its lower 1993 level, TPES would have to grow by an average of about 2.5 per cent a year in the high case, or 1.4 per cent a year in the low case, to reach the same 2010 levels.

The quality of Poland's energy statistics is high. The current data collecting system focuses on state enterprises and is therefore growing inaccurate, but the authorities are aware of the problem and plan to revise their system and methods so as to incorporate the changes brought on by the transformation of the economy.

ENERGY END-USE AND EFFICIENCY

The energy intensity of the Polish economy fell by some 15 per cent from 1985 to 1989, and by another 7 per cent in 1990, mainly as a consequence of steep declines in energy-intensive industrial production. The following year saw an increase in energy use per unit of GDP of about 7 per cent: industry continued to contract, but growth in various private sector activities pushed energy use upwards. However, in 1992 the declining trend reasserted itself and in 1993 energy intensity was back at its 1990 level.

Comparing the energy consumption per unit of GDP in Poland with the energy intensity of OECD Europe, using official energy use and GDP figures and official exchange rates, indicates a ratio of between 6 and 7 to 1. Adjusting for conceptual differences and assumed measurement inaccuracies, and using purchasing power parity exchange rates, reduces the ratio to 2-3 to 1.

Most of Poland's industry is very energy inefficient. This situation reflects various legacies of central planning, such as the focus on meeting production targets and the absence of competition and incentives to cut costs. Since 1989 Polish governments have given more attention to energy efficiency issues than did their predecessors, and shown a clearer understanding of the nature of the problem. However, the slow pace of privatisation of larger industrial enterprises, the stability of, or, in some cases, declines in, real energy prices to industrial end-users, a lingering lack of interest in energy efficiency by enterprises and a shortage of funds, limiting companies' possibilities to replace energy-inefficient equipment, have contributed to making progress on this front rather modest.

Apparently, structural change within the manufacturing sector had a small dampening effect on the energy intensity of the sector as a whole, whereas energy intensity changes at subsector level have pushed the energy intensity of the sector upwards. While some components of industry's energy use vary in proportion to production, others stay the same even if output plummets; such components account for a high share of industrial energy use in Poland, as state owned enterprises tend to be engaged in all sorts of social activities.

By OECD standards, Poland's transport sector accounts for a small share of the country's energy use and road transportation represents a small share of total transportation. The sector is expanding, however, and the road transport subsector is growing faster than the rest of the sector. The number of passenger cars has increased rapidly in recent years. Average passenger car fuel intensity fell by nearly 20 per cent during the 1980s, but this decline, which stemmed from a switch to smaller cars, may have bottomed out. Poland's energy use for transport looks set to continue to grow.

The residential sector accounts for three-fourths to four-fifths of TFC in "other sectors". Residential energy use is in turn dominated by space and water heating. About 40 per cent of Poland's dwellings are served by district heating systems. The remainder rely on coal-fired central systems or single dwelling coal stoves. Many different water heating systems are in use. Gas is used to an increasing extent, and electric storage heaters have a considerable market share, but so have district heating systems, coal-fired boilers and coal stoves. Household use of coal and heat is a significant source of energy overconsumption.

A pent-up demand for better housing may lead to a gradual switch from smaller to larger apartments and from apartments to detached dwellings. Poland's building codes are being updated. The main problem with respect to the residential sector is to find ways and means to retrofit the country's generally poorly insulated and energy-inefficient buildings.

Electricity use per capita is considerably lower in Poland than in OECD countries. The low level of penetration of electric equipment more than compensates for the low efficiency of the equipment in use. Rising incomes, however, will permit acquisition of more appliances, and although the average energy efficiency of Poland's stocks of TV sets, freezers, etc., will increase, it is expected that the use of household appliances and of data processing and communication equipment in the commercial sector will account for a growing share of Poland's electricity consumption.

ENERGY SUPPLY

Main Institutions and Ownership Structure

The Mazowiecki Government inherited an energy sector whose main enterprises were subordinated to the MoIT. The local heat production and distribution companies were exceptions, linked to the Ministry of Physical Planning and Construction.

The running of the energy and fuel industries was left to boards such as the Hard Coal Board and the Electricity and Brown Coal Board; in the case of gas, to the fully integrated POGC; for heat, to regional and local authorities; and, in the case of liquid fuels, to various state enterprises in charge of individual links in the oil product supply chain. Energy prices were set by the Ministry of Finance after consultations with the industry and physical planning ministries and the core energy sector enterprises. Subsidies were paid by the Ministry of Finance and regional or voivodship authorities.

The industries forming the energy sector have since been restructured and reorganised to varying degrees. Only some ancillary functions have been privatised so far, but several major enterprises in the solid fuel, electricity, heat and liquid fuel industries have been turned into Treasury owned joint stock companies so as to place them under commercial law, encourage them to adopt better accounting practices, abolish their Employee Councils, liberate and strengthen their management and, more generally, allow workers and management time to acquire the skills and the spirit necessary to survive in a fully fledged market environment. In most cases the Government intends eventually to sell part of the shares in these companies to the private sector.

Until 1989 the **coal** industry was organised on the principle of centralisation of decision making powers. The hard coal mines and their administrative superstructure were subordinated to the Planning Commission, supervision of the industry was the responsibility of the Hard Coal Board, and domestic distribution and exports were in the hands of two state owned monopolies, CZW and Weglokoks.

In 1989 the Ministry of Coal Mining was abolished and in 1990 the individual coal mines – 70 in all – were established as independent state owned enterprises with the right to market their own output. The Hard Coal Board became a link between the MoIT and the individual mines. Since then 46 mines have been grouped into six joint stock companies, 11 have been incorporated in a holding company, seven are to be closed and six are being kept outside the new structure. The Hard Coal Board has been transformed into a joint stock company, renamed the State Hard Coal Agency and charged with advising local and central authorities on coal issues and providing services to the operating units. CZW was renamed Weglosbyt; it and Weglokoks were re-established as joint stock companies and their monopolies were abolished.

Since 1990, when the Electricity and Brown Coal Board was liquidated, the core institution in the **electricity** industry has been the Polish Power Grid Company (PPGC). This joint stock enterprise buys electricity from the country's 28 public generation companies and from the industrial autoproducers that account for some 10 per cent of Poland's net installed generation capacity. PPGC resells the power to 33 local public distribution companies. In addition, three lignite mines are considered part of the electricity sector. PPGC manages the high voltage transmission grid and is responsible for dispatching. The local distribution companies are responsible for the local grids and operate some smaller combined heat and power (CHP) and heat-only boilers. These last companies and some of the CHP companies have been turned into joint stock companies while the electricity-only generators have been retained as state enterprises.

Heat is supplied mainly by public power plants and CHP plants, centrally located heat plants owned by the public power industry, industrial enterprises and district heating enterprises operating a large number of heat-only boilers. These last companies are responsible for heat distribution, a function that was further decentralised in 1993 when the 50 district heating enterprises, many of which ran several, un-integrated networks, were broken up into 473 companies in charge of one network each. These companies represent a variety of owner-ship forms and degrees of decision making independence; some are municipal utilities but have some financial independence, some are joint stock companies, some are owned by housing co-operatives and some are private.

The **gas** sector is more or less synonymous with POGC, a state owned enterprise reporting to the MoIT. With 23 separate affiliates, POGC covers the entire natural gas chain from exploration, development and production to transmission, storage and distribution, manages Poland's onshore crude oil production and is in charge of gas imports.

There is no such integrated company in the **liquid fuels** sector. Poland's modest oil production is in the hands of POGC (onshore) and a joint stock company named Petrobaltic (offshore). Oil imports have been demonopolised and partly privatised; a joint stock company called Ciech, which used to be the sole buyer of crude as well as products from abroad, is still a large operator, but other public companies and many private firms have entered the business. A state owned enterprise named Przedsiebiorstwo Eksploatacji Rurociagow Naftowych (PERN) is responsible for all crude and product pipeline transportation. Seven refineries organised as joint stock companies supply the bulk of the country's product needs. Wholesaling and retailing are split between Centrala Produktow Naftowych (CPN), a state enterprise, which lost its monopoly position in 1990; a large number of private operators, including some foreign oil companies; and some of the other public oil sector companies.

Supply of Individual Energy Forms

Poland's recoverable **coal** reserves are estimated at 65 billion tonnes. Of this total, about one-fourth is regarded as mineable given the present state of technology. At current rates of exploitation, the ratio of mineable reserves to production exceeds a century.

Hard coal production increased steadily from 1950 to peak in 1979 at 201 million tonnes. During most of the 1980s output fluctuated around 190 million tonnes. Most was consumed domestically; exports totalled about 30 million tonnes a year. Production levels during this period did not reflect economic rationality. The industry was not given incentives to maximise profits. Instead it was used to further other economic and social goals. These goals called for a maximisation of employment and thus coal output.

In the late 1980s production started to decline. In the wake of the changes in policy orientation in 1989 the decline became steeper, not so much because of the adoption of free market policies or the incipient restructuring of the coal industry as because of declines in domestic coal consumption following the introduction of economic reforms and the ensuing economic downturn. Output fell to 130 million tonnes in 1993. Exports dropped to 19 million tonnes in 1992, but rebounded to 25 million tonnes the following year.

Labour productivity in the Polish coal industry is low even by European standards. In 1991 coal output per employee was 400 tonnes, as against 630 tonnes in Germany and 1 520 tonnes in the United Kingdom. The shedding of workers, which has been in progress since the late 1980s, has been smaller, in relative terms, than the declines in output. The long term restructuring programme for the coal industry is intended to increase average productivity to 940 tonnes a year by 2000.

The coal industry's processing facilities are technically obsolete, and inadequate in terms of the volumes they can handle. Mines had no incentives to deliver good quality coal under the old pricing system, but since 1990 efforts have been made to increase the proportion of coal being washed.

The industry may be able to increase exports in real terms while maintaining commercial viability, but only if it manages to reduce its marginal costs. The development of exports in a commercially rational fashion is a strong argument for more rapid rationalisation of production.

Electricity is produced mainly from solid fuels. In 1993, hard coal plants accounted for 62 per cent of Poland's public generating capacity of 29.4 GW, lignite plants for 31 per cent and hydro plants for 7 per cent. In terms of actual gross public electricity generation, the thermal plants accounted for an even higher share, 97 per cent.

There is no immediate need for additional capacity. In 1993, maximum demand corresponded to about 70 per cent of Poland's total installed generating capacity of 32.8 GW (autoproducers included). This situation mainly reflects a very rapid build-up of capacity during the 1970s and a drop of 10 per cent in final electricity demand from 1990 to 1993.

There is, however, a pressing need to upgrade and rehabilitate existing plants, many of which are obsolete and uneconomically small. Some 60 per cent of the capacity in place is more than 15 years old and 40 per cent is more than 20 years old. In addition, during the 1970s and 1980s maintenance expenses were kept at a minimum. PPGC estimates that more than 20 GW of capacity needs rehabilitation and about 3.5 GW should be retired by 2005. Installing pollution control equipment and upgrading and expanding transmission and distribution systems are also urgent tasks. All in all, the Polish electricity industry needs invest-

ments of around US$ 8 billion by the end of the decade.

PPGC favours integration of the Polish system with the western European UCPTE system, as such a move would improve Poland's security and quality of power supplies. Since the beginning of 1994 the country's utilities have maintained the parameters set by UCPTE.

Five lignite mines produce almost exclusively for adjacent power plants. In 1993 they delivered 68.1 million tonnes, implying – since annual output in the late 1980s was 72-73 million tonnes – that lignite production has held up much better than hard coal production. The MoIT foresees a decline in lignite mining of some 20 per cent by 2005, as developed sites will be exhausted and new mines may not be defensible on economic grounds; while lignite produced from existing mines can compete with coal at today's hard coal prices, lignite produced from new mines would have to be priced far too high to be competitive.

Like the hard coal mines, the lignite mines are heavily overstaffed. Miners have protested the Government's plan for a combined electricity and lignite sector restructuring as pointing towards layoffs.

District heating networks supply 53 per cent of Poland's total residential heating needs. In 1993 public power plants and CHP plants represented about half the country's total heat supply capacity. Heat plants operated by the district heating enterprises accounted for a little less than a third of capacity, autoproducers for 10 per cent and heat plants owned by the public power industry for 8 per cent.

The average efficiency of heat production varies from 78 per cent for the public power and CHP plants to less than 50 per cent for the small, local heat plants, which often are in bad technical shape. There is a lack of automatic control systems, and almost no measuring of delivered heat. Another widespread problem is pipe corrosion, leading to leaks, failures and interruptions in supplies: water losses from district heating systems are about four times higher in Poland than in western Europe, and heat losses are estimated to range from 10 per cent to 45 per cent.

Poland is about 40 per cent self sufficient in **gas**. Four types of gas are produced: high methane natural gas, low methane natural gas, coke oven gas and manufactured (town) gas. The coke oven and town gas supplies are gradually being replaced by natural gas. Poland's gas production fell by about a third from 1988 to 1992, but increased slightly in 1993 and is expected to grow by some 40 per cent by 2000 before stagnating and starting to decline again some years into the next century.

POGC remains the country's only producer of high and low methane natural gas, but its formal monopoly was abolished in 1991 and since then two licensing rounds have been held. Foreign companies were invited to prospect for and eventually develop fields with a view to selling the gas in the domestic market but at international prices. As a general rule they found the terms satisfactory, and several participated.

In spite of the presence of companies like Exxon, Shell, British Gas and Amoco at the licensing rounds, however, Poland is not regarded as a highly attractive prospect. Onshore resources are estimated at only 158 bcm (mid-1994), and the territory available for licensing, given POGC's position, is already relatively well explored.

Poland imports gas only from Russia. Government forecasts point to a rapid increase in import needs, and security of gas supply is high on the energy administration's agenda. Natural gas could in principle be imported from the United Kingdom, Norway, Algeria and Iran in addition to Russia. For cost reasons, Iran and Algeria seem to be options only for the very long term. Various pipeline projects to connect Poland with the North Sea producers are under consideration.

One project that may diversify Poland's gas imports at least from a technical point of view is Europol, involving a new pipeline system from western Siberia (eventually from the Yamal Peninsula) via Belarus and Poland to western Europe. POGC and Russia's Gazprom have formed a joint venture to build the segment of the system on Polish territory. Russia plans eventually to export 67 bcm of gas per year on this system, of which Poland would have an option to buy 14 bcm. At this stage, however, it is unclear if and when this option will materialise.

Poland has four underground gas storage facilities with total working capacity of 620 million cubic metres and combined withdrawal capacity of 6.5 million cubic metres a day. Some 17 000 km of transmission pipelines and 68 000 km of distribution pipelines serve 2 800 localities and over 6 million customers. POGC plans to add some 45 000 to 60 000 km by 2010.

Regarding **oil**, Poland's domestic crude oil and condensate production is small scale, and the country's dependence on imports for between 98 per cent and 99 per cent of its crude supplies is not expected to decline significantly.

Until 1989 Poland imported crude and products almost exclusively from the Soviet Union. Crude was received on the Druzhba (Friendship) pipeline and products by ship. Since then, however, the country has managed to diversify its oil imports to a remarkable extent. In 1993 Poland received about 56 per cent of its crude supplies and most of its product supplies from countries other than Russia[1]. Moreover, the country has put the necessary infrastructure in place to be able to get all its oil from other countries, if need be.

Imported crude is refined at Poland's seven refineries, whose combined distillation capacity of about 17 million tonnes exceeds Poland's product consumption. However, as not even the two most modern refineries at Plock and Gdansk are very sophisticated by western standards, the composition of their output corresponds to a decreasing extent to the structure of product demand; Poland has a deficit of motor fuels and an exportable surplus of heavy products.

Polish authorities are concerned about this growing discrepancy and about the refineries' ability to compete when current product import restrictions are phased out by 1997 according to agreements with the European Union. Polish officials have for years been considering various restructuring and privatisation plans for the oil refining and distribution sector, one aim of which would be to increase investments in the refinery subsector. Recently there have been calls for an extension of the transition period granted by the EU.

A number of companies are involved in supplying refined products to end-users. State owned CPN is

---

1. The share of Russian oil in Poland's crude imports during the first quarter of 1994 was reportedly as low as 28 per cent.

the market leader, but private Polish entrepreneurs and a handful of foreign companies have built up considerable capacity in the motor fuel markets, and the bigger refineries are feeling their way into the wholesaling and retailing businesses. The private retailers, whose numbers have mush-roomed, are so far the only private element of significance in the Polish energy sector.

ENERGY PRICING

In socialist Poland, energy prices were set by the central Government. As they were conceived of mainly as social policy instruments, they were kept artificially low – well below economic costs. This was particularly true for coal, electricity, gas and heat. The energy industries received subsidies enabling them to maintain high cost production.

Half-hearted attempts at reforming energy prices during the 1970s and 1980s did not have much of an impact on real price levels. Since 1990, however, energy prices and pricing systems have undergone real changes.

In 1991 the Government sent a letter of intent to the World Bank in which it outlines its energy pricing policy as follows: "The Government's strategy is first to raise official prices to households to parity with official prices to industry. In a second step, we will shift all electricity, gas and heat prices from direct price control to indirect supervision, i.e. as part of a regulatory framework for energy networks. A second phase of price adjustment [to full economic cost] will then take place within this framework, starting [at the] end of 1992."

For various reasons this policy has been implemented more slowly than envisaged. Most prices are still below their economic levels.

Prices and Pricing Principles for Individual Energy Forms

Coal prices have since 1990 been set on the basis of two formulas, one for steam coal and one for coking coal. These formulas relate the prices of all steam and coking coal types and qualities produced in Poland to the prices of a reference steam coal and a reference coking coal.

In conditions of perfect competition, the reference price should be somewhere between the import parity price and the export parity price of coal of the same quality, i.e. (in June 1994) between US$ 20 and US$ 40 a tonne. The current steam coal prices are within this range and appear at first sight reasonable. However, factors related to supply costs on the one hand, and to the structure of the industry on the other, indicate that prices may be unstable.

Electricity prices have since early 1991 only kept up with the general rate of inflation, to the detriment of the electricity companies' earnings. In 1993 prices were 40-50 per cent below economic costs. There is broad agreement that further real price increases are necessary, and the Ministry of Finance has responded with a plan to raise prices to cost-covering levels, but only very gradually.

Heat price developments have allowed a reduction in the ratio of subsidies to total costs of heat supplies from 78 per cent in late 1991 to about 27 per cent at the beginning of 1994. The Ministry intended to implement nominal price increases amounting to about 65 per cent during 1994, so that from 1995 the district heating systems in about half of the voivodships would not need further subsidisation. The remaining systems would receive subsidies for two more years. The process of aligning prices to costs has thus advanced further for the district heating sector than for, say, the electricity and gas industries. However, there is a risk that phasing out state subsidies will increase the pressure on municipalities in areas where heat prices are above average.

Gas import prices have risen more than sixfold since 1990, and nominal gas prices charged to Polish end-users have, on balance, increased even faster. However, since early 1992 prices paid by households have been stable in real terms, whereas prices paid by industrial consumers declined in real terms from January 1990 to January 1994 to about a third of their level at the outset of this period. At present they broadly cover POGC's operating costs, but do not generate funds for replacement of capital or system expansion. Following increases in the first quarter of 1994, households paid some 40-60 per cent of the price that would have reflected costs completely, while industry paid 60-80 per cent.

Regarding oil product prices, the Ministry of Finance decides on maximum motor fuel prices after having consulted with the MoIT and the state owned enterprises in the refining and distribution sector. Other refined product prices have been liberalised. Motor fuel prices converted to US dollars at the official rate are 40-50 per cent lower in Poland than in OECD Europe, mainly because of excise tax and margin differences. Fuel oil prices to industry are somewhat closer to international levels. The maximum prices are underpinned by a system of motor fuel import quotas, licences and permits, and by relatively high import duties. These restrictions were put in place as a response to declines in the refineries' throughput in 1990 and 1991.

STRUCTURAL AND OWNERSHIP CHANGES AND REGULATION

Planned Structural Reform and Ownership Changes

In March 1993 the Economic Committee of the Council of Ministers adopted a three stage **hard coal mining** restructuring programme whose objectives are to bring the coal industry back to profitability, to maintain the competitiveness of Polish coal on world markets and to design and implement an investment strategy for the industry.

The first stage, covering 1993, encompassed measures to halt the accumulation of losses and thus save mines from bankruptcy. The Government undertook to adjust coal production to market needs, attack overstaffing problems and increase productivity, while moving prices towards cost covering levels and beginning financial restructuring. Stage two, covering 1994-95 and involving a mine closure programme, aims at adjusting production levels and increasing productivity levels further. Another target is to clear the debts of the industry. The goal of stage three, covering 1996-2000, is to maintain minimum profitability levels despite deteriorating geological and mining conditions and real wage increases.

The biggest obstacle to the intended restructuring and rationalisation of the coal industry is the social and political implications of the job losses that will follow from the planned mine closures. The Government has committed itself to financing the technical and social costs of the closure programme. Furthermore, the programme includes undertakings to avoid group dismissals, establish social security arrangements, create new employment in the mining districts and assure job training. The question is whether the Government has retained sufficient incentives for decision makers on all levels to push ahead with restructuring.

For the **electricity** industry, there is agreement to turn the hard coal and lignite power plants into state owned joint stock companies and thereby complete the commercialisation of the industry, but continued struggle over what restructuring moves to make next. A suggestion to merge the 33 constituent parts of the distribution business into 12 to 15 entities met with so much resistance that it was decided to leave the number of companies unchanged. A proposal was made in the spring of 1994 to create two holding companies out of the major hard coal generating plants and three holding companies out of the lignite plants and adjacent mines, in the hope of striking a balance between the need to centralise financial resources and the perceived benefits of increased competition between generators. This plan triggered strong protests, a lignite miners' strike and a discussion on whether the envisaged structure would indeed force the companies to become more competitive.

PPGC has proposed phasing in competition in the power sector. During phase one, intended to last to 1997, generators would sell power to PPGC on contracts covering gradually declining shares of their capacities. Phase two (1998-2008) would be characterised by competition among generators for short term contracts with PPGC and the introduction of a pool mechanism to create competition in dispatching. From 2009 generators would contract directly with distribution companies; the role of PPGC would be reduced to administering the grid and the power pool.

District heating is the responsibility of the Ministry of Physical Planning and Construction, but the plants supplying heat to the district heating systems are supervised by the MoIT, and for local planning purposes they report to municipalities or voivodships.

The reorganisation of the district heating industry at the municipal level has been carried out in a legal vacuum and with scant concern for economic implications. The new energy law will provide a legal framework for the organisation and running of the industry, but because of delays it will come too late to have any influence on the first round of decisions on the structure of the sector. Eventual inconsistencies between the provisions in the energy law and the new layout of the industry will have to be remedied by adjusting the latter.

There is furthermore a risk that some of the new district heating companies may prove to be continually short of financial as well as human resources, and thus unable to undertake the necessary investments to become efficient and profitable.

As for the **gas** sector, the Government has adopted a plan to restructure POGC in stages. First, various support units are to be commercialised and partly privatised, i.e. set up as separate companies with a POGC shareholding of less than 50 per cent. As a second step, the exploration and drilling companies are scheduled to be subject to the same reform. The third step, for which no deadline has been set, will be to separate out the production companies. Finally, the downstream gas business will be unbundled into a transmission company and distribution companies.

With these reforms the Government hopes to achieve a separation of POGC's current core and ancillary activities, transparency of accounting in general and clear dividing lines between the accounts of the upstream and downstream businesses, improved cost control and a more precise allocation of authority and responsibilities.

The debate on how to restructure and to what extent to privatise the **oil** refining and distribution industry has focused on setting up a Treasury owned holding company to function as an integrated national oil company holding shares in the refineries, CPN and various transportation, building and service companies together with private Polish and foreign investors. An interministerial working group charged with preparing a plan for the sector has submitted its conclusions to the Council of Ministers, but the plan had by early 1995 not yet been presented to the Sejm.

Energy Industry Regulation

Two pieces of legislation will provide a framework for the necessary regulation of the Polish energy sector: the Geological and Mining Law of 4 February 1994 and the energy law, which is to replace the outdated Energy Management Act of 1984 but which by early 1995 had not yet been submitted to the Sejm. The mining law regulates the ownership of and right to explore for and extract natural resources. The energy law will contain provisions for the supply and use of energy and fuels. More detailed terms of operation within the different energy industries will be issued in the form of common secondary legislation applying to companies and licences individually.

Successive draft energy laws have contained principles for price setting and provided for unbundling of accounts and for establishing an independent Energy Regulatory Authority empowered to:

- issue, amend and withdraw licences to enterprises desiring to operate in the energy field;

- approve and control the observance of energy and fuel prices and tariffs;

- prevent energy enterprises from abusing monopoly or dominant positions;

- set quality standards for the energy industries' services;

- assess complaints and resolve disputes;

- decide on conditions for third party access to power or gas grids;

- impose fines on violators of principles provided by the energy law;

- gather, process and publish information on energy management and energy efficiency issues.

However, the degree of the ERA's independence is in some doubt. The president of the regulatory body will be appointed, and apparently may be removed at will, by the Prime Minister. The Council of Ministers may suspend the ERA's decisions for up to six months if they are found to endanger the energy security of the Polish state, and the Sejm may eventually do so for longer periods. Moreover, the ERA's mandate with regards to prices will apparently be limited to checking on companies' observance of the principles, terms and detailed tariffs decided by the MoIT in the cases of electricity and gas, and by the Ministry of Physical Planning and Construction in the case of heat; the agency will only have the right to be consulted by the ministries when the latter are working out these parameters.

ENERGY AND THE ENVIRONMENT

Parts of Poland are known to be among the world's most polluted areas. Heavy, energy-intensive industry accounts for a high share of GDP, and enterprises are only now beginning to feel price and competition pressures to improve the efficiency of their energy use. Obsolete technology and the high share of coal in TPES are other factors. During the 1980s the Government introduced fees on emissions and fines for violating standards. These instruments had little effect, however, as fee and fine levels were kept low and the only real priority was to keep production levels up regardless of costs, including damage to the environment.

Poland's main energy-related environmental problems are:

- air pollution stemming from coal burning by power and heat producers, industrial enterprises and households, from coal mining (which causes emissions of methane) and, increasingly, from traffic;

- water pollution related to coal mines' dumping of saline water into the Vistula and Oder rivers and refinery emissions of insufficiently treated water;

- solid waste generation from coal mines and power plants.

The Ministry of Environmental Protection, Natural Resources and Forestry is the chief state authority for environmental protection. Various national councils serve as advisers to the Minister. The State Environmental Protection Inspectorate is charged with supervising economic units affecting the environment. Organs at voivodship level issue permits, collect fees and carry out various measurement and control activities.

Reform policies adopted in 1990 included energy price increases, measures designed to enhance competition and lead to general efficiency improvements, a revision of the system of environmental fees and fines and a tightening of Poland's ambient air quality standards. The short term effects of these steps were obscured by other factors, however. Emissions of most pollutants declined, but mainly because of industrial contraction due to lower domestic and foreign demand for Polish goods. More recently, however, there has been some structural change, substitution of cleaner fuels, improvement of operation and maintenance procedures and price driven energy saving, with the result that emissions of certain pollutants have kept declining in spite of economic recovery.

The outlook for emissions appears uncertain as the energy price adjustment process has slowed – among the network-based energy forms, only district heating prices have continued to appreciate in real terms – and the environmental fees and fines have remained stable, or even declined slightly, since 1992.

Poland's energy related environmental policies are focused on coal production and use. Measures either in place or nearly so include reduction targets for mines' sulphur dioxide (SO_2) and dust emissions, salt water discharges and solid waste. Longer term programmes include installing clean coal technology and pollution abatement equipment. For oil, there are targets referring to the proportions of unleaded or low lead gasoline and low sulphur diesel and gas oil to be sold in the years ahead, and to refineries' emissions to water and air.

The power/CHP industry accounted in 1992 for more than half of all SO_2 emissions and high shares of all NO_x and particulate emissions. Large power and CHP plants have been equipped with high stacks and pollution abatement equipment, which have improved their environmental performance considerably. However, they are still far from meeting the standards that will be in force from 1998.

The Polish Government and the country's expanding private sector face an enormous challenge in mobilising the necessary funds to clean up Poland's environment. The Government will be neither able nor willing to foot the bill. The Polish capital market is still small, as is the banking system. To be willing to lend money, foreign banks will want government guarantees or very sound projects, and foreign investors still face bureaucratic and legal hurdles, scepticism about privatisation and, in many cases, low revenue. In the short to medium term, i.e. up to 2000, environmentally motivated investments may fall short of what would be needed just to mitigate the most serious pollution problems.

CHAPTER 3

REFORM POLICIES AND ACHIEVEMENTS SINCE 1990

CHALLENGES AT THE OUTSET

The economic transformation programme prepared during the autumn of 1989 by the Solidarity-led Government that came to power in September, was launched in what was not yet a market economy but no longer a planned economy. The share of material inputs subject to central allocation had declined from 45 per cent in 1986 to 22 per cent in 1988, and a number of prices were subject to only limited controls. However, companies had not been made fully responsible for their destinies; they received state subsidies, there was no pressure to make them pay their debts and bankruptcy proceedings had never been enforced. Thus companies were very susceptible to Employee Councils' demands for wage increases. During 1989 excess demand conditions became acute, and by October that year the annualised level of inflation exceeded 16 000 per cent.

The new Government had to decide very quickly on a programme to combat hyperinflation in the context of a wider agenda to transform the Polish economy into a real market economy. It opted to combine a strong stabilisation package with immediate liberalisation of prices and trade, while developing a set of structural reforms to be implemented over time. This meant that initially stabilisation and liberalisation measures would affect an economy that in other respects remained stuck in the heritage of central planning.

**Polish Prime Ministers
Since the Fall of Communism**

September 1989 – November 1990: Tadeusz Mazowiecki

November 1990 – October 1991: Krzysztof Bielecki

October 1991 – June 1992: Jan Olszewski

June 1992 – October 1993: Hanna Suchocka

October 1993 – February 1995: Waldemar Pawlak

March 1995 – : Jozef Oleksy

STABILISATION POLICIES AND RESULTS

The Government's first steps included:

- liberalising most prices (though not all energy and fuel prices, as later chapters will show);

- abolishing most restrictions on trade so as to "import" competition;

- making the zloty convertible and pegging it, at least temporarily, at a fixed value in terms of foreign exchange;

- introducing nominal wage controls in the form of a tax on wage increases above a statistically determined norm, the so-called popiwek tax;

- tightening monetary and fiscal policies.

The results came fast. Prices jumped by an average of 80 per cent during the first two weeks of January 1990, but inflation dropped to about 16 per cent during February as demand declined and companies started to curtail or even reverse price increases and cut production. Inflation averaged less than 5 per cent a month during the rest of 1990. Consumer prices increased by about 550 per cent for the year as a whole. Real wages fell by 42 per cent during January 1990 and by an average of 29 per cent from 1989 to 1990.

GDP declined by an estimated 11.6 per cent from 1989 to 1990, dragged down by a fall of 25 per cent in industrial production. Official unemployment increased from 0.3 per cent at the beginning of 1990 to about 6 per cent at the end of the year. Some regions and population groups fared relatively well, while others – people in north-eastern Poland, women, young people – suffered heavily from the scarcity of jobs. Real consumption levels declined, but not by as much as apparent real wage levels. In the first place, "real" real wages had never been as high as apparent real wages; many of the goods and services that Poles citizens could nominally afford were in chronically short supply. In the second place, small private businesses started to mushroom in 1990, and their contributions to households' incomes were probably under-recorded for quite some time after the transformation had started.

Fiscal discipline was part and parcel of the agreement between the Mazowiecki Government and the International Monetary Fund (IMF). In 1989 public spending exceeded public revenue by zlotys (Zl) 3.6 trillion, the equivalent of 3 per cent of GDP. The Government's targets for 1990 included a deficit equivalent to 1 per cent of GDP. During the first months of the year, however, inflation boosted revenue so much that 1990 ended with a surplus equivalent to 0.5 per cent of GDP.

Mainly because exports responded well to the large depreciation of the zloty in 1989, the current account swung from a deficit of US$ 1.4 billion in 1989 to a surplus of US$ 0.7 billion in 1990.

Developments in 1991 were marked by a collapse in intra-CMEA trade and sharply rising prices for imported energy. GDP declined by an estimated 7.6 per cent while consumer prices increased by 76 per cent. Industrial production dropped by

about 17 per cent, and in some branches of industry – engineering, metallurgy – output declined by more than one-fourth. In an end-use perspective, domestic absorption increased slightly as wage indexation caused consumption to rebound by 6 per cent, while capital formation, including stock building, fell by nearly a fifth. Registered unemployment escalated to almost 12 per cent by the end of the year.

Cutting down on subsidies, which during the 1980s amounted to roughly 40 per cent of total annual budget expenditures, has been a recurrent theme in the post-1989 governments' programmes. In 1990 subsidies were reduced to 26 per cent of expenditures, and in 1991 their share was only 9 per cent. Nevertheless, the latter year ended with a budget deficit equivalent to 3.8 per cent of GDP. The tax system proved increasingly inadequate in the face of mounting social security payments and debt service.

Hard currency exports continued to increase, but as hard currency imports jumped by nearly 50 per cent, Poland's trade surplus was wiped out and its current account showed a deficit of about US$ 1.4 billion. The effects of devaluations of the zloty during 1989, on 1 January 1990 and in May 1991 were petering out. In October 1991 the Government stopped trying to maintain a fixed rate for the zloty and switched to a pre-announced crawling exchange rate regime.

In April 1991 the Government reached the first of several agreements on Poland's foreign debt. The Paris Club member countries accepted to write down their claims on Poland – at that time around US$ 32 billion – by 50 per cent if Poland stayed on good terms with the IMF and if the London Club member banks accepted a similar write-down of their claims.

In 1992 Poland became the first of the European economies in transition to achieve economic growth: GDP increased by an estimated 2.6 per cent. Parts of industry remained in the doldrums, but others, especially those dominated by smaller companies, showed signs of learning how to operate in a market environment. Real wages decreased by some 3 per cent while industry labour productivity increased by 13 per cent. The construction, trade and service sectors had already started to recover in 1991. Unemployment continued to increase, though at a somewhat slower rate; by December 1992, it

Figure 3.1
Macroeconomic Indicators

Industrial Production and Real Wages
(Indices, averages for 1989 = 100)

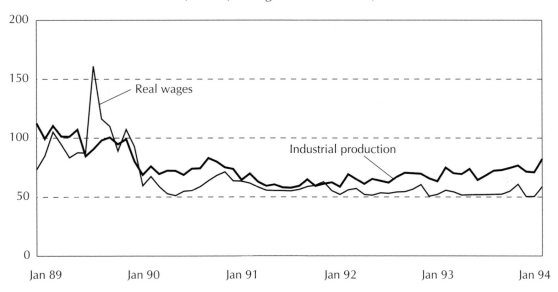

Note: "Real Wages" are represented by earnings in "material branches and municipalities" deflated by the consumer price index.

Consumer Price Changes, Registered Unemployment
(%)

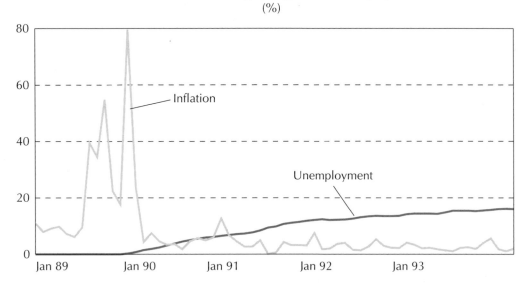

Sources: OCDE, Short-Term Economic Indicators

amounted to 13.3 per cent of Poland's registered working population. While private consumption stagnated, public consumption grew strongly, and though total capital formation continued to decline, gross fixed investment started to pick up. Consumer prices increased by 43 per cent. Energy price increases and tax changes accounted for about one-sixth of this rise.

The budget outcome for 1992 was a deficit equivalent to 6 per cent of GDP. A change of government caused delays in the economic policy decision making process – the Suchocka administration's budget was accepted by the Sejm only in June.

Hard currency exports increased by about 10 per cent and imports by 6 per cent in 1992, resulting in a hard currency trade surplus of around US$ 0.5 billion and contributing to a current account deficit of about US$ 0.3 billion.

Poland's economic recovery gained strength in 1993. Industrial sales continued to pick up, contributing to growth in GDP of 3.8 per cent. The unemployment rate reached 16 per cent. Real wages declined slightly while labour productivity in industry improved by 9.6 per cent. Consumption increased by 4-5 per cent and gross fixed investments by nearly 3 per cent. Inflation was 35 per cent.

The budget for 1993 was intended to stabilise the deficit in nominal terms. A large number of measures, mainly on the income side, were put in place. A 6 per cent surcharge on imports was introduced, the narrowly based turnover tax was replaced with VAT and the indexation of pensions was cut by 9 per cent. As a result, the deficit fell to 2.8 per cent of GDP.

Declining hard currency exports and surging hard currency imports combined to produce a hard currency trade deficit of US$ 2.3 billion and a current account deficit of the same order of magnitude. Imports increased by nearly 18 per cent, partly because of temporary excess demand and expectations of tax and exchange rate adjustments, but also as a reflection of changes in the structure of the economy. Financing the current account deficit posed no major problems: Poland's hard currency and gold reserves declined by no more than US$ 0.5 billion during 1993. Since then, the Government has managed to complete the restructuring of its foreign debt – in March 1994 the country got a deal with its London Club creditors giving it a 42.5 per cent reduction on its US$ 13.2 billion bank debt and stretching repayments over 30 years.

The recovery continued at an even faster pace, and became more broadly based, in 1994. GDP increased by an estimated 5 per cent in real terms.

Investments were up by 11 per cent in January-June (year-on-year) while industrial sales by private companies jumped by 37 per cent. Labour productivity levels improved considerably. Exports increased by about 24 per cent and imports by some 12 per cent from 1993 to 1994, leading to a fall in the trade deficit from US$ 2.3 billion in the former year to about US$ 0.8 billion in the latter. Inflation did not come down very much, however; consumer prices rose by about 32 per cent in 1994.

The excess wage tax (the popiwek) lapsed at the end of March 1994. Wage controls were reintroduced in July, but only for the remainder of the year. Enterprises that are current on their tax and social security payments will be allowed to choose between:

- entering into a management contract, including permissible wage increase clauses, with their so-called founding body in the administration;

- entering into an agreement with the local tax chamber specifying wage limits;

- continuing to work with the popiwek as it was practised in 1993-94, i.e. with a link between the expected ratio of gross profits to wages and permissible wage increases;

- continuing to work with a modified version of the original system whereby the so-called Tripartite Commission, established in 1993, decides on permissible wage increases.

Enterprises in arrears on their tax or social security payments must continue with the fourth option.

There were worries about the consequences of abolishing wage controls, but after a jump of 15 per cent in March, nominal wages resumed their gently increasing trend; real wages and salaries declined by 1.4 per cent in the first half of 1994.

Unemployment appears to have levelled off at some 16.5 per cent. This is cold comfort, however, to the worst hit regions and population groups. Small farmers who used to support their incomes by working part time in industry have emerged as the biggest problem group. Most of them have lost their jobs outside their farms and are finding it impossible to compete in the markets for agricultural produce.

The Government had to tighten its monetary policies during 1994 as large inflows of capital led to a faster than expected accumulation of reserves. The budget deficit turned out to be somewhat smaller than forecast as expenditure remained on target while revenue exceeded expectations.

STABILISATION PROBLEMS AND CHALLENGES

Steadfastly adhering to stabilisation objectives, the post-1989 Polish governments have come a long way towards creating a foundation for sustainable economic growth. Current trends are, on balance, encouraging. However, it will take continued efforts to secure what has been achieved and continue the recovery.

Inflation has been brought down to a level where it easily gets stuck, according to other countries' experiences. The budget deficit, although not very big relative to GDP by international standards, remains a point of political contention.

The Government is under heavy pressure to deal with the social costs of the transition to a market economy. Social security expenditures are set to increase further. However, if financed by borrowing on market terms, incremental expenditures may make the Government's debt burden unsustainable. Its domestic debt amounted at the end of 1993 to more than Zl 350 trillion or 23 per cent of GDP. Poland's gross foreign debt at the time was estimated at close to US$ 44 billion; the interest payments on this debt will amount to about US$ 1.2 billion a year for several years. The Government's total debt service in 1994, an estimated Zl 103 trillion, was more than one-fifth of total budget expenditures in 1993.

In the view of the OECD, Polish government spending needs a thorough restructuring. The present structure does not appear to support growth. The existing pension system is unsustainable beyond the end of the decade. Infrastructure investment remains too low. Changing policies in this area presupposes, however, that suitable regulatory mechanisms are in place. Poland's tax system has been restructured, but it is now characterised by high marginal rates of both personal and corporate tax, which may encourage distortionary behaviour on the part of taxpayers. The Government should consider several measures,

particularly a discontinuation of double taxation of dividends, better inflation adjustment for enterprises and a lowering of taxes on long term capital gains relative to taxes of income.

In the area of monetary policy, the OECD recommends consideration of more ambitious inflation targets. Anti-inflationary policies may lose their credibility if they appear to be based on a very gradualist approach. A tightening of targets would require, among other things, reducing the pre-announced crawling devaluation of the zloty, ending the practice of unannounced devaluations, maintaining positive real interest rates on zloty deposits and reducing the budget deficit further.

Table 3.1
Projections for the Polish Economy
(% except where noted)

	1994	1995	1996
Inflation	32.2	23.0	18.0
GDP growth	5.0	5.5	5.0
Export growth (in foreign currency)	24.0	15.0	12.0
Import growth (in foreign currency)	12.0	14.0	14.0
State budget deficit/GDP	2.7	3.3	2.5
Registered unemployment	16.2	15.5	15.0
Current account (billion US$)	-0.9	-0.9	-1.4

Source: OECD

STRUCTURAL CHANGE

The emphasis given to structural reform by the post-1989 Polish governments has varied, reflecting difficulties in maintaining consensus about the way forward. Some changes in the rules of the game have been implemented quickly and firmly. Other reforms have proceeded much more slowly than anticipated.

Most prices, and the bulk of Poland's foreign trade, were liberalised in early 1990. The ability to acquire and dispose of property, and freedom of entry into most activities, were institutionalised at the same time. These changes have led to an explosive growth in the number of private

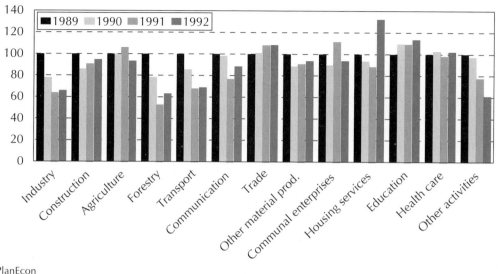

Figure 3.2
Output Changes by Sector
(Index 1989 = 100)

Legend: 1989, 1990, 1991, 1992

Categories: Industry, Construction, Agriculture, Forestry, Transport, Communication, Trade, Other material prod., Communal enterprises, Housing services, Education, Health care, Other activities

Source: PlanEcon

companies, which now account for more than half of GDP and almost 60 per cent of total employment.

As a consequence of the introduction of market forces and private ownership on a large scale, there has been a reallocation of resources, mainly from industry to trade and services.

The relative positions of the individual subsectors and branches of the industry sector have changed too. As shown in table 3.2, metallurgy and engineering have lost much more ground than, for instance, the fuel and energy industries.

Poland is approaching the OECD countries in terms of some aspects of its economic structure, but still has a long way to go.

The post-1989 governments have by and large limited themselves to pursuing indicative industry policies, in spite of calls from hard-pressed industries and their representatives in the state bureaucracy for a more activist role. The governments have initiated studies and moved on certain sector or branch organisation issues, usually following a strategy of consolidating large numbers of firms into a few holding companies (the chapters on the coal, electricity and oil industries provide examples). In this way possibilities have been created for stronger firms to cross-subsidise weaker ones. Direct funding

requirements have been modest, and politicians have been relieved at least temporarily of the burden of having to close unviable entities.

In some areas later governments have moderated the Mazowiecki Government's liberalisation measures. In 1990, Poland had one of the world's most open foreign trade regimes. Since then,

Table 3.2
**Individual Industries' Shares
of Total Industrial Production**
(%)

	1985	1990	1993
Fuel and energy	14.6	15.6	21.8
Metallurgy	9.4	12.5	6.9
Engineering	25.0	24.6	20.8
Chemicals	8.6	9.8	9.0
Construction materials	3.8	4.1	4.1
Wood and paper	4.3	4.9	5.7
Light industry	11.5	7.9	6.9
Food	20.5	18.6	22.8
Other industry	2.3	2.0	2.0
Total	**100.0**	**100.0**	**100.0**

Source: Economist Intelligence Unit

however, various import restrictions suspended by the Mazowiecki Government – mostly tariffs, but also some quota arrangements – have been reactivated to support domestic industries (the oil sector is an example). In other cases it has proved more difficult than anticipated to remove the remnants of the pre-1990 regimes, e.g. to free on schedule those prices that remained under government control. Moreover, because of the growth in unemployment, extra social safety net support is being provided. However, it remains a government tenet that companies will have to rely mainly on their own resources and access to private financial sources for investments and technical restructuring.

The Government expects foreign direct investment inflows to underpin Polish enterprises' restructuring efforts and create jobs. Inflows have so far fallen short of expectations. During 1989-93 they totalled about US$ 1 billion. Investors' interest picked up towards the end of this period; nearly US$ 600 million arrived in 1993. From 1989 to 1992, most foreign investments were the result of purchases by foreign firms of privatised enterprises, but since 1993 greenfield investments have become more significant. Surveys show that foreign investors have been concerned mainly about increases in taxes and customs duties, anti-competitive behaviour, and the bureaucracy and other problems surrounding the acquisition of land.

While the Government has generated sector plans and initiated the establishment of holding companies, the Anti-Monopoly Office has tried to identify and remove obstacles to competition. Occasionally it and the Government have been at loggerheads. In some government restructuring plans, competition has been treated as a marginal issue. The Anti-Monopoly Office is not empowered to override government policies, but has tried to influence government thinking on rules and mechanisms in securing competition.

Regarding enterprises' attitudes and behaviour, there has been a marked improvement in financial discipline. In general, state owned enterprises have stopped expecting to be bailed out by the Government. There is a widespread realisation that the era of cheap, automatically granted credit is over. The level of non-performing loans held by banks has stabilised. Moreover, inter-enterprise credit has not increased abnormally and firms are now very active in seeking payment from each other. Running counter to these developments, tax arrears have increased. Especially some large electronics, mining, shipbuilding and steel enterprises are trying to force subsidies out of the state in this way.

Financial discipline is only one characteristic of a functioning market economy, however, and in several important areas, the post-1989 Polish governments have not progressed as rapidly as most local and foreign observers thought possible four or five years ago. Above all, it has proved much more difficult and time consuming than expected to turn state owned firms into private companies. Interest groups have been well organised and effective, and the political consensus in key policy areas has been fragile.

A Ministry of Privatisation has been established, but a few particularly complicated or sensitive processes involving commercialisation and restructuring as well as privatisation are conducted by other government bodies. The MoIT is charged with developing new organisational forms and ownership and management relations for the coal and gas industries. An interministerial committee is deciding on the transformation of the downstream oil business.

All state owned enterprises "belong" to so-called founding bodies, most of which are in the MoIT. Privatisation is to be voluntary, not forced upon either managers or workers. The privatisation of an enterprise should thus start with a request from its director and workers.

There are many possible routes to privatisation. One observer[1] suggests that what has happened and is happening in Poland should be classified in the following way:

1) *Self-transformation* of the co-operative sector by the removal of both central bureaucracy and central allocation of inputs.

2) *Small privatisation* through the sale or leasing of small portions of state-owned assets, e.g. shops.

3) *Medium-sized privatisation* involving small to medium-sized state enterprises, using either

---

1. Stanislaw Gomulka: "Poland: Glass Half Full", in Richard Portes (ed.): Economic Transformation in Central Europe: A Progress Report, London 1993.

the Act of Privatisation of State Enterprises – essentially employee and/or management buy-outs, a popular means of "privatisation from below" – or liquidation under the State Enterprise Act, the enterprises being closed and their assets auctioned off.

4) *Classic privatisation* along western lines through auctions of shares with special purchase rights reserved for employees, and sales to foreign investors.

5) *Mass privatisation* through the allocation of 60 per cent of the shares in large enterprises to some 15 "National Investment Funds", which are essentially investment trusts, and then the distribution for nominal fees of the shares in these funds among a large number of small investors. The remaining 40 per cent of the shares would be divided between the Treasury (30 per cent) and employees (10 per cent).

6) *Organic or growth privatisation* through the natural contraction of the state sector and the organic growth of the private sector under the new, competitive conditions.

Routes 1 and 2 were put into effect immediately after the Solidarity-led coalition assumed power in September 1989. They became the most effective means of privatisation in 1990. Route 3 came to prominence in 1991, involving about 400 enterprises through the Act of Privatisation and 500 enterprises through liquidation; there are about 6 000 enterprises in this size category. Route 4, the "British approach", proved very time consuming as it involved careful valuation of each enterprise; it has been used for only a few privatisations. These, however, have underpinned the establishment of a share market and a stock exchange. Route 5 has taken some time to open, but looks set to become an important vehicle for further privatisation of medium-sized companies. Route 6 has been functioning all along, which is why the private sector has shown as much dynamism as it has.

Had it not been for the emergence of new private companies, the status after five years of trying to privatise the bulk of the Polish economy would have been far from satisfying, not only because so few of the bigger state enterprises have been affected but also because not all of those ownership changes that have taken place have

The Booming Polish Stock Market

The Polish stock market rose to fame during 1993 when the Warsaw Stock Exchange (WSE) index increased twelvefold. In 1991 when the WSE was established, shares worth Zl 0.3 billion were bought and sold. In 1992 the turnover amounted to Zl 2.3 trillion and in 1993 it was Zl 77.5 trillion. The impetus for the 1993 boom came from two sources. One was a dip in domestic bank interest rates, which prompted savers to find a new home for their money. The other was a surge in foreign investors' appetite for shares in the now 23 listed companies.

Undaunted by the September 1993 elections, investors continued to flock to the WSE. However, events during 1994 have illustrated the problems of staying on track for a small market packed with more or less inexperienced players.

When shares in Bank Slasky were offered for sale, they were quoted at 13 times their nominal subscription value. Then it turned out that most of the 800 000 Poles who had applied for the shares were unable to trade them because of long delays in getting shares registered. Practically the only shareholders able to sell were the bank's employees.

Nonetheless the WSE index continued to increase until 11 April, when confidence suddenly evaporated and share prices plummeted to their end-December level. Observers had expected such an adjustment, as it was felt that price-earnings ratios had become unsustainable.

These setbacks do not spell the end of the Polish stock market. On the contrary, the number of listed companies increased strongly during 1994. Through 1993 most of the capital raised on the exchange went straight to the state Treasury; now capital is raised through share issues to the benefit of the companies themselves. Polish authorities preparing further bank privatisation will anchor share prices to avoid another Bank Slasky affair.

The Polish Securities Commission has a difficult task safeguarding the interests of investors largely unfamiliar with shares and share trading and with the companies they are buying into, but the WSE looks set to play an increasingly important role in channelling savings to formerly state owned companies in need of investment funds.

led to the desired changes in governance and management conduct.

So far no part of any energy/fuel industry has been privatised. However, some enterprises have been incorporated with the intent of making shares available to the private sector later, others are scheduled to be incorporated and eventually privatised, and "route 6" has been opened for entrepreneurs interested in establishing themselves as wholesalers and/or retailers of oil products. Finally, private companies are providing services to the state owned energy producing, exporting, importing, transmitting and distributing companies, as shown in later chapters.

As it appears that the Government will be stuck with a large number of enterprises – and thus with the responsibility for the functioning of large segments of the Polish economy – for quite some time, it has to give very high priority to the task of making these enterprises function as efficiently as possible. And, piece by piece, over the course of 1992-94 a wide ranging policy package was developed.

One early measure was the launching of an enterprise debt restructuring programme. The idea was that state owned enterprise debt should be restructured in a decentralised manner through negotiations between the enterprises and their bank creditors. The programme instructs the banks to monitor the business plans and performance of their indebted clients, i.e. to fulfil some of the functions of a true owner. However, it affects only a limited number of large state owned enterprises, and it represents only a very partial solution to the governance problem even for those enterprises. In the Polish context an improvement in governance requires a clarification of management responsibilities and a clearly defined route to privatisation, as uncertainties in this area have contributed to poor corporate performance.

The Suchocka Government's response was the Pact on State Owned Enterprises. Recognising the powers of the Employee Councils to obstruct any effort to make managers change their attitudes and behaviour, the pact aimed at giving workers sufficient interest in their enterprise's future privatisation that they would refrain from wage maximising practices and decapitalisation. Against giving up some influence in their as yet state owned enterprise, workers would be guaranteed

free shares and a role in the supervision of the future private company.

According to the Government's proposal, workers and managers would have to decide on the mechanics of the privatisation no more than six months after adopting the pact. Regardless of the choice of method, workers would acquire 15 per cent of shares free of charge, and be guaranteed a third of the seats on the future private company's supervisory board. If the parties failed to agree on a privatisation programme, the enterprise would be commercialised compulsorily.

The pact was finalised in early 1993, but Poland's legislators had not managed to pass much of the legal framework for its implementation when the Sejm was dissolved a few months later. The Parliament elected in September 1993 has returned to the issue. In June 1994 the Pawlak Government adopted a policy document – "Strategy for Poland" – which, however, differs in some respects from the pact.

Successive governments have pursued a policy of incorporating state owned enterprises. Turning an enterprise into a state owned joint stock company involves placing it under commercial law, dissolving its Employee Council and strengthening its directors' incentives and authority to act responsibly, in the hope of providing a better basis for any restructuring that may be needed prior to privatisation. This policy, which has embraced various energy enterprises, has now been elevated to medium term strategy: the Government envisages the compulsory incorporation of around 1 000 enterprises and the establishment of a regionalised state Treasury to oversee them.

There are certain problems with this strategy, the most fundamental of which is that it does not represent a solution to the problem of governance, as the state will hardly be able to fulfil the functions of a true owner. The regionalised Treasury would have to be non-political and would need considerable resources to be able to monitor and eventually correct the business plans and performances of its mass of companies. Other countries' experiences do not indicate that such government bodies are easily established. Nor are Poland's own experiences very encouraging; there is no convincing evidence that the incorporations that have taken place have improved enterprise performance.

Moreover, by de-emphasising early privatisation the proposal does not help resolve the key problem facing enterprises: uncertainty about their future status. And by suggesting that all enterprises should be treated the same way, even though many are dragging their feet while others have shown a capacity to adapt, the Government risks bringing positive developments to a halt.

RESEARCH AND DEVELOPMENT

Basic and applied research is carried out mainly by:

- laboratories subordinated to the Polish Academy of Sciences (PAN);

- universities and high schools;

- some 300 specialised research centres attached to ministries, which account for about 60 per cent of total public research [2].

Some rationalisation of the structure of institutions has taken place, and scientific projects are selected and funded differently today than in communist times.

Formerly, the Government allocated funds to basic research mainly through PAN and the Ministry of Science, Higher Education and Technology, and to applied research through the other ministries. This structure led to duplication of efforts, losses of economy of scale, low efficiency and wasted resources. It did little to foster co-operation between researchers and industry, encourage researchers to develop solutions to practical problems or provide for uptake of new technology.

In January 1991, a new body – the State Committee for Scientific Research (KBN) – was

---

2. The MoIT, for instance, controls 60 "scientific and research" institutions, three central laboratories and 64 R&D units.

established. KBN has a hierarchical structure. At the top there is a committee charged with laying down a science policy for Poland and supervising the work of the rest of the organisation. Under this committee are two commissions – one for basic research, the other for applied – responsible for preparing a framework budget and establishing criteria for its use. These commissions are sub-divided into a total of 12 groups dealing with different sciences and economic sectors and branches, and charged with working out detailed budgets, assessing applications from institutions and individual researchers, allocating money and checking on research results. KBN has a staff of about 230 full time employees.

KBN supports science by i) providing core funds for statutory R&D activities to selected research establishments; ii) supporting investments in R&D infrastructure such as buildings and equipment; iii) channelling research funds to institutions and individual researchers on the basis of project proposals and applications; iv) subsidising R&D programmes deemed to be of national importance; v) subsidising international scientific and technological co-operation under inter-governmental agreements; and vi) subsidising support activities such as technology information campaigns. In 1993, the funding of statutory R&D activities accounted for nearly 45 per cent of KBN's total funding. The share of research grants in KBN's outlays was 17.7 per cent while those of investments in infrastructure, subsidies for programmes of national importance and subsidies for support activities were 11-13 per cent each. International co-operation accounted for 2 per cent of the total.

KBN's research priorities, in addition to quality, are that projects should meet observed societal needs so that the results may be used, that links between sciences should be strengthened and that private co-financing by parties interested in the results should be forthcoming.

The setting up of KBN implied three major reforms:

- The state financing of scientific work was completely centralised; PAN and the ministries no longer have anything to do with the funding of their own researchers.

- The scientific community was given consider-able say over the allocation of research money –12 of the 19 members of the top committee and 58 of the 75 members of the two commissions are scientists elected by their colleagues [3].

- Competition for funds, and standardised, strictly scientific (as opposed to political and ideological) criteria for evaluating applications, were introduced. Institutions have been classified into four groups – using an elaborate system of bibliometric indicators and such criteria as the number of scientific degrees awarded – entitled to state funds to very different degrees.

These reforms have not gone down equally well with everybody involved. There is much resentment of the new system in the institutions that no longer allocate research money, and doubts about its long run viability also exist among KBN officials.

The OECD holds that radical reform was needed, and that the new system represents major improvements over the old one – but also that parts of it should be considered transition arrangements. There are strong arguments for re-establishing KBN as a policy making body and setting up a limited number of research councils to manage funds; under present circumstances the KBN leadership may be distracted from its strategic tasks by its executive ones. There are also dangers inherent in having a body dominated by scientists elected by fellow scientists to decide on how to spend limited funds; narrow professional interests, conservatism and egalitarianism may creep in and result in biased decision making and an unwillingness to concentrate resources as forcefully as appears necessary.

Financial constraints have tightened progressively since reforms were introduced. In nominal terms, public spending on R&D increased from Zl 6.13 billion in 1991 to Zl 8.93 billion in 1993, i.e. by 46 per cent; but as prices rose by more than 90 per cent from the end of 1991 to the end of 1993, real spending declined by nearly one-fourth, and as a proportion of GDP it fell from 0.75 per cent to 0.58 per cent. Gross domestic spending on R&D – budgeted spending plus some

3. All holders of Ph.D. degrees are qualified to vote; in practice, university professors make up 80 per cent of the electorate.

extrabudgetary and private money – has dropped from 1.5 per cent of GDP in 1985 to 0.75-0.8 per cent today.

The 1994 R&D budget amounted to Zl 11.6 billion, and spending plans for 1995 add up to Zl 14.36 billion. Nominal outlays to science are intended to increase slightly ahead of inflation. The figures indicate a will to stop the decline in the research funding/GDP ratio, but do not promise an immediate reversal of trends.

Polish authorities hope that the research centres attached to the ministries will be able to fund themselves to an increasing extent by selling their services to industry. For the time being, however, few Polish companies can afford to buy R&D in the market. Some of the best Polish research institutions have managed to attract foreign customers, but as the bulk of the institutions focus on issues of limited interest abroad or are unable to compete with consultants from other countries, this is unlikely to become a general solution to the sector's financing problems.

Like other funds, research funds are used more efficiently now than before. At the same time, however, Poland needs a dynamic scientific community much more now than when the country led a sheltered life within the CMEA. The OECD finds the present level of spending on R&D far too low for an industrialised country the size of Poland. Particularly disturbing are the brain drain problems of the country's research institutes. The OECD advises the Government to give higher priority to science, take a closer look at the salary levels of researchers and consider other incentives to make the best researchers stay in their laboratories instead of moving to industry or trying their luck abroad.

The most important institutions involved in energy related R&D are:

- the Institute of Fluid-flow Machinery, Gdansk (reporting to PAN);

- the Departments of Electrical and Mechanical Engineering at the Technical Universities of Warsaw, Gdansk, Gliwice, Lodz and Wroklaw;

- the Institute of Energy, Warsaw (reporting to MoIT);

Table 3.3
Composition of Public Spending on Energy Related Research, 1993 and 1994
(%)

	1993	1994
Core funding for statutory activities	28.2	35.7
Research grants proposed by applicants	43.5	35.8
Targeted projects co-financed by industry	28.3	18.4
R&D programmes of national importance		10.1
Total	**100.0**	**100.0**

Source: Jacek Marecki, Technical University of Gdansk

- the Institute of Power Engineering, Warsaw (reporting to MoIT);

- the Institute of Atomic Energy, Warsaw (reporting to MoIT);

- the Institute of the Oil and Gas Industry, Krakow (reporting to MoIT);

- the Central Institute of Mining, Katowice (reporting to MoIT).

Among the KBN groups, the most interesting from an energy point of view are the Group for Electrical and Power Engineering and the Group for Mining, Geodesy and Transport under the Commission for Applied Research.

In 1993 KBN allocated Zl 77.7 billion (US$ 3.8 billion at an exchange rate of Zl 20 500/US$) to energy related research. In 1994 the figure was Zl 90 billion (US$ 3.9 billion at a rate of Zl 23 000 to the dollar). Table 3.3 shows how the money was allocated.

Generally, priority is given to projects that may enhance the international competitiveness of Polish industry, raise the living standard in Poland and contribute to the protection of the environment. More specifically, research areas are: upgrading and rehabilitating existing coal-fired power plants; integrating the electric power system with the UCPTE system; developing new baseload power plants with a combined gas-steam cycle; increasing the share of co-generation in district heating systems; and improving the thermal performance of buildings to reduce heat loss.

CHAPTER 4

ENERGY BALANCE DEVELOPMENTS

RECENT CHANGES IN TPES, TFC AND ENERGY BALANCE OF TRADE

Poland's **total primary energy supply** increased by averages of 8.2 per cent a year during the 1950s, 4.7 per cent a year during the 1960s and 4.2 per cent a year during the 1970s. As supply was based on coal produced domestically and oil and gas imported from Russia at subsidised prices, the country's energy consumption habits were not strongly affected by the world oil price shocks of 1973-74 and 1979-80. Pressure for structural changes and energy efficiency improvements started to build only when the CMEA trading area fell apart and Russia started to align its fuel export prices to former allies with world market prices. The income elasticity of Poland's energy use is only now beginning to decline.

It was thus not because of price developments that TPES fell by some 8 per cent in 1981, but because of political unrest following the emergence of Solidarity, culminating with the Jaruzelski take-over and leading to a dip in economic activity. Growth rates picked up towards the middle of the decade, but in 1988 the level of political tension increased again, and the economy started to slide: the system of central planning was rapidly deteriorating and there was not yet any adequate institutional, legal and mental framework for its replacement by market mechanisms. In 1989 TPES dropped by 4.5 per cent, and in 1990 – the year of economic "shock therapy" – it plummeted by 18 per cent. The next two years saw further TPES declines of 1.6 per cent and 1.0 per cent, but in 1993, when the economy started to pick up, energy use increased by an estimated 1.6 per cent. Preliminary data for the first half of 1994 show a drop in total energy use of a little over 4 per cent (year-on-year) despite continued growth in GDP, presumably reflecting a mixture of random weather and temperature fluctuations and the fact that the potential for energy savings in the Polish economy is beginning to be realised.

The energy intensity of the Polish economy fell from an estimated 2.11 toe per 1987 US$ 1 000 in 1985 to an estimated 1.69 toe per 1987 US$ 1 000 in 1993 [1], that is by a total of 20 per cent or an average of almost 3 per cent a year.

Most of the decline took place in 1988-90. As energy use in OECD Europe was 0.29 toe per unit of GDP in 1985 and an estimated 0.25 toe per unit of GDP in 1993, Poland gives the appearance of having used 7.3 times more energy than western Europe to produce one unit of GDP at the beginning of this period, and 6.8 times more at the end of it. However, as Poland's GDP may be under-reported and as the use of official exchange rates for international energy intensity comparisons is debatable, it is a more widely held assumption that Poland's energy use per unit of GDP is two to three times higher than that of OECD Europe.

---

1. Zlotys converted to US$ at official exchange rates.

Figure 4.1
Total Primary Energy Supply, 1988-93
(Mtoe)

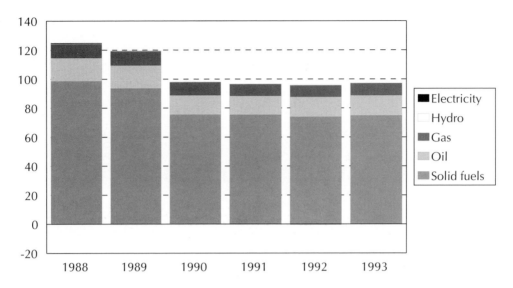

Source: CIE, IEA Secretariat

Table 4.1
Changes in Energy Use, First Half 1993 to First Half 1994
(Mtoe, %)

	Energy use first half 1993 (Mtoe)	Energy use first half 1994 (Mtoe)	Change (%)
Total	**49.34**	**47.29**	**-4.2**
Solid fuels	38.3	36.24	-5.4
Liquid fuels	6.87	6.93	+0.9
Gaseous fuels	4.24	4.13	-2.6
Hydropower	0.09	0.10	11.1
Other electricity	-0.16	-0.11	-31.3

Source: CIE

In 1985, Poland's energy use per capita was about 20 per cent higher than that of OECD Europe. In 1990, however, the relationship was reversed, and in 1993 Poland was about 8 per cent below OECD Europe in this respect.

Poland's primary energy supply has always been dominated by coal. In the early 1970s the solid fuels share in TPES was 80-82 per cent, in 1988 it was about 79 per cent and in 1993 it was an estimated 77 per cent. All of Poland's major power plants burn hard coal or lignite, the district heating systems are based mainly on coal, and industry, service enterprises and households use coal directly. The oil share has increased from 11-12 per cent in the early 1970s to 13 per cent in 1988 and 14.6 per cent in 1993, reflecting fairly rapid growth – albeit from a small base – in gasoline and diesel transportation. The gas share has increased from 6 per cent in 1971 to 7.7 per cent in 1988 and an estimated 8.4 per cent in 1993 due to fairly rapid growth in the distribution pipeline network and household gas use. Poland does not have nuclear power plants and hydroelectricity production amounts to only a few tenths of a per cent of TPES. The structure of

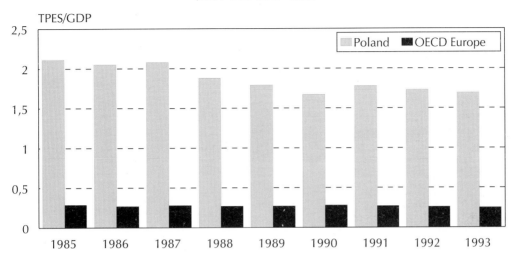

Figure 4.2
Energy Intensity Developments, 1985-93
(toe/1 000 1987 US$)

Based on of official TPES and GDP figures and official exchange rates.

Source: IEA Secretariat

Poland's primary energy supply is thus very different from that of OECD Europe.

The fuel structure of Poland's **total final energy consumption** has changed slightly more than the corresponding structure of TPES. The share of coal in TFC declined from 52 per cent in 1971 to about 40 per cent in 1989 and 36 per cent in 1993, indicating that the prominence of coal in TPES is underpinned mainly by the rigidity of the structure of the electricity and heat industries' fuel supplies. The share of electricity increased from 7 per cent in 1971 to 12.6 per cent in 1990; since then it has declined by one percentage point. The share of

---

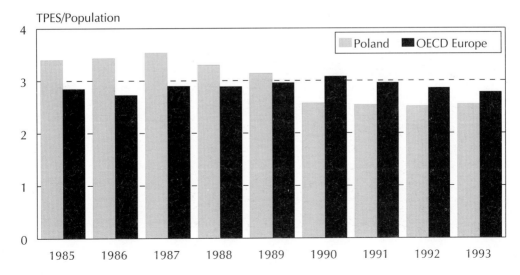

Figure 4.3
Energy Use per Capita, 1985-93
(toe/capita)

Source: IEA Secretariat

heat has held steady at 22-25 per cent throughout this period of more than two decades, reflecting the importance of heat in the Polish TFC picture and the fact that household energy use fluctuates less with overall economic conditions than does the productive sectors' energy use. The oil share increased from 13 per cent in 1971 to 17.2 per cent in 1989 and 18.6 per cent in 1993. The gas share increased from about 7 per cent in 1971 to almost 12 per cent in 1990 before starting to decline to an estimated 9.6 per cent in 1993; industrial gas consumption fell by around 50 per cent from 1986 to 1993, and since 1990 this trend has more than outweighed the continued growth in household gas use.

Industry's share in TFC has come down from 47 per cent in 1971 to 37.5 per cent in 1988 and 32.6 per cent in 1993, i.e. to the present level of OECD Europe. Industrial energy use fell by more than 30 per cent from 1989 to 1992. The branch structure of industry's energy consumption has changed somewhat since Poland embarked on its transformation to a market economy, but there are as yet only weak and inconsistent signs of a reallocation of energy resources from heavy industry to the lighter, consumer goods oriented branches. The transport sector's share in TFC increased from about 11 per cent in 1989 to 13.4 per cent in 1993.

The sectoral composition of Poland's TFC deviates from that of OECD Europe with respect to the shares of road transportation, the residential sector and "other sectors". Driving accounts for a much higher share of Poland's TFC today than it did 20 years ago, but it is still markedly less important, from a fuel use perspective, in Poland than in OECD Europe. Although growing rapidly, Poland's fleet of private cars is still small compared to the size of the population. Truck transportation is increasing as a percentage of total goods transport as a result of structural changes in the economy and high tariffs and loading, reloading and unloading costs for rail, but again, the base is comparatively small. Residential energy use is also much less important, in relative terms, than in OECD Europe; while Poles' apartments and heating systems are less energy efficient, housing units are smaller and appliances scarcer than in western Europe, and the latter factors more than outweigh the former. The share of "other sectors" is bigger in Poland than in OECD Europe mainly because the agricultural sector, public administration and army are larger and less energy efficient.

In terms of its **energy balance of trade,** Poland moved from a surplus of about 9 million tonnes of oil equivalent (Mtoe) in 1973, then corresponding to some 9.5 per cent of TPES, to a deficit of

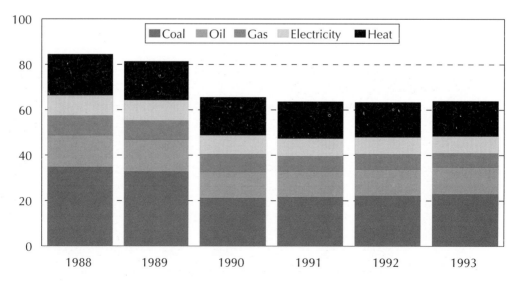

Figure 4.4
Total Final Comsumption, 1988-93
(Mtoe)

Sources: CIE, IEA Secretariat

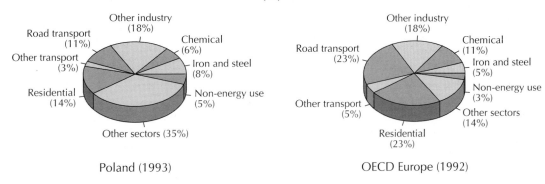

Figure 4.5
TFC Structure by End-use Sector
(%)

Poland (1993)

OECD Europe (1992)

Sources: CIE, IEA Secretariat

3.9 Mtoe in 1993, corresponding to about 4 per cent of TPES. The balance showed a declining surplus through the 1970s, turned to an 11.2 Mtoe deficit in 1981, increased towards zero in 1983-85 but worsened to a deficit of 5.2 mtoe in 1987. Since then the deficit has moved more or less in parallel with TPES, giving a stable ratio of net imports to total supply. However, data for the first half of 1994 show a small surplus of about 0.3 Mtoe on the energy balance of trade.

Poland is a significant net exporter of coal, but depends on imports for nearly all of its oil and almost 60 per cent of its gas. The hard coal industry has seen its net exports dwindle from almost 25 Mtoe in 1979 to about 15 Mtoe in 1993, but the net exports to production ratio has been relatively stable at around one-fifth. Poland's net crude oil and refined product imports doubled during the 1970s, but declined in the early 1980s and again in the early 1990s, and although they

Figure 4.6
Net Energy Exports, 1971-93
(Mtoe)

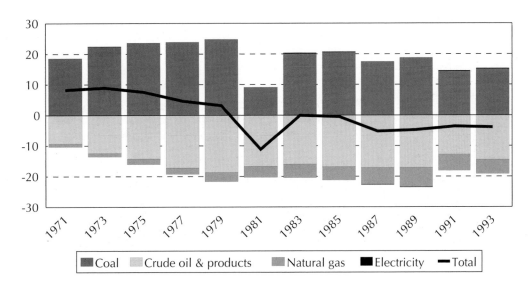

Sources: CIE, IEA secretariat

increased by 9 per cent in 1992 and by 3 per cent in 1993, they were still far below their 1979 peak. Net gas imports increased by more than 400 per cent from 1971 to 1989, but have since declined by 26 per cent. Poland's trade in electricity has never been very significant relative to its power production and consumption and does not exhibit any clear trend; in 1993 the country exported about 0.7 Mtoe of electricity and imported about 0.5 Mtoe, leaving it with a surplus corresponding to less than 3 per cent of its final electricity consumption.

FUTURE ENERGY CONSUMPTION

Driving Forces

Poland's future energy consumption will as a matter of definition depend on the rate of growth in the economy and the rate of decline in energy intensity. The latter variable will in turn reflect changes in the structure of the economy and in the energy efficiency levels of individual sectors and industries.

These driving forces may be interlinked in that high economic growth reflecting a high level of investment will facilitate a reallocation of resources from more to less energy intensive activities and a replacement of less energy efficient processes, equipment and buildings in the expanding sectors. The income elasticity of energy demand is not only as a general rule lower in more developed economies than in less developed ones, but it may also vary inversely with the pace of economic growth in one economy.

The Government may strengthen this link, which tends to dampen the effects of economic growth on energy consumption, through its investment and income tax policies and by means of direct regulation. The income elasticity of energy demand can hardly be made zero or negative, though, not even in a country like Poland where the potentials for structural change and "autonomous" – i.e. non-price driven – energy efficiency improvements are huge.

Poland's energy consumption could grow at different rates under the same assumptions on economic growth and on public investment,

income tax and regulatory policies depending on how domestic energy prices develop and on the price elasticity of energy demand. The latter may vary from zero, when consumers are not billed according to their energy use or are unable to respond to price signals by regulating their energy use, to significant negative figures. International energy price developments, the Polish Government's exchange rate policies and above all its policies on domestic energy prices and metering and billing systems will thus exert a strong influence on the country's future energy consumption.

Another important issue is how fast economic developments and import, tax and other government policies allow the population to adopt western lifestyles, e.g. in the area of private transport and in the use of appliances.

Provided that the Government carries on with economic reforms in general, and with price liberalisation and the encouragement of competition in particular, the energy intensity of the Polish economy will come down. Businesses exposed to international competition will be forced to lower their input use per unit of output towards the levels of their foreign competitors. Other sectors will be enticed by domestic competition, and perhaps by tax incentives and direct regulation in the form of standards, to follow suit. The process may be slow, however, as buildings and many capital goods have long lifetimes.

With structural change and substitution processes related to price and convenience premiums, the structure of Poland's TPES will approach that of OECD Europe. All parties, including the Polish coal industry, see the share of coal in TPES declining. With respect to structural change, there is reason to believe that industry will continue to lose ground to transport and commercial services. Privately owned cars will become even more widespread, and as more roads and service stations are built, driving distances will increase. The number of commercial vehicles will probably increase too, as domestic and international trade picks up. These factors point to relatively high rates of growth in consumption of motor fuels. The supply of commercial services is still embryonic compared with the situation in the west, pointing to relatively rapid growth in electricity use. Heavy industry will probably contract more than light industry, with additional declines in coal use as a result. Businesses and households will switch from coal to electricity and gas when relative prices, adjusted for the cleanliness and other advantages of the latter alternatives, cease favouring the status quo, and funds for switching become available. Moreover, the share of power and heat producers' incremental fuel demand devoted to gas is expected to grow rapidly.

In spite of these tendencies and possibilities, however, Polish authorities expect coal use to continue to increase in absolute terms, not only in the electricity and heat industries but for the country as a whole. For the foreseeable future, Poland will therefore remain a very coal intensive economy.

Energy Consumption Scenarios

In a policy paper submitted in late 1992 and updated in 1993, the MoIT presents two TPES scenarios. A low growth case has primary energy supplies in 2010 exceeding their level of 1990 by 23 per cent, implying average annual growth in 1991-2010 of about 1 per cent a year. A high growth case combines circumstances that make TPES increase by 46 per cent from 1990 to 2010, i.e. by a little less than 2 per cent a year. Starting from its lower 1993 level, TPES would have to grow by an average of about 1.4 per cent a year in the low scenario, and by 2.5 per cent a year in the high one, to reach the same 2010 levels.

It is assumed that GDP grows by an average of 2 per cent a year in the low scenario and by 4.2 per cent a year in the high one. Taking GDP developments in 1991-93 into consideration, the Polish economy would have to grow by 2.4 per cent a year in the low case and by 5 per cent a year in the high case in 1994-2010 to reach its 2010 "target" levels. The energy intensity of the Polish economy is seen as decreasing by 21 per cent in the low scenario and by almost 35 per cent in the high scenario – that is, by an average of 1.2 per cent a year in the former and by 2.1 per cent a year in the latter. As TPES per unit of GDP was almost exactly the same in 1993 as in 1990, so that three years were "lost" in this respect, the targets imply a need to achieve energy intensity reductions of 1.4 per cent a year or 2.5 per cent a year during the rest of the scenario period.

The combined hard coal and brown coal share in TPES declines from 73.8 per cent in 1990 to 67.5 per cent in 2000 and to 61.9 per cent in 2010 in the low case, or to 68.9 per cent in 2000 and 63.3 per cent in 2010 in the high case. The gas share increases from 9.4 per cent in 1990 to between 13.1 per cent (low case) and 13.7 per cent (high case), while the liquid fuels share increases from 15.4 per cent to between 18 per cent and 20.2 per cent.

As for TFC, industry's share is seen as declining from 42 per cent in 1990 to 35 per cent in 2010 in the low scenario, and 37 per cent in the high scenario. The transport sector's share is expected to increase only marginally, from 15 per cent in

Table 4.2
TPES Scenarios
(million tonnes of coal equivalent)

		Low		High	
	1990	2000	2010	2000	2010
Total	**143.7**	**163.2**	**177.2**	**181.8**	**209.7**
Hard coal	87.9	92.7	92.1	107.8	115.3
Brown coal	19.2	17.5	17.5	17.5	17.5
Natural gas	12.7	17.9	23.2	21.9	28.6
Liquid fuels	22.0	30.3	35.8	29.3	37.8
Nuclear power	0.0	0.0	0.0	0.0	0.0
Others	1.9	4.9	8.6	5.1	9.6

Source: MoIT

1990 to 16 per cent (low) or 17 per cent (high). Consequently, other sectors' shares are seen as increasing from 43 per cent in 1990 to 49 per cent/46 per cent in 2010.

Recommendations

- **While both these scenarios appear possible, it might be advisable to examine the energy and fuel implications of an even wider spectrum of GDP growth rates, energy intensity developments and fuel substitution processes, in view of the uncertainties surrounding the outlook for the Polish economy and the applicability of parameter values derived from other countries' experiences, and considering the potential for structural change and energy efficiency improvements.**

- **Accurate long term forecasting of demand for energy and fuels is taking on greater importance as Poland goes down the path of reform. Erroneous forecasts of demand for electricity and gas could have particularly serious consequences. To enable the companies in charge of these industries to undertake the necessary rigorous planning and reduce the uncertainties in the present forecasts, the Government needs to move forward as quickly as possible to secure a stable framework of regulation and pricing.**

THE POLISH SYSTEM FOR ENERGY STATISTICS

Data Collection Arrangements

Polish energy statistics, characterised by outstanding breadth and depth, are probably the best in central and eastern Europe. The task of collecting and processing energy statistics is performed by three institutions:

- GUS, the Central Statistical Office, which has the legal power to impose statistical reporting obligations and which approves of surveying projects, performs the collection and preliminary verification of individual questionnaires and, with CIE (see below), publishes the main results of statistical enquiries;

- CIE, the Energy Information Centre, which is responsible for planning surveying projects and formulating statistical enquiries and which develops energy statistics methodology, compiles national energy balances, completes questionnaires for international organisations and publishes specialised statistical publications;

- ORGMASZ, the Institute of Organisation and Management in Industry, which is charged with verifying and aggregating collected data and which develops software for energy data processing.

The survey system has been in place since the early 1980s, when it covered about 80 per cent of Poland's TPES. As it was designed for use by central planners, and was a survey of all state owned enterprises, it is being rendered obsolete by the economic restructuring that has occurred at rapid pace since the late 1980s. The growth in the number of private businesses has made it impossible to continue surveying all economic entities. A transitional model now in use does not differentiate between state owned and private enterprises, but as the criterion for a company's reporting obligation is the size of its workforce, the energy consumption of small enterprises is not surveyed at all, with the result that the system covers only about 50 per cent of TPES, and the share is falling.

CIE, a productive, dynamic company, has been a pioneer in adapting energy statistics from the central planning system and CMEA classification to the international definitions and methodology used by the IEA and other organisations. The huge task of reaggregating historical statistics to meet international standards has been completed, with GUS participation, for 1988-92. The task will need to be carried back to 1961 if Poland joins the OECD and IEA and hence needs to be presented on a comparable basis with other Member countries. It is understood that final consumption data for the 1960s and 1970s would have to be estimated and would be characterised by a high degree of uncertainty.

Reform

Adaptation of the questionnaires to incorporate changes to the system of classification of economic activities, changes to the survey coverage and new legislation will combine to keep pace with the restructuring of the economy.

A new statistics law, scheduled to be passed in 1995, will redefine confidentiality of individual enterprises' submissions as absolute, outline new penalties for poor completion or failure to complete questionnaires, and clarify such areas as the legal ownership of data. The law will permit GUS to adjust the requirements for statistics to national needs annually by submitting the requirements for the next year to the Council of Ministers for approval. The requirements will become law upon acceptance by the Council, legally obliging the requisite companies and individuals to report. This flexible system will allow the Council of Ministers and GUS to fine-tune their requirements with relative ease, while subjecting them to public scrutiny.

The proposed new energy law will provide for the creation of an Energy Regulatory Authority, which will be also empowered to collect certain energy data. The details of the rules that will govern the relationship among GUS, CIE and the ERA have not been decided yet. CIE may be integrated in the ERA as its statistical division. Another alternative is that, while remaining an independent company, CIE will perform statistical tasks on the basis of contracts with the ERA.

A two-level annual survey will replace the existing arrangements. Some 4 000 major energy supplying and using enterprises will provide detailed questionnaires using the NACE [2] economic classification of activities. To cover smaller commercial entities, a further survey using a simpler questionnaire will be undertaken with some 12 000 suppliers and consumers. Together, the two surveys will provide a detailed picture of energy consumption throughout the country. As the economy continues to change, the samples and questionnaires will probably be adjusted and in all likelihood reduced.

Recommendations

The survey sample sizes and the detail with which energy statistics are collected in Poland go some way beyond what is generally required by OECD Member countries' governments. Although the current system is increasingly outdated, the authorities have a clear, comprehensive plan to change their methods of collection so as to take economic transformation into account. In time, as the economic restructuring continues and government involvement in the energy sector is reduced, government bodies will compete more strongly for the resources available for statistics collection. GUS, CIE or the ERA may then be obliged to re-examine the energy statistics system, particularly the data collection procedures, with a view to identifying possibilities for cost reductions.

- **Concentrating on energy suppliers and reducing the frequency of surveying of energy consumers would be a major way to save money without a disproportionate loss of coverage and reliability in statistics.**

The quality and experience of Polish energy statisticians and the integrity of the statistics produced are already equal to the best in OECD Member countries.

- **A prime aim of the rationalisation of CIE and the data system should be to preserve and use the professionalism available and to employ the best survey techniques so as to meet, at reduced costs of source data collection, the requirements of national and international data recipients, particularly the international organisations.**

- **The national oil market monitoring would benefit from a strengthening of oil statistics collection and processing. The aim should be to provide national and international users with monthly oil statistics in a format compatible with IEA standards.**

Data on emissions of harmful substances related to energy sector activities are collected and processed by CIE and the Ministry of Environmental Protection independently. CIE calculates emissions by applying coefficients to its energy production and consumption data. The Ministry obtains emissions data from inspectors monitoring pollution sources in individual voivodships.

---

2. Nomenclature Générale des Activités Economiques dans les Communautés Européennes.

- Both approaches should be continued, as they are well established and complementary; any discrepancies should serve to put the institutions on the track of weaknesses in their systems and methods.

Whatever data the pollution inspectorate gathers on quantities of fuels consumed by major industries in the voivodships should be shared with CIE, to the improvement of both systems.

CHAPTER 5

ENERGY END-USE AND EFFICIENCY

Research by the Lawrence Berkeley Laboratory in the Unites States and by Poland's Energy Information Centre has produced an improved picture of energy consumption by the major consuming sectors in Poland: industry, transport, residential and services, and agriculture. CIE's surveys regarding energy use by specific equipment and activities within each sector provide a basis for analysing the efficiency with which energy is consumed, which in turn can contribute to the development of policy initiatives for improving energy efficiency. Continued improvement in this area is welcomed.

ENERGY INTENSITY [1]

While estimates vary, most studies of the energy intensity of the Polish economy conclude that Poland uses two to three times as much energy to produce a unit of GDP as does OECD Europe. Such comparisons can only be approximate because of difficulties in estimating GDP and in expressing GDP in a common currency (with conversion factors based on exchange rates yielding substantially different results than those based on purchasing power parities), as well as differences in end-use structures – e.g. in the share

of energy intensive industry output in GDP – and climate. However, regardless of the vagueness that such factors produce, it is clear that the legacy of the centrally planned economy – artificially low energy prices, lack of metering for heat, lack of market discipline to encourage cost-effective investments for reducing energy costs, priority on production goals, monopolistic supply systems – has produced an economy noticeably lacking in incentives for improved efficiency. Furthermore, a fledgling financial system with limited lending experience for efficiency, combined with the high cost of borrowing, discourages much-needed investments that could lead to improvements in the efficiency of energy use.

On an economy-wide basis, the intensity of energy use in Poland declined by about 6 per cent between 1989 and 1993, as the reductions in energy demand (TFC fell by 21 per cent, electricity demand by 17 per cent and district heating use by 9 per cent) exceeded the fall in GDP (13.8 per cent). Examination of the various sectors reveal details of these changes.

Industry

Industry represents about one-third of TFC in Poland. The concentration of energy-intensive

---

1. Unless stated otherwise, the quantitative and analytical information presented in this first section is drawn from Stephen Meyers *et al.*, "Energy Use in Poland, 1970-1991: Sectoral Analysis and International Comparison", Lawrence Berkeley Laboratory, University of California, Berkeley CA, July 1994, and Stephen Meyers, Lee Schipper and Jurgen Salay, "Energy Use in Poland: An International Comparison", Energy: The International Journal, June 1994.

industry is relatively high; ferrous and non-ferrous metallurgy, pulp and paper, chemicals and building materials accounted for 30 per cent of manufacturing value added in Poland in 1990 – much more than in western Germany, France, the United States or Japan. This, combined with the relatively poor efficiency of the associated processes, produce a level of industrial energy intensity several times higher than that of most OECD countries. The low process efficiency is apparently due to ageing capital stock and inadequate attention to sound management practices, driven by a lack of financial incentives. In 1988, over 80 per cent of Poland's capital stock in industry was more than five years old, compared with 40 per cent in western Germany. A 1986 study concluded that the energy required to produce a tonne of steel in Poland was 25-50 per cent higher than in western Europe. The share of open hearth furnaces was 25 per cent in 1991, compared with 2 per cent in western Europe and 8 per cent in the United States, where the more up to date basic oxygen and electric arc furnaces predominate.

After economic restructuring began in 1989, industrial output (measured as value added) fell by 24 per cent in 1990 and 12 per cent in 1991, reflecting reduced production and a net shift away from heavy industry. While these changes were accompanied by reduced energy use, intensity rose by 7.6 per cent, reflecting a deterioration of efficiency; many plants were being run at reduced levels of capacity utilisation but continuing to use the same amount of energy for light, etc. While this general trend masks some cases where efficiency improvements have been made in response to higher prices, there appears to have been little investment in more efficient technology as plant managers have been consumed with more immediate questions of survival and marketing.

In 1992, a decline in manufacturing energy use combined with an increase in manufacturing value added reduced energy intensity, suggesting that the effects of restructuring and price increases were beginning to take hold.

Residential/Services/Other

The "other sectors" category (residential/services/other) accounted for 49 per cent of TFC in 1993.

Of this, residential consumption represented close to a third. Some 75-80 per cent of residential energy use is for space and water heating, with 10 per cent for cooking and 10 per cent for such uses as lighting and refrigeration. Space and water heating are heavily dominated by coal and heat, both of which are consumed inefficiently. For example, the heating requirement of Polish dwellings in the late 1980s was estimated at 220-260 kJ per square metre per degree-day – about twice that of Western European dwellings at the time.

Residential and service sector energy use fell in 1990, apparently in response to increasing coal prices, some stockpiling of coal in 1989 and increased use of non-commercial fuels such as wood. A similar response with respect to electricity price increases appears to have occurred. Conversely, district heating use was virtually unchanged: it is billed according to dwelling size, not use, and most individuals do not have control over their consumption. Energy use in buildings increased by 7 per cent in 1992 despite warmer weather; coal use accounted for most of the rise.

Electricity use per capita in the residential sector is relatively low compared with OECD Europe. There are two underlying factors: low penetration of electric equipment, and low efficiency of the equipment used. For example, the combined ownership of refrigerators and freezers is about 1.2 per household, compared with 1.4-1.5 in OECD Europe, and Polish models tend to be much smaller than their western counterparts. Other appliances, such as clothes washing machines, are less widespread in Poland, and clothes driers and dishwashers are almost non-existent. As appliances increase in penetration, electricity demand in this sector is expected to increase substantially. The degree of energy efficiency of these appliances will have significant consequences for aggregate growth in electricity demand.

Even though energy prices have not yet reached cost-based levels for residential consumers, price increases have significantly outpaced income growth, to the point where the domestic energy bill represents close to 10 per cent of average household incomes (it is of course much more in the case of low income residences). This is two to three times the share in OECD Europe, and has resulted in a substantial level of non-payment of energy bills – estimated at up to 25 per cent for electricity and heat. Consumers who do not pay for energy services have very little incentive to save, a point discussed further in Chapter 7.

Transport

Transport energy use per capita in Poland is well below that of western Europe, the United States or Japan. Per capita auto ownership is also substantially lower, although recent data suggest a pronounced increase in car ownership (primarily used vehicles imported from western Europe; see Chapter 9). Per capita use of buses and rail is substantially higher in Poland than in either the west or the former Soviet Union. Data uncertainties limit the extent to which conclusions can be drawn regarding the efficiency of transport in Poland. In 1989, Polish automobiles apparently required some 8-9 litres/100 km, compared with 12 litres/100 km in the United States, 8 litres/100 km in Denmark and Italy, or 10.5 litres/100 km in western Germany. Efficiency of buses and passenger rail appears to be within the range of that in western countries, while freight – dominated by rail because of the intensive movement of heavy goods (e.g. coal), and largely electric – is somewhat less efficient (as measured in MJ/tonne-km).

ENERGY EFFICIENCY POLICIES AND ACTIVITIES

Government Initiatives

The Polish Government recognises the importance of improving energy efficiency throughout the economy. It correctly observes that efficiency improvements will result from its efforts to orient the economy in general, and the energy supply system in particular, towards a more market based system – including bringing energy prices to a level that reflects full costs. These changes will take time, however, and they will need to be preceded and supplemented by additional efforts – efforts that now are largely lacking from government policy initiatives.

The planning document "Poland's Energy Policy and Outline of the Program by 2010" acknowledges the importance of improved efficiency, but does not provide specific policy measures to realise efficiency gains. The November 1994 version of the draft energy law predominantly concerns reforms of the supply system. While some of these reforms will contribute directly to improved supply efficiency and reduce barriers to improved end-use efficiency, very few initiatives are specifically designed to accelerate or enhance the uptake of more efficient end-use equipment. The sections of the draft that address improved efficiency (see box) are generally in the form of "enabling legislation" that suggests, but does not guarantee, that ordinances designed to implement the proposals will follow (ordinances do not require parliamentary approval).

Expertise and policy guidance on energy efficiency matters reside with a few quasi-governmental or private organisations. Although energy efficiency is nominally the responsibility of the Energy Department in the MoIT (with the Ministry of Physical Planning and Construction responsible for the district heating distribution systems and energy codes for buildings), no official government unit has responsibility for developing, planning and implementing (or overseeing the implementation of) a coherent energy efficiency policy. The new National Energy Conservation Agency, created three and a half years after being authorised by the Sejm in November 1990, has neither the authority nor the resources to carry out these tasks [2].

Recommendation

- **The Government should establish a formal policy unit with direct responsibility for developing energy efficiency policy. This unit could be formed from an existing body, such as the National Energy Conservation Agency. It should be given sufficient responsibility and resources to enable it to develop credible proposals and garner support. Programme implementation could be carried out and/or overseen by this unit.**

---

2. The National Energy Conservation Agency is a joint stock company, not a state agency. The three main shareholders are the Bank of Domestic Economy, the National Agency for Industrial Development and the National Fund for Environmental Protection and Water Management. The Ministries of Industry and Trade, Physical Planning and Construction, and Environmental Protection are expected to buy in as shareholders.

Articles of Draft Energy Law Relating to Energy Efficiency

Description

Art. 12   Consumers running a business and obliged to keep books should maintain separate accounts for energy/fuels, if such costs exceed 2 per cent of total costs.

Art. 18   Enterprises engaged in transmitting or distributing electricity or gaseous fuels through a grid shall consider opportunities to improve the efficiency of energy use, as well as opportunities for system modernisation and extension, in their development of plans.

Art. 26   Energy enterprises shall publish information regarding energy efficiency improvements, and shall gather and process information regarding energy management.

Art. 50   Tariffs for electricity, heat and gaseous fuels may include costs of co-financing projects and services intended to reduce energy and fuel use by consumers, providing these are cost-effective relative to new supply.

Art. 53   The design, production, import, construction and operation of installations and equipment should ensure efficient use of energy and fuels (consistent with safety and reliability concerns).

Art. 54   Manufacturers and importers of equipment shall include energy requirements relative to equipment output as part of their technical specifications. This information shall be displayed by means of a label on the product. The MoIT may decide on performance requirements and conformance procedures for specific items through ordinances.

Art. 55   Equipment that does not meet the requirements referred to in Article 54 will not be allowed onto the domestic market.

The Ministry of Physical Planning and Construction runs the sole existing efficiency initiative, a programme begun in 1992 for the thermal renovation of co-operatively owned buildings, budgeted at Zl 1.5 trillion (about US$ 75 million) per year. The funds, channelled through voivodships, can cover up to 80 per cent of the costs of insulating walls, weatherproofing windows, installing controls and meters, renovating and insulating distribution pipes, and related measures. The tracking of these funds has been limited so far, and measurement of results virtually non-existent.

Initiatives through Non-governmental Organisations

Energy efficiency initiatives have been undertaken by the Polish Foundation for Energy Efficiency (FEWE), the Polish Energy Conservation Foundation, the National Fund for Environmental Protection and Water Management, and the Environment Protection Bank.

FEWE, a private, non-profit organisation, was established with assistance from three US institutions: The Agency for International Development (USAID), the Environmental Protection Agency and Pacific Northwest Laboratory. It is largely self-supporting. FEWE undertakes studies on energy efficiency potential and programme development and provides input to the energy policy process, particularly through comments on the draft energy law and involvement with local authorities.

The Polish Energy Conservation Foundation, part of the Polish Development Bank, is a non-profit institution with activities aimed at "limiting and rationalising energy use as well as developing renewable resources". Funding is provided by domestic and foreign banks, the state, equipment suppliers and energy service companies. The foundation is active in most sectors, although its focus has largely been on public information and the training and licensing of energy efficiency auditors. It used to pay half the cost of audits for industrial plants in exchange for a commitment that cost-effective measures would be taken; this auditing service is now being provided on a commercial basis. The foundation also helps companies prepare loan applications for commercial banks.

The National Fund for Environmental Protection and Water Management receives funds from environmental fees and fines related to air emissions, as well as mineral rights concessions and extraction fees. Its budget was Zl 4.5 billion in 1993. The fund has dealt with energy efficiency only indirectly, its primary focus being pollution control. There have been discussions of supplements to this fund that could be used to finance energy efficiency projects more directly.

The Environment Protection Bank (Bank Ochrony Srodowiska) is a joint stock company that supports activities connected with environmental and water management, including energy efficiency.

Initiatives through Foreign Aid

Bilateral and multilateral financing and aid organisations have provided assistance directed towards energy efficiency improvements. These efforts tend to focus largely on information and training, audits of industrial plants and conversion of residential heating systems to incorporate metering and controls (Table 5.1). Three programmes targeted at improved institutional

capabilities for promoting end-use efficiency within the electricity and district heating systems are of note. The first is the World Bank's power sector loan, which includes a component for the institutional development of demand side management (DSM) capabilities within the Polish Power Grid Company. The second, funded by USAID, involves identifying cost-effective electricity efficiency measures and developing a cost of conserved energy curve for these measures and a pilot project in industry. The third is funded by the European Union's PHARE programme; it involves developing a least cost master plan for Warsaw based on the electricity, district heating and natural gas grids.

ENERGY EFFICIENCY OPPORTUNITIES

This section discusses opportunities for improving the efficiency of energy use in Poland, and recommends policy initiatives that the Government may want to consider in order to both accelerate and enhance the effects of existing and proposed energy sector reforms. The types of measures proposed are described in general terms, since detailed specification needs to be based on careful consideration of the changing institutional and economic backdrop of Poland's energy sector, and on a thorough cost-benefit analysis of approaches.

Table 5.1
Ongoing Energy Efficiency Projects with Bilateral and Multilateral Funding

Donor country/ organisation	Project type	Sector	Funding level	Initiated in
EU/PHARE	Training & technical advice (TA)	District heating, electricity, natural gas		1994
World Bank	Investment, TA	Electricity		1992
Netherlands	Training, TA	Buildings	US$ 0.37 million	1992
Norway	TA	Industry	US$ 0.33 million	1993
Sweden	Training, TA	Energy management		1993
Sweden	Training	Power & heat production	US$ 0.17 million	1993
UK	Policy support	Municipal	US$ 0.01 million	1992
USA	Investment	Industry	US$ 1.5 million	1993
USA	Policy support	Utility DSM		1993
USA	Investment, TA	Residential & commercial		1993

Source: OECD Register, end 1994

Moreover, while these policy initiatives are intended to be complementary – most IEA Member countries have discovered that a mix of measures has the greatest likelihood of success – there are trade-offs with regard to the level of emphasis that might be directed towards a particular programme type. For example, efficiency standards for refrigerators could eliminate the least efficient models from the market, while a utility DSM programme could steer consumers towards the more efficient models available. The determination of where to set limits through standards would in turn influence the level of DSM activity; however, such a determination would be the focus of much more detailed analysis.

General

Although specific policy responses vary according to national circumstances, IEA Member countries have recognised a valid role for government intervention in the area of energy efficiency, as the market will not always take up efficiency measures deemed economic. In addition to ensuring that prices reflect costs and that markets operate as freely as possible, sector-specific policy tools typically include: the provision of information on the energy consuming characteristics of equipment; audits of homes, commercial buildings and factories; recognition and commitment activities in co-operation with industry; financial incentives for selected measures; and performance requirements for selected equipment. These policy tools are designed to address the market impediments that discourage consumer uptake of more energy-efficient practices and equipment, where the benefits of such policies exceed their costs.

The argument for a coherent set of government policies is particularly compelling in countries like Poland, where consumers have had relatively limited experience with energy price increases and options for responding to prices (e.g. a range of equipment choices with different efficiency characteristics). Access to capital to finance energy efficiency investments is also limited. Most importantly, decisions regarding equipment selection and operation are often disconnected from the energy use consequences – those responsible for investment or consumption decisions are often not those paying the energy bills.

This issue, familiar in the west as a principal/agent or tenant/landlord problem, is usually the basis for policy responses such as standards, which remove the possibility that builders or equipment purchasers will make inefficient choices. The problem is particularly acute in countries like Poland, where for decades experience with individual ownership and accountability has been non-existent, and it is optimistic to assume that increased prices and open markets will in themselves be sufficient to produce the efficiency improvements needed to help satisfy the Government's environmental and economic objectives. Much time will pass before consumers become aware of, and gain control over, the energy cost consequences of their decisions on appliances, building materials, industrial process equipment and the like. Furthermore, the eventual demand for greater efficiency may not be articulated to suppliers in a way that leads to widespread availability of more efficient equipment. In the interim, factories will have been built and equipment choices made, all with long term implications for energy use that may frustrate economic growth and environmental objectives.

Thus, it is important for the Government to consider supplementing and supporting the development of market mechanisms for improved efficiency with various types of approaches that could prevent lost opportunities. At the same time, these approaches should be flexible and temporary; they should not represent a sup-planting of one set of subsidies and distortions with another.

During the transition period in which energy prices are rising to their liberalised levels, below market prices will continue to impose a heavy cost to everybody, either through direct government outlay or in the form of subsidies. There may well be less costly means of serving the same goals, however; in a number of cases, energy efficiency measures would cost less than the current fuel price support.

Another barrier that could easily be remedied is that energy efficiency technology produced outside Poland is subject to an 11 per cent import duty and 22 per cent value added tax. These reduce further the financial rewards associated with the equipment and discourages its penetration, particularly when energy prices are below cost based levels.

Recommendations

- **The Government should consider and develop ways to couple financial incentives for consumers to improve energy efficiency with a more rapid progression to cost based price levels. This would help smooth political difficulties in achieving the goal of cost based energy prices, and could be targeted to the lower income segment of the population. The effort could be financed by reducing subsidies applied to (or engendered by) the current pricing structure, such as budgetary support to tenant associations for heat costs, and/or by increased revenue from energy taxes applied to various fuels.**

- **The high level of unpaid district heating and electricity bills suggests a financing strategy that would reduce the accounts receivable burden on these systems and possibly increase the likelihood of at least the smaller bills being paid. Additionally, at least while energy prices are reaching market or cost based levels, the Government could consider reducing or removing VAT on imports of energy efficiency products.**

- **However, reliance on financial support to promote efficiency improvements, whether in the form of direct subsidies or tax incentives, should be seen as temporary. The ultimate goal will be to convince equipment producers and importers to supply more efficient equipment, and to steer consumers towards the more efficient end of the range.**

The most effective energy efficiency programmes are generally based on a sound understanding of underlying energy consumption patterns and the barriers preventing more efficient use of energy. Moreover, such programmes are carefully monitored and evaluated to ascertain whether they should be improved, modified or phased out. Although energy statistics in Poland tend to be in better shape than in many countries in the region, a heightened focus on end-use data and a better understanding of consumer operating and purchase decisions will aid programme development and design. Yet, the development of end-use data for programme planning and the continuing collection of data for evaluation is both resource and time intensive. The introduction in the meantime of a variety of visible, pilot-scale programmes, accompanied by broad dissemination of the results,

should give the Government an opportunity to select for further development those programmes that offer the highest likelihood of success while additional end-use data are being collected and analysed.

Recommendation

- **The Government should continue and extend its data collection and evaluation efforts in order to improve the design and implementation of energy efficiency programmes. These programmes should be designed to allow evaluation of results. At the same time, a broad range of pilot-scale programmes should be introduced in order to gain experience in programme design and implementation, and to fortify the level and quality of end-use data.**

The private sector should be an important element of any concentrated effort to improve energy efficiency. In this regard, the Government can take steps to help form, develop and promote a vibrant energy services industry. The industry should offer technical expertise in energy auditing and engineering, and be able to develop energy efficiency projects and attract private financing. Even in OECD countries the energy services industry is a growing but toddling business that could be fortified, promoted and advanced through government support.

Recommendation

- **The Government, independently or with financial assistance, could establish a training and accreditation system to certify capabilities and provide a government "seal of approval" with which companies could assure potential clients of their credibility. The Government could also take steps to make energy users aware of this source of energy efficiency expertise and support, and could provide potential clients with a check-list of items they should expect to see as part of a performance contract.**

District Heating

As in most countries of central and eastern Europe and the former Soviet Union, urban areas in

Poland are served extensively by district heating networks that are very inefficient, even those supplied by CHP plants. Losses in transmission and distribution of heat (see Chapter 7 for details) are substantial. Moreover, most users are charged by floor space rather than consumption, and the virtual absence of control devices means they could not reduce their heat use even if they were motivated to do so. Although the prices charged for district heating have increased by a factor of about ten in real terms since 1989, they are not, in general, sufficient to cover the costs of the individual systems. Through a relatively complicated mechanism, the Ministry of Finance and, in some cases, municipal budgets provide funds to "top off" the payments by consumers. In 1993, the Ministry of Finance provided an estimated Zl 2 trillion (US$ 100 million) for heat to co-operatively owned buildings; additional amounts were provided by municipalities for municipal buildings. Even assuming tenants could control their consumption, either through improvements to the building shell or by modulating the heat supply to the unit, the state and local authorities, not the tenants, would be the primary beneficiaries. Hence there may be ample incentive for the state and municipalities to support efficiency investments to reduce their own outlays, at least until such time as the system is changed.

Assistance to the district heating systems has focused on improving the efficiency of heat production and delivery, not end-use [3]. While efficiency improvements in the supply delivery system are needed, steps to optimise a system that is serving inflated and inefficient demand may eclipse much more cost-effective investment opportunities that would be available through reducing this demand.

A study was recently performed on four adjacent 11 storey apartment blocks in Krakow [4]. The first building was set aside as a control, the second was retrofitted with a temperature sensitive, variable speed drive circulation pump, the third got unit by unit control valves and meters, with heat charged on the basis of actual use, and the fourth was weatherised, using measures satisfying a three year payback criterion. The fourth building realised the greatest savings – about twice that of the third building.

The experiment was run for only one season, limiting the opportunity for any investment decision. Because of this and other factors, it is perhaps not an adequate basis for policy development. The results suggest, however, that while prices do influence consumption decisions, price signals alone do not induce consumers to undertake all cost-effective measures for saving energy. In addition, several of the measures in the fourth building were applied to the ceiling and basement – something tenants of individual units are less likely to undertake irrespective of the strength and clarity of the price signal. Thus, split incentives between owner and tenants account for a large share of unexploited energy savings potential. Finally, some tenants in the third building appeared to increase consumption, suggesting that the units had been underheated.

Recommendations

- **The Government could examine ways to increase the penetration of heat meters and controls, since their absence is a primary impediment to understanding and improving energy use, irrespective of progress towards more cost based pricing. At the same time, the configuration of most heating systems suggests that net energy consumption may not be reduced significantly unless comprehensive controls are provided throughout the system.**

- **The Government should evaluate the current system of financial support to residential district heating users to determine how state and voivodship outlays can be reduced through improved thermal performance of buildings. The Government should furthermore consider ways to target loans to district heating systems so as to improve end-use efficiency in addition to reducing heat losses in production and distribution.**

Electricity

Although electricity prices for household consumers have increased by 300 per cent in real

---

3. Ironically, the most efficient systems are in a financial position qualifying them for assistance loans while the least efficient systems cannot cover their costs and thus do not qualify for the necessary credit to invest in efficiency improvements.
4. See Wisnewski, Ross *et al.*, "Energy Price Incentives in a Planned Economy", Proceedings ACEEE 1994 Summer Study on Energy Efficiency in Buildings, Pacific Grove, CA.

terms since 1989 (prices for industrial customers have remained constant), they remain some 50 per cent below cost based levels (see Chapter 7 for details). Moreover, although the incentives to consumers to save electricity are somewhat more pronounced than for heat – meters are more widespread, as is the ability to control use – bills are typically sent about four times per year, providing little immediate feedback regarding the effects of consumption decisions. A USAID study[5] identified cost-effective electricity efficiency opportunities of about 25.4 TWh available from programmes that could be implemented through 2000; these savings would be competitive with power from existing stations estimated to cost US$ 0.048/kwh, of which US$ 0.027 is for energy and US$ 0.021 for pollution abatement. (The savings potential is 9.4 TWh if pollution abatement costs are ignored.) The primary measures include more efficient lighting, refrigerators, motors and industrial processes. According to the study, DSM programme administration costs and conservative assumptions with regard to penetration rates would reduce the savings to 1.7 TWh per year by 2000, representing slightly less than 2 per cent of 1991 electricity sales.

Whether this potential will be realised, or possibly even exceeded, depends on the roles assumed by the Government and the electric utilities, which in turn depend on how the latter are organised. As Chapter 7 explains in more detail, the electricity system consists of 28 generation companies, one transmission company (PPGC) and 33 distributors. Like their counterparts in most OECD countries, the various segments of the electricity supply industry in Poland have very little incentive to seek out cost-effective end-use efficiency investments that would compete with supply investments, largely because this would run counter to their financial interests. Costs undertaken by distributors directed towards improving end-use efficiency are not recoverable. Furthermore, there is no provision for lost net revenue (average revenue in excess of short run costs) associated with reduced sales brought about by efficiency programmes. Most distributors are not collecting all their costs in any case – a presumably temporary circumstance that has prompted the distribution company serving Warsaw to seek ways to reduce demand in order to avoid having to upgrade the distribution system.

The current intent is to reorganise the electricity supply industry in three phases, with increasing levels of competition in generation, and with PPGC dispatching generating units on a merit order basis and selling the power (adding a regulated transmission charge) to the distribution companies. The distributors would retain exclusive supply monopolies in their respective franchise markets. In the third phase, the distributors as well as large customers served at transmission voltage would be able to contract directly with one or more generating company instead of having to purchase from PPGC.

Recommendations

- **The Government should require the electricity distribution companies to plan and operate their systems on the basis of least cost principles that include consideration of demand and supply side resources. The appropriate least cost approach will depend upon the organisation and regulatory regime adopted. If distributors are to retain exclusive franchises to serve customers, the Government could encourage the companies to pursue end-use efficiency by eliminating restrictions that prevent utilities from passing on to consumers the costs of end-use efficiency investments, as specified in Article 50 of the draft energy law. Even in the current situation, in which some utilities are losing money as business costs outpace their latitude to raise prices, price increases could be granted to allow the recovery of cost-effective investments in end-use efficiency.**

- **Furthermore, the Government or the proposed independent regulatory body could introduce rate making mechanisms that eliminate financial losses to the distributors resulting from reduced sales and thus encourage utilities to seek out the least cost approach, including demand side options. End-use efficiency "resources" could be provided by private sector participants through competitive bidding, with the costs**

---

5. "Demand-Side Management in Poland, Part 1: National Assessment" prepared by RCG/Hagler Bailly Inc., Washington DC, December 1993.

and other attributes of the resource compared with supply costs. A similar requirement could be considered for PPGC with regard to customers served at transmission voltage. If the Government introduces competition in electricity supply (through third party access), the requirement that distribution companies operate on a least cost basis should be re-examined. It may be more appropriate to consider including a fee per kilowatt-hour in the wires charges to form the basis for a government-administered energy efficiency fund, available by competitive bid to utilities and private energy service companies.

Residential and Commercial Sectors

The efficiency opportunities for the residential and commercial sectors tend to be related to buildings – apartments, homes, offices, schools – or equipment such as lights, refrigerators, air conditioning systems and computers.

Buildings

New residential buildings constructed in Poland must comply with building codes regarding the thermal characteristics of walls, roof, windows and basement slabs. These codes were formulated in 1954 and revised in 1972 and 1982. A new standard, with more stringent requirements for wall and roof/ceiling insulation, was introduced in 1991. It applies to existing buildings undergoing renovation as well as to new buildings. This standard is itself being revised and may eventually be based on overall energy performance per square metre. Code enforcement tends to be a problem, however, so it is not always clear whether requirements for thermal insulation and other measures are satisfied.

A much more pervasive problem is the energy requirements of existing residential buildings, particularly the prefabricated apartment blocks built during the 1960s and 1970s, which tend to be more poorly insulated than their counterparts in the west. The challenge lies in devising ways to bring about retrofits to these buildings, particularly when it is not clear with whom the motivation and responsibility for improved efficiency reside. Table 5.2 characterises the various types of residential buildings with respect to location (urban versus rural) and ownership (rental versus owner-occupied).

About 25 per cent of residential units are co-operatively owned, 20 per cent municipally owned, 15 per cent owned by state enterprises and 40 per cent private. Roughly two-thirds are characterised as urban. While these factors alone do not always tell an unambiguous story regarding the incentives for residents to save energy, a few general observations can be made.

In general, owner-occupiers will be more motivated than renters to improve the overall quality of the unit. These include owners of private buildings (which tend to be in rural areas) as well as almost half the occupants of co-operative buildings. The latter are more likely to be in urban areas and served by district heating, which as has been noted tends to provide limited opportunity and incentive for consumers to control their energy use. In some cases co-operatives are responsible for purchasing their own fuel, giving them collectively an incentive to reduce energy losses throughout the building,

Table 5.2
Characteristics of Residential Buildings

Housing type	Number in 1992 (thousands)	Per cent urban	Per cent owner occupied
Co-operatives	2 975	99	45
State enterprise	1 480	60	99
Private	4 795	35	95
Municipal	2 028	95	10

Source: Stephen Meyers *et al.*: 'The Residential Space Heating Problem in Eastern Europe: the Context for Effective Strategies", unpublished draft.

including common areas; financing, however, remains a barrier. Municipal buildings tend to be urban, and inhabited primarily by renters. While the incentive for and ability of tenants to act is limited, the municipality could reduce its own financial outlay for heat price support by investing in thermal renovations. The same basic conditions apply to housing of which a state enterprise is the landlord and provider of basic services such as heat.

At present, there is very little turnover of existing housing. Even if information were available regarding the energy requirements of properties and charges were based on actual use, the housing market is far from mature enough for such information to be reflected in selling prices. And it is not clear whether lending institutions would formally recognise the first cost premium and attendant reductions in energy bills associated with a more efficient home. On a limited basis, the two principal mortgage banks, the Polish/American Bank and BudBank, are considering modifying the lending requirements associated with home loans to take current energy costs into account. This requires, in addition to basing charges on actual use, the development of an audit/rating programme so that energy requirements of properties can be objectively established.

Although commercial buildings, particularly those with western co-financing, are somewhat better built than new residential buildings, they are not necessarily operated or maintained more efficiently. The types of policy measures the Government could consider for commercial buildings include codes for new buildings, the development of design centres demonstrating more efficient building design techniques, commercial audit programmes and required retrofits upon sale of existing buildings, and recognition/commitment activities for retrofits of existing buildings to improve thermal performance.

Recommendations

- **Since prospective buyers of existing property are unlikely to be able to evaluate its energy requirements due to lack of information stemming from the limited penetration of heat metering, the Government could examine and evaluate the trade-offs associated with requiring efficiency retrofits of property upon**

sale. **Such requirements have been employed selectively at municipal level in certain OECD countries, where new construction is low but turnover of existing property is high, and the link between the market price and the energy requirements of property is weak or non-existent. Alternatively, a mechanism could be considered by which the amount lent for the purchase of a property could include money for investment in energy efficiency retrofits identified through a mandatory audit at the time of sale. This additional money could be repaid through the savings derived from the investments, and possibly guaranteed by the Government in order to reduce risk to lenders.**

- **The Government could support comprehensive audits of buildings and information campaigns associated with common cost-effective measures. These would give consumers information on how energy could be used more efficiently. The Government could also consider establishing a labelling system for residential and commercial property. This would help consumers understand the energy consumption implications of their purchases. Moreover, financial institutions could consider the energy expenditures projected for existing property and use this information in establishing loan limits for prospective buyers. A revolving fund could be established by some mortgage and commercial banks to finance energy efficiency improvements, with the loans repaid through the related savings to replenish the fund.**

Lighting and appliances

Residential electricity use is dominated by lighting (55 per cent) and refrigerators (21 per cent), while commercial use is dominated by lighting (54 per cent). The 1993 USAID study estimated that 10.5 TWh could be saved by 2000 by using compact fluorescent lights in place of conventional incandescent bulbs. The question is how to bring these savings about. The most common approaches in IEA countries are various types of information and financial incentive programmes, typically carried out by electric utilities, designed to educate customers regarding the benefits of more efficient lights and to influence their purchases accordingly. A proposed pilot programme awaiting approval from the Global Environment Facility (GEF) would provide some US$ 3.5 million in financial incentives to manufacturers of compact fluorescent lights (there are now three) to take advantage of the price-plus-VAT effect and increase the lights' competitiveness as they move from manufacturer to distributor to retailer. This could increase the penetration and associated energy savings of such light-bulbs.

The savings potential offered by more efficient refrigerators was estimated at 2.8 TWh by 2000. Utility organised DSM programmes are one way to encourage customers to invest in more efficient models. Alternatively, the Government could consider the development of performance standards for all refrigerators produced in or imported into Poland. A number of OECD countries have introduced or are considering such standards, which can be developed administratively or voluntarily, depending on the responsiveness of manufacturers and importers. Recent programmes in some OECD countries (e.g. the United States and Sweden) have led to the introduction of more efficient refrigerator models by aggregating otherwise dispersed consumer demand for greater efficiency and asking suppliers to respond to a competitive bid for providing the equipment.

Recommendations

- **The Government should evaluate the trade-offs associated with efficiency standards or other approaches for improving the efficiency of equipment such as refrigerators and freezers in the residential sector and computers, fax machines and printers in the commercial sector. This type of equipment may represent the largest share of growth in electricity consumption in Poland. While the costs associated with the efficiency improvements are relatively small, experience in OECD countries has shown that the improvements are not likely to be made without some sort of government involvement, either through administrative standards (e.g. for refrigerators) or the development of co-operative agreements or organised purchases (e.g. for computers). Article 54 of the draft energy law would give the MoIT the authority to establish standards for equipment via ordinances.**

- **The Government should consider a labelling system for consumer products to help consumers understand the energy consumption implications of their purchases and evaluate**

energy costs of competing products. Article 54 of the draft energy law would allow the MoIT to establish an energy labelling programme for equipment via ordinances and prohibit the sale of non-complying equipment.

Public Sector

Government purchases of equipment, such as computers, represent one area in which user-specified efficiency improvements can be brought about, as shown through the US and Swedish programmes mentioned above. The Government is in position to put the markets for many types of equipment on the desired tracks, aggregating buyers as well as being a large volume purchaser able to reduce manufacturers' risk. This idea might include collective purchase decisions involving the state, voivodships and municipalities. Similar types of consumer groupings could be considered among governments in the region – e.g. the Czech and Slovak Republics, Hungary and Romania. Such efforts would also achieve the objective of having government provide exemplary support of its efficiency policies. Other services still largely within the public domain, such as schools and hospitals, could be included. Incentives to localities might also be considered, to facilitate changes in the accounting and administration of schools and hospitals to encourage trade-offs between capital budgets (efficiency investments) and operating budgets (energy savings).

Industry

The industrial sector is a sensible target for government energy efficiency policy, based on the savings potential identified through the studies discussed above. For example, the USAID study estimated cost-effective savings of 9.5 TWh a year in this sector, primarily through more efficient motors, adjustable speed drives, improved lighting systems, improved maintenance and optimised production procedures. IEA Member countries have introduced a wide range of policy instruments directed at this sector even where prices are cost based and even though plant managers are often viewed as being motivated to save energy so as to be more competitive.

By western standards the Polish industrial sector is not stable, and its instability is expected to continue as costs of inputs (e.g. energy and raw materials) and markets for finished goods adjust in response to reform measures, and as new ventures are begun. While it would be ill-advised to treat the sector as stable and make efficiency investments guided by static assumptions regarding savings persistence, neither will it do to wait for the shake-out to be complete before looking for efficiency opportunities. The latter approach would probably result in continued operation of inefficient equipment in existing plants or the installation of inefficient new equipment, while the former would most likely generate investments that would prove unnecessary either because efficiency improvements would have taken place on their own accord, or because the investment is lost when a moribund factory closes.

Several policy options could combine flexibility and responsiveness with low capital outlays and hence low financial risk. These include: government sponsored audit programmes, emphasising follow-up; recognition and commitment activities involving company or branch level co-operation in the establishment and achievement of energy efficiency targets; and performance standards for equipment (e.g. motors and lighting systems). Article 12 of the draft energy law would require businesses whose energy costs exceed 2 per cent of total costs to record energy consumption. This would be an important first step in introducing awareness of the importance of energy as a factor input. As IEA Member countries have recognised, a mix of approaches tends to provide the flexibility and balance sought by industry.

Recommendation

- **The Government should consider developing recognition and commitment programmes with industrial branches and/or individual companies. Such programmes would involve the joint establishment by government and industry of energy efficiency goals, and procedures for measuring the results. One possible approach would be for the Government to co-finance audits of industrial plants and recommend efficiency investments. It would be the responsibility of the industry to undertake the measures and evaluate and report the results to the Government. Alternatively, the Government could allow accelerated depreciation of qualifying measures for tax purposes.**

In all IEA Member countries, environmental considerations are prodding governments to explore a wide range of measures, and improved energy efficiency is seen as an important element in this regard. The Polish Ministry of Environmental Protection has established a system of fees for emissions of various pollutants, including SO_x, NO_x and particulates (see Chapter 11). Emitters must satisfy the stricter of two different emission limits: grams/GJ based on fuel input, or absolute atmospheric concentrations. Even though the fees are low (well below the EU levels for these pollutants), the limits based on atmospheric concentrations should encourage emitters to seek a broad range of compliance options, including improved efficiency. However, the limits based on grams/GJ of fuel input do not provide an incentive for improved energy efficiency, since they are not based on the amount of fuel required to produce a unit of output. Thus, energy efficiency measures that would reduce overall emissions for a given level of product output, be it a tonne of steel or kilowatt-hour of electricity, would not satisfy the financial demands of the emission fees. There are several ways to align the financial incentives with a wider range of measures available to the emitter. One example would be to establish product-specific performance measures (e.g. GJ/tonne of steel), which could be combined with the grams/GJ system to recognise and reward improved efficiency.

Recommendation

- **The Government could examine ways to include options for encouraging consumers to improve energy efficiency as part of the Ministry of Environmental Protection's system of emission limits and fees. The per-unit emission limits, to the extent that they apply in a particular situation, do not provide an explicit reward for improved efficiency. A way of recognising efficiency improvements by a particular plant (or by another plant, under a tradable permit plan) could help achieve the Government's environmental goals more cost-effectively.**

Transport

Given the rapid growth observed and expected in this sector, inadequate attention has been paid to measures designed to limit the proliferation of inefficient vehicles and the expansive growth of vehicle-kilometres travelled. This sector continues to challenge IEA governments to find ways of increasing vehicle fuel efficiency and encouraging the use of public transport. Further analysis is required before specific policy measures can be suggested for Poland, but, in general, the Government could consider some of the approaches employed in the west.

Recommendation

- **The Government could evaluate the trade-offs associated with efficiency standards or other approaches for improving the efficiency of vehicles. Article 54 of the draft energy law seems to cover this possibility, as it authorises the MoIT to determine requirements for equipment via ordinances. However, the article is sketchy. The Government could also consider ways to improve and encourage public transit, such as the provision of bus-only lanes; a tax on gas guzzlers combined with a rebate for more efficient models; and labelling. Finally, Polish gasoline taxes are low by European standards: raising them before car ownership booms could encourage the purchase of more efficient cars.**

CHAPTER 6

COAL

The profound transformation of Poland's political and economic system that began in 1989 has created uncertainty about the hard coal industry's viability and role in the emerging market economy. As hard coal is of great importance to the national economy, the industry's restructuring and rationalisation raise sensitive political, social and economic issues.

Some key indicators demonstrate the coal sector's great significance. In 1993, hard coal covered two-thirds of Poland's TPES, a much higher proportion than in OECD Europe countries. The coal industry accounts for a significant share of GDP and coal export revenue is the mainstay of the country's foreign exchange earnings, despite the magnitude of the fall in coal exports in the 1990s. At the end of 1993, the industry employed about 320 000 people (out of a total national labour force of 7-8 million), nearly all of them in Upper Silesia.

The sector faces increasingly serious problems: high costs, scarcity of funds for investment, overstaffing and lack of alternative employment opportunities, deteriorating geological conditions and significant environmental consequences. The restructuring of the industry, which has begun, must adequately address these issues if the industry is to remain viable and retain its importance to the economy.

INDUSTRY OVERVIEW

Until around 1990, the hard coal industry had a strictly centralised structure. The Hard Coal Board oversaw the industry; the mines and their administrative superstructure were subordinated to the Planning Commission; and coal exports and distribution were in the hands of two state owned monopolies, Weglokoks and CZW. Since then, the industry's structure has undergone frequent change in the attempt to transform it from a monolithic, inefficient organisation, welded to a culture inherited from the communist age, into a more competitive business.

In 1989 the Ministry of Coal Mining was abolished and in 1990 the 70 individual coal mines were established as independent enterprises with the right to market their output independently, both domestically and abroad. The Hard Coal Board was to function as a link between the MoIT and the individual mines. Later, this institution became the State Hard Coal Agency, a centralised institution charged with overseeing the industry on behalf of its owner, the Government.

Early in 1993, a further reorganisation took place with the aim of strengthening the industry administratively and financially so as to ease the restructuring efforts but at the same time to avoid monopolistic conditions in the domestic market. Most of the mines were grouped into six joint stock companies and one holding company. After an interim merger, Weglokoks and CZW were established as joint stock companies in 1993 and their monopolies abolished.

State Hard Coal Agency

The State Hard Coal Agency was established on 1 August 1990 as a joint stock company wholly owned by the state Treasury and supervised on its behalf by the MoIT. It was formed from the planning and technical services of the Hard Coal Board.

The agency's principal role is to advise local and central government; its most important customers are the MoIT and the Ministry of Environmental Protection. It also provides services to the operating units in the sector, to the coal companies and to manufacturers of mining machinery and equipment. It is paid for its services on a fee basis.

At present, its main task is to support the restructuring programme through technical advice and monitoring. In this, its main clients are the MoIT and the mining companies. It also worked with foreign consultancies in 1994 and expects to expand this activity in 1995. As of June 1994 the company had a staff of 198, about 145 of whom were professionals.

Coal Companies and Mines

When the Hard Coal Agency was formed, the mines were separated as individual state enterprises. This was done as a reaction against previous centralised decision making. However, the structure proved unsatisfactory; company level decision making and independent negotiations between mines and power stations led to keen competition among the mines, and overcapacity drove prices down to a level that threatened the financial viability of the enterprises.

Accordingly, legal action was taken to group a majority of the mines into seven joint stock companies during 1993. The first six were established in April that year, incorporating 49 of the 70 mines. The joint stock companies were entirely owned by the state Treasury and supervised on its behalf by the MoIT. Integrated

into these companies, the mines lost their legal identity.

A seventh company, formed in June 1993, incorporated 11 more mines. It is described as a holding company (Katowice Holding Company), but in fact its legal form is identical to the others, with the individual legal identity of each mine not preserved. The main differences between the six joint stock companies and the holding company are in the areas of internal organisation and in incentives arising from the allocation of revenue. The coal companies' revenues are distributed among the mines to cover their costs while, in the Katowice Holding Company, revenues are distributed according to the value of the coal produced by each mine. Unlike the former method, this gives an incentive to the mines to reduce costs and allows them to compete with one another.

Eleven mines were not included in this structure, and continue to be individual enterprises under state ownership:

- Bogdanka in the Lublin area, geographically distinct from the others; it has good economic prospects and may form a holding company with the power stations in the area, which are its customers;

- Budryk, a mine under construction, originally included in one of the coal companies but later separated into a distinct joint stock company;

- two other mines in Upper Silesia with poor economic prospects and depleting reserves which will begin closure soon;

- four mines in Lower Silesia and three in Upper Silesia that had begun closure before the formation of the coal companies.

With these and other recent changes, the current structure, as far as the organisation of the mines is concerned, is:

Six coal companies	Katowice Holding Company	Independent mines - State Treasury companies	Mines under closure
49 mines	11 mines	4 mines	7 mines

When the companies were formed, many ancillary activities previously carried out by the mines (provision of housing, sports facilities, holiday resorts and other social functions) were separated into joint stock companies, which have been privatised. The transformation of the mines into joint stock companies was carried out under the Act of Ownership Transformation of Some Companies of Particular Importance to the National Economy, passed on 5 February 1993, which covers a variety of strategic industries. The regrouping of the coal mines caused some concern on the part of the Anti-Monopoly Office but its members were eventually persuaded that unrestrained competition would lead to social disruption and violence.

Weglozbyt (CZW)

CZW was created after World War II as a distribution company for coke, hard coal, brown coal, briquettes and other solid fuels. It originally handled all aspects of coal trade, including stock, exports and management of coal at ports. In 1952, another company, Weglokoks, was separated out and assigned responsibility for export sales. CZW has been in charge of brown coal trade at various periods; it was last relieved of this responsibility in 1988. For a short time, 1989 through March 1990, CZW was again joined with Weglokoks. On 5 February 1993, CZW was changed to a joint stock company, as was Weglokoks, under the Act on transformation of strategic industries; the company was registered on 1 July 1993. It has since adopted the name Weglozbyt (its old telex address) as a more identifiable and "user friendly" title. Two-thirds of the members of its supervisory board are nominated by the MoIT and one-third by staff.

Up to 1989, CZW managed the trade of hard coal on domestic markets and export markets, although in the former case the direct seller was Weglokoks. CZW determined the allocation of coal volumes and types to the domestic and export markets and, in the former, to the various sectors. It was responsible for balancing quantity, quality and type of coal in all markets. It carried out the financial settlements between mines and their customers and paid the transport costs involved. It also kept statistics required by the Government.

From 1 January 1990, CZW's obligatory role in coal trade was lifted. Each coal mine was then allowed to sell freely in the market. This caused great difficulties for CZW. Because new intermediaries came onto the market – at one time an estimated 1 000 traders were active – sales through CZW fell dramatically. These changed market circumstances obliged the company to market more aggressively and cut costs. As a consequence, some 50 per cent of its staff was discharged.

The situation eased slightly when CZW became a joint stock company. Some of its departments were abolished or transferred to Weglokoks (for example, transport settlements). In addition, the process of staff reduction became simpler because new rules made it possible for enterprises reducing the scope of their activity to declare people redundant. CZW, under great competitive pressure, took advantage of these rules.

The now rechristened Weglozbyt does not sell to power stations; its customers are industry and smaller traders who sell to households and small consumers. Prices for sales to industrial consumers are freely set, but old price lists issued by the Ministry of Finance are still used as reference. Competition is still strong, though statistics are not available on the breakdown of the market between Weglozbyt and other traders. Weglozbyt's competitive advantages lie in its experience, knowledge and reputation, its large capital base and its ability to offer high quality technical support on coal quality control, handling, preparation and combustion. Weglozbyt also manages a large, well equipped stockpile of 1.5-2 million tonnes (Mt), the largest in eastern Europe.

Weglokoks

Weglokoks was formed on 1 January 1952 as a state enterprise to sell hard coal, brown coal, coke and other solid fuels in foreign markets. Initially it was also responsible for the import of natural gas and, at one time, of electricity, but it lost these functions in the mid-1970s.

The founding body of Weglokoks was the Ministry of Foreign Economic Relations. For about 15 months, covering 1989 and the first quarter of 1990, the company was absorbed into CZW and transferred to the MoIT. On 1 April 1990, Weglokoks became an independent state enterprise under the MoIT and on 1 September 1993 was registered as a joint stock company. Its transformation into a joint stock company was provided for by the same Act as for the mines, but the date of registration was a little later. There is some thought, at a later stage of restructuring, of giving 50 per cent of the shares in Weglokoks to the coal producers and 25 per cent to the staff, with the remainder staying with the state.

Weglokoks originally had a monopoly of foreign trade based upon the Act on State Monopoly in Foreign Trade. At that time, the Central Planning Agency drew up the plans for allocation of coal to domestic markets and to export. Of the foreign trade, about 50 per cent was to CMEA countries, with payment in roubles. Most of this was rather poor quality steam coal fines to the Soviet Union. The remainder was screened coal for households, also of somewhat poor quality. Exports outside the rouble zone were of the highest quality products.

When the coal mines became independent, they acquired the right to trade freely on domestic and foreign markets and Weglokoks' monopoly of foreign trade was broken. The independent mines could trade directly, through Weglokoks or through other traders. Weglokoks had had a general licence to trade, but since 1990 every export contract has had to be covered by an individual licence. Licences were originally issued on a quarterly basis to ensure adequate supplies for the domestic market, but this created problems for exporters so licences are now valid for the duration of the contract.

The main purpose of the licensing system was to check for exports at excessively low prices and to discourage competition between Polish producers on export markets. In this, it does not appear to have been successful; competition developed and prices in the domestic market fell. Independent mines began to compete with Weglokoks for export by land freight to neighbouring countries – eastern Germany, Czechoslovakia, Hungary, Ukraine – where they could get better prices than in western Europe. The export monopoly had enabled Weglokoks to keep prices up and extract a large part of the geographical rent, but with competition, this rent was lost. Some estimates put the loss to the Polish economy at US$ 200 million over two years.

In mid-1992, Weglokoks attempted to institute new relations with the coal mines and it has since reached agreements with the mining companies covering Weglokoks' demand for coal for export for eight to ten years. The contracts cover 367 Mt of coal over the period to 2003, starting at around 25 Mt per year and rising to 40 Mt or so. This agreement will help Weglokoks maintain its position as the second largest coal exporter in the world (after Australia's Broken Hill Proprietary).

Weglokoks seems to expect the markets in neighbouring countries to grow only slowly and it thinks that substantial increases in exports will depend upon increased seaborne shipments. In this situation, Weglokoks can negotiate better rates and arrangements with railways and harbours than individual producers can, and it hopes by this means to persuade producers of the advantages of co-operation and market discipline. Weglokoks' experience and greater understanding of markets appears to have been an important influence in changing the behaviour of the mines. Co-operation is encouraged by the composition of Weglokoks' supervisory board, which comprises the seven chairmen of the coal companies, five members elected from the company staff, two members from the MoIT and one from the Ministry of Foreign Economic Relations.

Co-operation from the mines was also stimulated by the low prices for steam coal on world markets and the realisation that prices on the domestic market, by then relatively high, might not be sustainable. Moreover, payment for exports is generally more reliable.

DEMAND

The dominant market for Polish hard coal is the domestic market, though significant (but marginal and decreasing) amounts have been exported and coal remains Poland's main source of foreign exchange. Hard coal has always formed the bulk of Poland's TPES; its share of nearly two-thirds in the recent past is much higher than that in western Europe. A major proportion of the coal sold domestically – 60-70 per cent in recent years – is consumed in the generation of heat and power; some 45 per cent of total electricity generation is based on hard coal.

Another sector of note for hard coal use is households, which account for more than 10 per cent of total consumption – again, a much higher share than is typical in western Europe. This sector has seen the biggest recent decline in use. Consumption dropped by almost 45 per cent from 1990 to 1992.

The ongoing transformation of the Polish economy has led to predictions of declining energy intensity and substitution of other fuels for coal. These in turn have led to declining expectations for domestic coal consumption. For example, while a 1990 MoIT analysis forecasts coal consumption in 2000 at around 143-146 Mt, a 1993 MoIT study suggests a range of 116-137 Mt, with a "minimum consumption" scenario and a "maximum consumption" scenario (Table 6.1).

Both scenarios show hard coal continuing to be of key importance to the domestic energy sector and economy (particularly in electricity generation), even though its share in TPES is set to decline gradually. Forecasts by other bodies confirm these expectations. The study demonstrates that if production capacity is cut back to the range of 130-140 Mt as planned, this will be sufficient to meet the expected domestic demand and reinforce the domestic market's importance for hard coal sales. The key assumption underlying these forecasts is that Polish coal prices remain competitive, i.e. below the import parity price.

The outlook for exports is more debatable. Provided that Polish export prices remain competitive, that the demand is there and that there are no adverse movements of the zloty against other currencies, a return to the levels of the late 1980s of around 30 Mt is feasible; the second stage of the restructuring plan assumes the stabilisation of economically justified exports at 28-30 Mt. However, as the maximum consumption scenario shows, the level of domestic production could well mean a decline in exports, particularly if the import and export parity price differentials are large.

The markets for Polish coal are western Europe, eastern Europe and the former Soviet Union. Traditionally, western Europe has accounted for about half of Poland's coal trade – with Scandinavia taking 50 per cent of this share – while eastern Europe and the former Soviet Union took the other half. Apart from a small amount of coking coal, there have been no significant exports to the rest of the world. Exports to the former Soviet Union have dwindled to almost nothing, though trade with the Czech and Slovak Republics continues.

It is more useful to classify the Polish export markets into three types:

- neighbouring countries accessible by land freight;

Table 6.1
Hard Coal Balance in Poland, Actual and Forecast
(Mt)

	1990	1992	Minimum consumption scenario			Maximum consumption scenario		
			1995	2000	2005	1995	2000	2005
Production	148	132	142	136	139	148	145	146
Imports	1	0	0	4	0	0	6	12
Exports	28	20	29	24	22	14	14	13
Domestic demand	121	112	113	116	117	134	137	145
of which: Power and heat	78	70	62	72	76	83	89	100
other industr	26	21	18	17	16	17	17	17
other sectors, incl. losses	17	21	33	27	25	34	31	28

Sources: Marian Radetzki, "Poland's Hard Coal Industry: Prospects after Completed Restructuring", SNS Energy occasional paper No. 58, Stockholm 1994; CIE (domestic demand data 1990-92)

- Baltic and Scandinavian countries accessible by small to medium-sized ships;

- the rest of the world.

With regard to neighbouring countries, Poland enjoys a geographic rent provided that its coal prices remain below the CIF prices of imports by these countries. The distribution of the rent depends upon this factor and the result of negotiations between the parties. There is some disagreement as to whether the market for coal in these countries is likely to be a source of growth for Polish exports.

In an optimistic scenario, even if the total market for coal in Europe remains stagnant, the growing Europe-wide pressure to eliminate coal subsidies, particularly in western Europe, will mean a reduction of production, with imports replacing a large part of the decline in output. In this scenario, Polish coal exports within a 500 km radius of Silesia should be competitive with other imported coal because of the possibility of deliveries by rail. The newly unified German market is seen as being of key importance because of its proximity and the possibility of rail transport without reloading.

The advantage of the Baltic/Scandinavian markets is that no Baltic ports are big enough for the large bulk carriers usually used for coal shipments to western Europe. Poland can supply coal to these countries economically in smaller ships, obviating the need for transshipment via non-Baltic ports.

Exports to the rest of the world would involve seaborne shipments; given the inland transport costs from the Silesian mines to Polish harbours as well as the cost of ocean transport, it is doubtful whether Polish prices could match those of low cost producers like Australia, Indonesia and South Africa. It is therefore surprising that Weglokoks appears to believe that increased export growth will depend upon seaborne shipments.

An equally plausible outcome is that the competitiveness of Polish coal in its main export markets will deteriorate further. The levels of productivity attained by some overseas exporters are unlikely to be matched by Polish coal, given the constraints on shedding labour, the status of the deposits and the conditions under which coal extraction takes place.

There may be temptation, related to concerns about foreign exchange earnings and social welfare, for the Polish Government to press for export sales even at a commercial loss as long as variable costs are covered and the labour used could not be usefully employed elsewhere. This policy would carry two main risks: delaying restructuring by diminishing the commercial incentives, and reducing the ability to finance much needed new investment because of lower profits.

SUPPLY

Reserves

Poland's hard coal reserves are classified by state of exploration and possibility of exploitation. As for the former criterion, reserves are divided into demonstrated and undiscovered. Demonstrated reserves are subdivided into measured, indicated and inferred, undiscovered reserves into prospective, prognostic and hypothetic.

The main division by possibility of exploitation is between economic and uneconomic reserves. Economic reserves are further categorised as recoverable or unrecoverable, and recoverable reserves are subdivided into "for extraction" and "losses".

Poland's huge coal reserves constitute by far the largest part of its indigenous energy resources. Recoverable deposits up to a depth of 1 000 metres are estimated at 65 billion tonnes. They are thought to consist of about 70 per cent steam coal and 30 per cent coking coal. The Upper Silesian basin alone has some 57 billion tonnes. Of the 28 billion tonnes in mines currently in operation or under development, around 15 billion are regarded as minable given the present state of technology. At current rates of exploitation, coal reserves are sufficient for almost a century, as Tables 6.2 and 6.3 show.

Production

Developments

Production of hard coal in Poland grew steadily from 1950 until 1979, when it peaked at 201 Mt.

Table 6.2
Proven Hard Coal Reserves, January 1993
(Mt)

Coalfield area	Geological	Recoverable	Industrial
Upper Silesia	77 010	56 860	15 646
Lower Silesia	9 764	7 596	408
Lublin	667	194	54
Total	**87 441**	**64 650**	**16 108**

Source: State Hard Coal Agency

Table 6.3
Hard Coal Reserves at Active Mine Levels, January 1993
(Mt)

Levels	Recoverable	Industrial
Active	11 867	6 918
In development	2 430	1 385
Below active/in development	13 785	7 028
Total	**28 082**	**15 331**

Source: State Hard Coal Agency

During most of the 1980s, output remained at about 190 Mt a year, the bulk of it consumed domestically. Between 1950 and 1990, the industry generated exports of around 30 Mt per year, but as the world coal market expanded after the first oil crisis, the country's share in global trade declined.

In communist Poland, production levels did not reflect economic rationality. The industry was used to satisfy other economic and social goals. It was given incentives to maximise output (and, implicitly, employment) rather than profit.

In the 1990s, production started to decline sharply. This was due not so much to the restructuring of the industry and the adoption of free market policies as to the dramatic reduction in domestic requirements following the steep decline in economic activity, higher real coal prices and the introduction of shorter work weeks with banning of Sunday shifts and virtual elimination of productive shifts on Saturdays. A succession of mild winters combined with these factors to produce a large coal surplus. Exports also declined over this period, primarily because a lack of export co-ordination resulted in Polish-Polish competition between individual mines in foreign markets.

Figure 6.1
Hard Coal Production, Sales and Exports, 1989-93
(Mt)

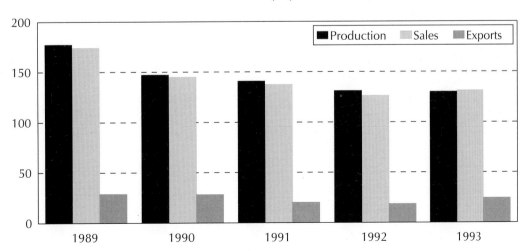

Source: Jan Piekorz, "The Transition to a Competitive Industry in the Polish Experience", paper delivered at World Bank Seminar on International Experience in Coal Industry, Washington DC, May 1994

Table 6.4 shows 1993 production broken down by mining companies/mines.

Extraction in 1994 was projected by the coal companies at 135.3 Mt: 108.3 Mt of steam coal and 27 Mt of coking coal. Total sales were forecast at 134.8 Mt – 107.1 Mt in the domestic market and 27.7 Mt in export markets. Figure 6.2 shows actual and forecast production levels from 1985 to 2010.

Table 6.4
**Hard Coal Production
by Coal Company/Mine, 1993**
(thousand tonnes)

Coal company/mine	Output
Bytom Coal Company	14 620
Rudzka Coal Company	12 756
Gliwicka Coal Company	17 205
Katowice Holding Company	23 621
Nadwislanska Coal Company	24 165
Rybnicka Coal Company	15 331
Jastrzebie Coal Company	15 211
Bogdanka mine	2 310
Jan Kanty mine	850
Porabka-Klimontow mine	1 014
Kopolnie mine	3 127
Total	**130 211**

Source: Piekorz, *op. cit.*

Location and number of mines

Poland's three coal mining regions are the Upper Silesian basin around Katowice/Gliwice at the Czech border; the Lower Silesian basin around Walbrzyck; and the Lublin basin in the south-east.

Upper Silesia is by far the most important of the three regions for hard coal. Of the 70 mines in existence in 1993, only four were in Lower Silesia and one, Bogdanka, in Lublin. The Lower Silesian mines are all due to be closed and no further collieries are planned in Lublin, where only one shaft has been developed.

Geological characteristics and production technology

Polish hard coal is fairly difficult to extract because of unfavourable geological conditions – tectonic faults, folding and inclination of the seams. Narrow seams are often exploited (particularly for

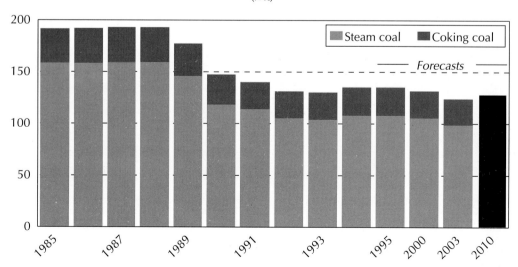

Figure 6.2
Hard Coal Production, 1985-2010
(Mt)

Source: State Hard Coal Agency

Figure 6.3
Location of Hard and Brown Coal Deposits

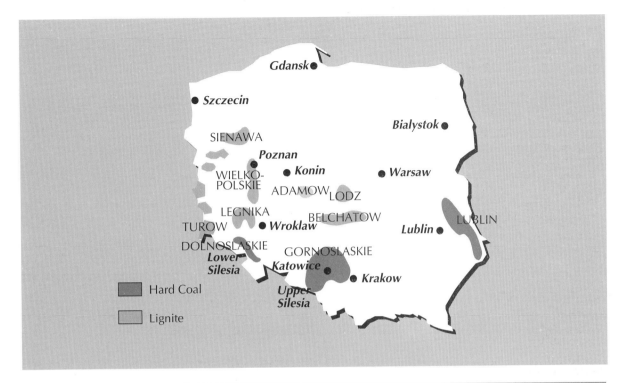

coking coal), extraction depths are high and rising, roof and floor conditions are difficult and miners are exposed to all kinds of hazards, such as methane, dust, fire and flooding.

Poland's hard coal deposits were laid down during the Carboniferous period. The area of productive deposits is 4 500 km² in Upper Silesia, 500 km² in Lower Silesia and 290 km² in the Lublin basin.

The spectrum of quality runs from anthracite and medium-volatile coking coal to high-volatile steam coal. The Upper Silesian basin has all types, the Lower Silesian only anthracite and coke, and the Lublin basin only steam coal.

Quality varies considerably. Ash content in mine-field reserves differs greatly, reaching 40 per cent in four mines, while sulphur content ranges from nearly zero to 5 per cent. The sulphur content of the run-of-mine coal is usually 0.5 to 1 per cent; the average sulphur content of washed coal is 0.7 to 0.9 per cent. Table 6.5 shows average coal quality in 1992 and 1993.

Average extraction depth has increased steadily as production has risen and older seams have been

Table 6.5
Hard Coal Quality in 70 Mines, 1992 and 1993

Year	Mean calorific content (kJ/kg)	Average ash content (%)	Mean sulphur content (%)
1992	23 909	15.7	0.77
1993	24 178	15.2	0.75

Source: Andrzej Karbownik, "Assumption and Status of the Reforms in Hard Coal Mining Sector", paper delivered at seminar organised by IEA, MoIT and CIE in Warsaw, 28-29 March 1994

Table 6.6
Evolution of Mechanisation, 1960-90

	Unit of measure	1970	1980	1990
Total year output	Mt	140.1	192.7	147.4
Operating longwall faces	number	961	716	738
Share of output from longwall faces	per cent	80.9	87.8	90.0
Faces with powered support	number	22	376	589
Share of output from faces with powered support	per cent	3.0	66.9	86.0
Daily output from faces with powered support	tonnes/day	797	1 249	1 054
Average daily output from faces	tonnes/day	484	921	880
Operating shearers	number	519	565	590
Share of double-ended drum shearers	per cent	6	74	94
Coal ploughs	number	65	69	97
Heading machines	number	10	276	456

Source: Polish Academy of Sciences Mineral and Energy Economy Research Centre, "Coal Mining Economy and Policy in Poland and Its Prospects in the Light of Overall Economic Reforms and of the Experience of Coal Industry in Germany and Great Britain", Krakow, 1992.

exhausted. In 1971 the exploitation depth averaged 406 metres. In 1992 it was 590 metres, and increase of 5 metres a year on average. Seam thickness ranges from 0.7 to 5 metres, with 6 per cent of seams being thicker than 7 metres. About 65 per cent of extractable reserves are in seams of 1.5 metres or more. The share of economic reserves in seams of 1.5-3 metres is expected to decrease and that of seams below 1.5 metres and above 3 metres to increase.

The effectiveness and productivity of coal exploitation will depend greatly on technical factors, especially the equipment and methods used at the coal face. Mining techniques in Poland are comparable to those in other European countries. Coal is mined from multiple seams through vertical opencast and blind shafts, and the production process is mechanised to a fairly high extent (although less than in Germany and the United Kingdom). Some 90 per cent of production is mined by longwall technique, mainly as longwall caving, and controlled gravity stowing is also used in inclined bedding.

Given the ever increasing output and, particularly, export targets of former governments, the coal mines were forced to mechanise. However, much of their equipment and technology are old and inefficient because of the persistent lack of investment over

the years. Table 6.6 shows the mechanisation development in Poland from 1960 to 1990.

Tables 6.7 and 6.8 give data for 1993.

Among the aims of the technical restructuring programme for 1994-95 are the introduction of fully mechanised mining longwalls with mechanised linings, combined cutter-loaders, conveyors with output of 2 500 to 4 000 tonnes per day per face and mechanisation of indirect product services to reduce the number of employees. On the basis of these aims and the planned mine closures, a significant increase in extraction concentration is forecast, highlighted by a reduction in the number of walls mined and an increase in mining output per wall.

Coal processing equipment in Poland is technically obsolete and inadequate in terms of volume. In the communist era, when the policy was to maximise the output of coal and electricity, the pricing system provided no incentive to invest in washers. Prior to 1990, only course and medium grain steam coal (>20 mm) was washed; most of the steam coal fines (<20 mm) burnt in power stations were used as run-of-mine coal (all coking coal has always been beneficiated because the pricing structure, different from that for steam coal, encouraged this). Mines had no incentive to

Table 6.7
Technique and Technology of Extraction, 1993

Specification	Unit of measure	Total	With caving	With hydraulic backfilling	With dry stowing
Production	thousand tonnes	130 210	112 300	16 312	1 600
Share	per cent	100.0	86.3	12.5	1.2
Average daily extraction front	metres	83 905	65 980	16 145	1 780
Mean daily output from one longwall *	tonnes/ day	1 100	1 310	668	649
Number of active longwalls *	number	498	432	60	6

* Not including mines under closure.

Source: State Hard Coal Agency

produce high quality coal because their targets were volumetric; indeed, delivering high ash content coal helped boost volume output.

Poland's 91 operating coal preparation plants have a total throughput potential of 70 000 tonnes per hour. They have the following characteristics [1]:

- 48 coarse grain washers for the preparation of coarse and medium grain sizes +20 (10) mm with throughput of 32 000 tonnes per hour and production potential of 448 000 tonnes per day;

Table 6.8
Basic Machines and Equipment, 1993

Type	Number in operation
Powered supports	46 000 sections
Shearers	469
Coal ploughs	32
Road headers	248
Loaders and floor loaders	694
Scraper conveyers	6 916
Belt conveyers	8 281
Suspended monorails	768
Floor train-units	56

Source: State Hard Coal Agency

- 32 coal washers for fractions 20 (10) - 0 mm with throughput of 14 000 tonnes per hour and production potential of 196 000 tonnes per day;

- 22 coking coal flotation sections 1 - 0 mm with throughput of 3 500 tonnes per hour and production potential of 49 000 tonnes per day.

There has been a substantial effort since 1990 to increase the amount of coal washed, particularly as most sulphur in Polish coal is inorganic and hence fairly easy to remove by washing. Moreover, all washers have closed water cycles, so there is no problem of contamination of water with fine material from the washers. Polish power stations' hard coal needs in 2000 are forecast at 50 Mt with a mean ash content of 14.5 per cent and average sulphur content of 0.7 per cent. With this in mind, the following investments have been envisaged by 2003:

- construction of 20 preparation and desulphurisation plants for fine steam coal processing;

- construction of 13 sections for fine steam coal coking;

- retrofitting of five fine steam coal washers.

It is not clear, however, whether this investment programme suits the capabilities of the generating plants. The average ash content of coal burned in Poland is currently around 22 per cent. Coal with 14.5 per cent ash, which would have a calorific

---

1. The number of individual washers does not add up to the number of coal preparation plants, as some plants have more than one washer.

Table 6.9
Results of Coal Preparation Plant Operations, 1993

Products	Per cent of net production	Calorific value (kJ/kg)	Ash content (%)	Sulphur content (%)
Total commercial (net) production, of which:	100.0	24 200	15.2	0.75
Steam coal concentrates 20 (10) - 0 mm	16.9	27 000	6.5	0.67
Steam coal concentrates 20 (10) - 0 mm	8.1	25 000	11.8	0.80
Coking coal concentrate 20 (30) - 0 mm	20.1	29 500	6.4	0.67
Middlings	3.4	21 600	22.9	0.74
Unwashed fines	51.5	21 300	21.5	0.83

Source: State Hard Coal Agency

value 23 per cent higher than the present average, may be outside the operating range of all existing Polish power plants. Moving to this level could necessitate reboilering of the entire generating stock. A combined assessment of investments in coal preparation and reboilering would be desirable.

The investments would be expected to result in a total production potential of 142 000 tonnes per day, a volume of washed fines of 40 Mt, calorific value of 21 000 to 27 000 kJ/kg, ash content of 10-15 per cent and sulphur content of 0.5-1.1 per cent.

Preparation plants for the Piast, Ziemowit, Czeczot, Wesola, Boleslaw Smialy, Pokoj and Wujek mines are perhaps the most pressing investment need. The quality of their raw stream coal fines puts these mines in a particularly difficult position. It is estimated that if these plants were built, the coal quality would be 24 000 kJ/kg, ash content below 8 per cent and sulphur content below 0.6 per cent.

Productivity trends

Labour productivity is much lower in European coal mining than in such exporting countries as Columbia, Australia and South Africa, primarily because most European mining takes place underground and under more difficult geological conditions.

Labour productivity in Poland is particularly low, however, even in comparison with the major western European producers. In 1991, coal output

in Poland was 400 tonnes per employee. The corresponding German and UK figures were 630 and 1 520 tonnes: the German coal industry was nearly 60 per cent more productive than the Polish coal industry, and the British output rate was nearly 280 per cent higher. Productivity levels in Poland have declined since the late 1980s because employment cuts did not match the decline in production.

The flip side of low productivity is excessive employment, and the industry is still to some degree suffering from the communist legacy of maximising output and job creation rather than cost-effectiveness. This legacy is being tackled but the pace of change has been slow because of the social implications of unemployment. Projections for 2000 indicate, however, that under the long term restructuring programme for the coal industry, productivity will rise substantially. Figure 6.4 compares the past, present and expected performance of the industry in terms of productivity.

Improving labour productivity is a means of attaining lower unit costs, not an end in itself. There is no point in striving for the lower labour/capital ratio of western European countries; such a policy would not make use of the comparative advantage offered by the lower cost of Polish labour.

Other options for raising productivity include better methods of organising work (for example, better shift working) and increased use of capital. The former option can certainly lead to significant productivity gains and should be applied at all economic mines. The major problem with the

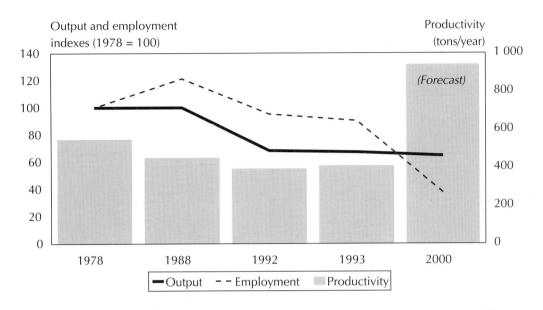

Figure 6.4
Hard Coal Productivity, 1978-2000

Output and employment indexes (1978 = 100)

Productivity (tons/year)

(Forecast)

Legend: ■ Output   - - Employment   ▨ Productivity

Source: Radetzki, *op. cit.*

latter option is that the true investment needs can as yet only be guessed at, given the inaccurate depreciation of the past, and even less is known about the extent to which these needs might be satisfied, in light of the scarcity of funds. Estimates for annual investment expenditure are in the range of US$ 400-600 million, but their accuracy and feasibility are debatable.

RATIONALISATION

The biggest obstacle to further restructuring and rationalisation and proposed closures is the social implications of job losses. Concomitant with the decline in production there has already been a fall in employment in the coal industry (Figure 6.5).

Pursuing policies that will lead to even higher levels of redundancy in coal mining areas raises obvious problems, and it is recognised that if the planned mine closures are to be successfully carried out, three conditions must be met: i) responsibility for financing of social and techni-cal costs of closure must be taken by the state; ii) a permanent redundancy benefit system

must be established and its financing secured; iii) new employment must be created in the coal mining regions.

For the second stage of the restructuring programme, an informal agreement has been reached between the Government and miners. Its salient features are:

- no group dismissals of underground hard coal miners;

- reduction of employment in active mines only through:

  – natural attrition or at the employee's request;

  – a freeze on recruitment of workers from outside hard coal mining;

  – voluntary use of the social safety net;

  – transfer of mine employees to new economic entities created on the basis of the mines' assets;

- no liquidation of mines apart from those already announced;

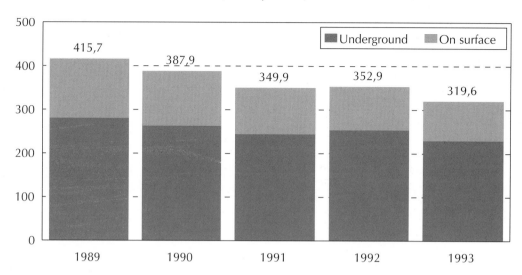

Figure 6.5
Employment in Hard Coal Industry, 1989-93
(1 000 persons)

Source: Piekorz, *op. cit.*

- a job offer at an active mine for each pit worker losing his job at a liquidated mine, or social safety net benefits if the miner prefers,

- other retraining and job creation programmes.

The pace of mine closure is therefore governed by the rate miners can be transferred to other mines as older workers leave these latter. As the average age of a miner in Poland is 26 years, this process will be quite slow. In addition, accelerated closure is limited by the scarcity of resources to finance unemployment benefits.

There is some slight incentive for early retirement. A miner can now retire three years before what would ordinarily be his first opportunity. An underground miner's first retirement option normally comes after 25 years; a miner choosing to retire early is paid for the three remaining years through a special budget line based on annual forecasts. Some 7 000 miners were expected to use this option in 1994; many miners, however, may prefer to work on, even past 25 years underground, because their pensions would be much less than their pay and alternative job opportunities are few.

Hence, the restructuring programme as it exists depends on fairly weak incentives to individual miners. As for the coal companies and mines,

under the informal agreement those that manage to reduce staff have to accept miners from a mine being closed. Some mines should, on economic grounds, be liquidated, but closure is the responsibility of their mining companies, and under the informal agreement they cannot act unless they can find other jobs for the miners – an extremely difficult task given the rate of unemployment in the mining areas.

In addition, because the coal sector is not competitive but rather is an organised market, it has been possible to pass on the costs of overmanning, and thus the operating companies have had no commercial incentives to reduce their workforce. As shedding labour is a difficult option, provoking industrial unrest, management tends to take the path of least resistance. However, recent signs of consumer resistance to full pass-through of costs indicate that commercial pressures to restructure may be building up.

It should also be noted that the present coal industry management has little experience operating in a market oriented environment and pursuing the new economic goals. Organisational structures, embedded habits and social inertia, together with the social responsibilities imposed by the Government on the hard coal industry, add to the difficulties faced by management. Extensive training in adapting to a market oriented economy is a key element for a successful restructuring. A training programme for senior management, funded by the PHARE programme, was carried out by a foreign consulting group in 1994. Other courses have been organised by the MoIT and the Energy Restructuring Group using Polish specialists. This co-operation should be continued and enhanced.

Halting the losses incurred by uneconomic mines could provide funds for more generous redundancy payments, but Polish employment law does not allow unique solutions to be created for certain types of workers – the three year mining leave arrangement is already an exemption. More importantly, there is no incentive for the Government to rationalise production: given the lack of other work, and the political problems attendant on announcing further job losses, it makes little difference to the authorities whether a miner is adding zero value inside or outside the industry. This will be the case until there are other, genuinely productive employment opportunities, and they may take some time to establish.

For productivity to improve significantly, sizable reductions in employment are needed. The State Hard Coal Agency's view is that the present production level of around 130-135 Mt a year could be sustained with half the existing workforce.

Due to the sharp decline in coal demand since 1989, there is overcapacity in the mining sector. Apart from the need to shed labour, capacity reductions are badly needed, particularly closures of uneconomic pits. However, the pace of mine liquidation is, once again, governed to a large degree by social constraints rather than economic considerations. The following programme of mine closures is planned:

I. Lower Silesian mines

Walbrzych mines: under closure process
Nowa Ruda: under closure process

II. Upper Silesian mines not integrated in coal companies

Saturn: under closure process
Sosnowiec: under closure process
Zory: i. partial closure during 1994-95

ii. incorporation in 1995 into the Borynia mine, Jastrzebie Coal Company

III. Upper Silesian mines integrated in coal companies

Barbara-Chorzow: under closure process
Paryz: under closure process
Pstrowski: under closure process
Siemianowice: i. partial closure during 1994-96

ii. termination of extraction in mine, 31 December 1996

iii. liquidation of mine in 1997

Table 6.10
State of Employment in Mines, 1993-95
(1 000 persons)

	As of 31 Dec 1993	As of 31 Dec 1994 (preliminary)	As of 31 Dec 1995 (forecast)
1. Total workforce	303.2	271.3	250.8
2. Reduction of which	–	31.9	20.5
due to natural departures and privatisation of surface facilities	–	24.9	17.7
due to voluntary use of the social safety net	–	7.0	2.8

Source: MoIT

IV. Mines restructuring through partial closure

Rymer: partial closure during 1994-95

Porabka-Klimontow: partial closure during 1994-95

Jowisz: partial closure during 1994-95 (decisions in preparation)

Jan Kanty: partial closure during 1994-95 (decisions in preparation)

As table 6.10 shows, total employment is the mining industry is forecast to decline by about 17 per cent during 1994 and 1995. Table 6.11 shows the estimated costs of this closure programme.

It is difficult to know how accurate the cost predictions in Table 6.11 will turn out to be and to what extent the technical, environmental and social costs have been analysed. A mining site that has been closed and restored will have a value for other uses, which should be subtracted from the closure costs but seldom is. A pilot study to develop an accelerated least cost closure programme for one mine was carried out in 1994; the results are not publicly available, but they are believed to show considerable scope for reducing the time scale and costs of closure while meeting all safety and environmental criteria.

One assessment of the costs of closing 17 mines came to a total of US$ 870 million or around US$ 50 million per mine, while another concluded that the total cost would be US$ 1.2 billion or US$ 70 million per mine. Social costs make up 12-14 per cent of these totals.

It is held that, because of the substantial excess capacity in the industry, the loss in output from these mines could be more than made up for by increased output from others to maintain the planned production level of around 130-140 million tonnes a year. This seems reasonable: while the average monthly output in 1993 was 10.8 Mt, the actual monthly output over the 16 months period ending in December 1993 ranged from a monthly high of 13.3 Mt to a low of 6.8 Mt. The 13.3 Mt was achieved in a five day work week, and so represents less than the full capacity limit.

It is estimated that the costs of the mine closure programme will be recovered within two to three years from the benefits of lower production costs (the benefits being the production costs of the closed mines less the costs of increasing output at working mines).

Table 6.11
Cost of Mine Liquidation, 1994 and 1995
(Zl billion)

		I	II	III	IV	Total mines	V	Total
Cost of physical liquidation	1994	722	395	614	342	2 073	0	2 073
	1995	585	609	961	197	2 352	0	2 352
Cost of social safety net	1994	128	75	160	60	423	164	587
	1995	188	56	174	45	463	90	553
Total	1994	850	470	774	402	2 496	164	2 660
	1995	773	665	1 135	242	2 815	90	2 905

Notes: I = Lower Silesian mines, II = Upper Silesian mines outside of coal companies, III = Upper Silesian mines in coal companies, IV = Partially liquidated mines, V = Mining Works Enterprise (PRG) and Shaft Construction Enterprise (PBSz).

The cost of social safety net has been calculated for:

a) 1 900 employees of mines and PRG for 1993,

b) 7 000 employees of mines (estimated) for 1994,

c) 1 000 employees of PRG and PBSz (estimated) for 1994.

Source: MoIT

ENVIRONMENTAL ISSUES [2]

Of the many environmental problems facing the mining industry, there are two priorities: saline water emissions and solid waste accumulation.

The three largest mines, Ziemonwist, Crenott and Piost, are on a list compiled by the Ministry of Environmental Protection of the worst polluters in Poland: they are obliged to solve the pollution problems they create or they will be forced to close. This would be unfortunate for the industry, as they are good, modern mines with horizontal bedding of seams producing 80 000 tonnes per day at low cost.

The saline water problem may be remedied by

- concentrating on higher seams with less water ingress, reinjecting water into deeper structures and sealing intrusions into operating longwalls;

- desalinating the remaining water pumped from the mines.

A desalination plant is already operating at the Dgbiensko mine using Polish technology depending on evaporation, based on heat generated from mine by-products. A second plant is in construction using reverse osmosis. New plants that will process 30 000 cubic metres of water per day are planned for the three principal mines; a feasibility study of the project has been prepared under the PHARE programme.

In the Katowice area, huge amounts of solid waste have accumulated on the surface as a result of past operations. The general trend today is to reduce the volume of solid waste by using minestone as construction material wherever possible, by reducing waste production, by changing exploitation techniques and by backfilling. Some waste from coal preparation plants is mixed with dry material and backfilled.

Environmental regulations require mines to pay a fee (now about US$ 1.5 per tonne) for all solid waste disposed of on the surface. Total environmental fees for the coal industry, retrospectively assessed for 1991-93, are about US$ 200 million, of which about one-quarter has been paid so far. The industry hoped by mid-1994 to have paid the rest by the end of that year and start paying on a current year basis by 1995.

The mines plan environmental investments accounting for 10-30 per cent of their total planned investments, the share varying by company. This level of environmental investment is far below what is necessary. It will be financed out of retained profits and from a fund managed by the Government and replenished by fees paid by industry for use of environmental resources.

Table 6.12
Environmental Fees Due and Paid by Hard Coal Mines, 1993
(Zl million)

Type of fee	Charged for	Fees due	Fees paid *	Indebtedness		
				Fees due	Interest	Total
Environmental fees	Qtr 1 of 1991 - 1993	3 253	606	2 647	770	3 417
Exploitation fees	Dec 1991 - Sep 1992	625	133	492	–	492
Total		**3 878**	**739**	**3 139**	**770**	**3 909**

* As of 30 September 1993.

Source: State Hard Coal Agency

2. See Chapter 11 for further details.

PRICES AND COSTS

Prices

Until 1990, prices took second place to the allocation of resources prescribed in industrial plans. Set by the central planners, prices had no economic significance and their levels did not cover the costs of production.

Since World War II, the system of coal pricing has been changed several times – in 1954, 1958, 1959, 1970 and 1990. Tables were published listing the prices of different qualities of coal measured by calorific value, ash and sulphur content. The steam coal price lists were designed to be consistent with the prevailing policy that steam coal should be burnt as run-of-mine coal; the price differential for washed coal did not cover the costs of washing, and consequently investment in washers was inadequate. For coking coal, a different pricing structure with a preferential for coal quality was established, and in consequence, all coking coal is beneficiated.

Price Formula for Steam Coal

$$S_e = r_e \times W_e \times C_e^b \, [Q_w^r/25\ 120.8 - (S_t^r - 1)/10 - (A^r - 12)/100]$$

Definitions:

S_e = price of steam coal, Zl 1000/Mg

r_e = index of price relation, dependent on coal size

W_e = index of price decrease, dependent on ash content range:
W_e = 1 for ash content = 5.0-12.0%
W_e = 0.98...0.82 for ash content of 12.1-21%
(index decreases by 0.02 for each 1% increase of ash content)
W_e = 0.8 for ash content of 21.1-45%

C_e^b = price of reference coal, Zl 1000

Q_w^r = heat content in coal as received, kJ/kg

S_t^r = sulphur content in coal as received, %

A^r = ash content in coal as received, %

Quality parametres of reference coal:

Heat content – 6 Gcal/tonne (25 120.8 kJ/tonne)

Ash content – 12%

Sulphur content – 1%

Moisture content – 8%

Remarks:

To get the price of any coal, enter the following values into the formula:

- Heat content in kJ/kg, rounded down to units, in the range 10 000-32 000 kJ/kg

- Ash content in %, rounded up to units, in the range 5.0 - 45.0%

- Sulphur content in %, rounded up to multiple of 0.2%, in the range 0.4-4.0%

Coal price rounded to Zl 100 according to rule

Power plants were designed to burn unwashed coal with high ash and sulphur contents. Since the ash content of Polish coal is generally high, there are power plants designed to burn coal of up to 33 per cent ash content. And yet, no matter how high the tolerance of the plant, the mines used to deliver coal of even worse quality; essentially the problem of waste was transferred from the mine to the power station.

In 1989 the new Government decided to abandon the former coal pricing policy, and in 1990 it introduced a new price list. Coal prices were calculated by separate formulas for steam and coking coal. The main feature of the formulas was that they allowed a complete price list to be created from a reference coal price level only: they gave the change in price of a given quality coal depending on how the quality parameters of

---

Price Formula for Coking Coal

$$S_k = r_k \times W_k \times C_k^b \, [1 - (A^d - 6)/50 - S_t^d/20 - (W_t^r - 8)/100]$$

Definitions:

S_k = price of coking coal, Zl 1000/Mg

r_k = index of price relation, dependent on coal type

W_k = index of price decrease, dependent on ash content range
W_k = 1.040; 1.038; ...0.945 for ash content of 4-9%
(index decreases by 0.002 for each 0.1% increase of ash content)

C_k^b = price of reference coal, Zl 1000

A^d = ash content in coal, dry basis, %

S_t^d = total sulphur content in coal, dry basis, %

W_t^r = total moisture content in coal as received, %

Quality parametres of reference coal:

Heat content – 7 Gcal/tonne (29 307.6 kJ/tonne)

Ash content – 6%

Sulphur content – 1%

Moisture content – 8%

Volatile matter content – 24%

Remarks:

To get the price of any coal, enter the following values into the formula:

- Ash content in %, rounded up to 0.1 %, in the range 4-9%

- Sulphur content in %, rounded p to 0.1 %, in the range 0.4-2.%

- Moisture content in %, rounded up to 0.5 %, in the range 6-11%

Coal price rounded up to Zl 100 according to rule

Sources, coal price formulas: Wieslaw Blaschke, Eugeniusz Mokrzycki, Stanislaw A. Blaschke, Zbigniew Grudzinski, Lidia Gawlik and Urszula Lorenz, Polish Academy of Sciences Mineral and Energy Economy Research Centre: "Coal Prices vs. Coal Quality in Polish Conditions of the Transition to the Market Economy", Krakow

that coal differed from those of the reference coal. The reference coal price level could be determined by the market situation or by negotiation but, once it was established, the structure of prices was given.

Because of a lack of homogeneity, quality distinctions are made between three categories:

- the average for all Polish coal (in 1993, 5 800 kcal/kg, 15 per cent ash and 0.75 per cent sulphur content);

- the "marker" steam coal (5 250 kcal/kg, 21 per cent ash, 0.9 per cent sulphur);

- the "reference" steam coal (6 000 kcal/kg, 12 per cent ash, 1 per cent sulphur).

This distinction between "marker" and "reference" coal is necessary; as no coal on the world market has such high ash and sulphur contents, no easy reference exists. The present marker price for Polish coal is US$ 32 per tonne and the reference price is calculated by fitting the parameters in the Polish formula to the characteristics of coal available on the world market and extrapolating to the characteristics of Polish marker coal. This is not really appropriate but it has been agreed after difficult negotiations, and none of the parties wish to renegotiate.

The basic aim of the formulas' design was to provide an incentive for better coal preparation. The intention was to give an 18 month to two year payback period for new investments in washers. The formulas were designed in such a way that the relationship between price and ash content described a three part linear function with a steeply declining section for coal with ash content between 12 and 21 per cent. In principle, this gave a strong incentive to improve the coal quality from the typical 20-22 per cent ash level down to 8-10 per cent.

The formulas were only partly successful in promoting benefication. Although the new system gave an incentive to the mines to produce washed coal, it gave no incentive to power plants to buy the more expensive coal; they reverted back to burning run-of-mine coal. There is an intention to revise the formulas to give a straight linear dependence on ash content so that the managers of the mining companies can decide for themselves what coal preparation plants to build and where to build them.

Price lists based on the formulas were issued by the Ministry of Finance in May 1990. In October 1991, following the lists ceased to be obligatory but the coal mines (later the coal companies) had to get the acceptance of the voivodship agency of the Ministry of Finance for any deviation. Since the third quarter of 1992, price changes have been, in principle, at the discretion of the company but in practice there is considerable informal agreement in price setting and production allocation, and all buyers and sellers continue to operate on the basis of the formulas because they are known and convenient. Rapid inflation undermined the utility of the lists but was dealt with by changing the reference price of coal; by December 1993, a multiplier of slightly more than eight was applied.

During the early 1990s domestic prices have basically been determined through regular negotiations between the coal companies and their major clients, with the MoIT often playing a role crucial for the outcome. Prices to the power stations, for example, are agreed between the mine companies and the power station managers, sometimes with the MoIT present. They are not the same for each power station; the price of coal for a given power station is the reference price modified by a factor indicating the contribution of coal to the costs of the station. The idea is not to disadvantage less efficient power plants.

In the final analysis, the price of coal to power stations is a political decision since there are significant economic and social implications. It appears that pricing decisions depend on the access of affected groups to decision makers – in the recent past, prices were set to the advantage of power stations, but more recently they have been adjusted to a level (around US$ 30-32 per tonne) that benefits the mines and may be more than the power sector can pay, unless electricity prices are increased to reflect the higher fuel costs.

Despite this semi-administration of prices, domestic coal prices in Poland have increased rapidly since 1990 through numerous ad-justments (although they were high enough to cover production costs only towards the end of 1993). The increases met with considerable resistance and the Government is now understandably wary, in view of the social implications, of over-rapid price alignment and

Table 6.13
Average Price of Coal Sold, 1993, 70 mines
(Zl 1 000)

	1992 average	1993 Quarter I	1993 Quarter II	1993 Quarter III	1993 Quarter IV	1993 average	per cent change from 1992
Total all markets	377.6	446.3	452.7	554.2	676.4	539.3	42.8
of which:							
home	358.2	443.9	442.2	582.5	676.1	536.0	49.6
power gen.	266.0	330.6	354.2	426.8	513.5	405.1	52.3
coking plants	470.9	588.0	629.7	823.8	915.1	741.9	57.5
export	488.8	523.1	494.0	517.2	678.3	548.5	12.2

Source: Karbownik, *op. cit.*

full market pricing. Table 6.13 shows the changes in average prices in 1993.

As prices reach levels where recorded production costs are being covered, the industry has halted the growth of its debt, and since September 1993 it has begun accumulating funds. It is felt that the present marker price levels of around US$ 30-32 per tonne will allow the industry to break even with no further need for subsidies, though the huge amount of indebtedness remains to be resolved.

In conditions of perfect competition, the domestic price should be somewhere between the import parity price (if it was above this level, consumers would wish to import) and the export parity price (if below, producers would wish to export) – between US$ 20 and US$ 40 per tonne in the current situation. Although it is difficult to say where within this range the price should settle, the level at the time of writing (late 1994) of around US$ 30-32 per tonne is within the range specified and, at first sight, appears reasonable. With proper rationalisation of production and a sufficient lowering of costs, these prices might be sufficient to ensure the industry's long term viability.

However, two countervailing factors threaten the stability of prices. First, it is almost certain that the true costs of production are still above recorded costs, and prices will need to rise even higher unless rationalisation lowers the real costs of production quickly. Second, the present price levels are difficult to reconcile with the overcapacity that has emerged.

Given the tight constraints on reducing labour, wages are almost a fixed cost. Effective competition between mine companies should drive prices down to their export parity level, or possibly even lower if export markets and infrastructure became saturated and coal had to be disposed of in the domestic market at short run marginal costs.

This eventuality is averted at present by a considerable degree of market organisation. Coal producers appear not only to agree price schedules jointly (with the aid of the MoIT) but also to allocate production levels among themselves, a practice obviously facilitated by the state ownership of the coal producers and their major customers. Further empirical evidence for the existence of this market structure is provided by the great difference in prices for domestic sales and exports. Broadly, the domestic market is supplied at a relatively high price and the remaining production is sold at export parity. This is only possible in theory with a degree of market organisation.

There are good reasons for not letting prices fall to the lower levels that would obtain under competition, but this degree of market organisation conflicts with other objectives, particularly the rationalisation of production. The present prices are not necessarily stable and may break down under the stresses of competition and the need to cover true production costs.

Costs

Given the present position of the Polish coal mining industry, it is imperative to get production costs down. As in the case of prices, cost considerations were of only secondary importance to volume targets prior to 1989. The problems in analysing the cost structures of the mining industry are numerous and stem from the quality and reliability of available cost statistics. To a large extent, these problems date from the communist era – the cost accounts of the coal industry are still heavily influenced by practices from that time. Thus any scrutiny of costs has to start with an analysis of exactly what costs are being recorded or omitted.

Figure 6.6 gives costs and their breakdown by category for the Polish hard coal industry for 1991-93. In addition, extraordinary cost items of US$ 171 million, US$ 220 million and US$ 288 million were recorded for 1991, 1992 and 1993, respectively.

The validity of these figures is questionable on at least four grounds:

- The low depreciation figures suggest that capital costs are greatly underestimated: in the days of central planning, the assets from investments

were often entered in the books at artificially low values. At that time, coal industry managers had an incentive to suppress costs via low depreciation, in view of the depressed revenue they received from low, centrally set prices.

- The mining industry is heavily indebted but it appears that the industry does not pay interest on much of the debt.

- The extent to which environmental costs have been fully incorporated into the accounts is highly uncertain. In the communist era, little or no attention was paid to environmental concerns. The "extraordinary" costs incurred by the industry were in part fines due for non-compliance with environmental regulations, apparently on a regular basis; it is misleading to classify them as extraordinary.

- Under the communist regime, there was a host of social expenditures undertaken by the mining industry, e.g. housing, health and recreation expenses, which do not appear in the accounts.

These factors all indicate that the true costs of the industry are substantially higher than the "book-keeping" costs of US$ 30-32 per tonne. Just how much higher is difficult to tell, given the conjecture

Figure 6.6
Costs and Breakdown by Category, Hard Coal Industry, 1991-93

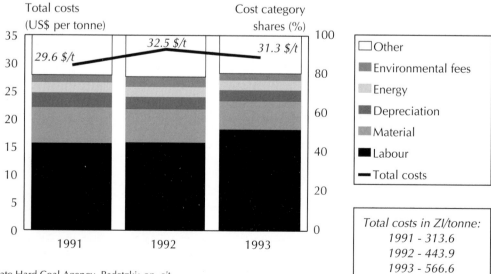

Sources: State Hard Coal Agency, Radetzki; *op. cit.*

and speculation that such an analysis necessarily involves, but several studies suggest an extra 20-30 per cent, implying that a cost range of US$ 36-42 per tonne would be nearer the mark.

The potential for future cost reductions will depend upon the progress of the rationalisation programme and how the issues of overcapacity, excess labour, low productivity, and investment are resolved. As Figure 6.7 shows, the mining industry now has a high cost production tail when mines are ranked by unit cost.

This high cost tail needs to be eliminated. Thus pit closures need to go beyond those planned for 1994-95 and more uneconomic mines need to be liquidated (though this is not to say that supply should be reduced at all mines where production costs are above prices received, because the cost curve depicted is not the short run marginal supply curve; since a major share of total costs is fixed, the short run supply curve lies below the cost curve shown). These factors will tend to reduce production costs, but will be offset to some extent by the investment needed for modernisation and other purposes.

Further closures would inevitably mean more miners leaving the industry, and those mines remaining in operation will also have to shed labour to increase productivity as mining equipment and techniques are modernised.

In any event, two other factors should help in cost reduction. The first is that the coal companies/ mines are to divest themselves of all non-core activities such as provision of housing and health; these functions are to be the responsibility of the Government or local authorities under the restructuring plan. The second is recent legislation giving more weight to the economics of extraction. The Geology and Mining Law passed by the Sejm in February 1994 and effective the following October rescinded the legal requirement that mines exploit thin seams even when it was uneconomical to do so. The new law introduced a system of operation consents under the Higher Mining Authority. The industry has already started to concentrate on the better reserves. In addition a revision of the rules for classifying industrial reserves implies a relaxation of the thickness and ash content criteria.

Future cost reductions will also depend greatly upon the evolution of real competition, as opposed to the present organised market. The incentives for players in the industry to reduce costs would be much greater in a competitive environment.

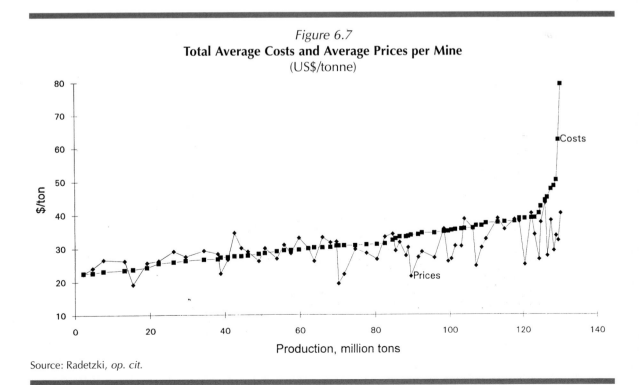

Figure 6.7
Total Average Costs and Average Prices per Mine
(US$/tonne)

Source: Radetzki, *op. cit.*

FINANCIAL CONDITION

Since the pre-1990 pricing policy meant that hard coal prices did not cover production costs, the mines needed large subsidies and could not accumulate funds for much needed future investment on a self-financing basis. This government policy of in effect giving the coal industry ever larger subsidies to ensure its viability was abruptly halted after 1990. Thanks to the current policy of eliminating subsidisation and making the industry entirely self-supporting, by the end of 1993 prices had been raised to levels where production costs were being covered and the accumulation of funds was possible (Table 6.14).

Prices did not reach break-even levels until September 1993, however, while subsidies were eliminated earlier. The result in the interim was a rapidly worsening financial situation and increasing indebtedness. This can be seen in Tables 6.15, 6.16 and 6.17.

A large part of recent losses have in effect been financed through non-payment of debt – of the US$ 2.37 billion gross debt owed in June 1993, unpaid taxes and fees to the Government amounted to US$ 540 million, unpaid bills to suppliers US$ 1.47 billion and loans from credit institutions US$ 360 million.

The coal companies clearly cannot carry out normal operations with this huge burden of debt. It is equally clear that solving the problem will require some form of public intervention; as long as the industry remains in state ownership, the authorities will have the ultimate responsibility for its losses. In fact, the losses should be viewed as unplanned, ex-post subsidies.

Table 6.14
Prices, Costs and Accumulation of Funds for 63 Mines, 1993
(Zl 1 000)

	Jan	Feb	Mar	Apr	May	Jun
Price	449.3	443.4	443.3	440.8	440.3	470.7
Cost	480.7	494.0	482.8	538.2	595.9	589.0
Accumulation	-34.1	-50.6	-39.6	-97.4	-155.5	-118.3

	Jul	Aug	Sep	Oct	Nov	Dec
Price	491.9	572.4	607.3	652.1	663.5	697.4
Cost	632.5	617.9	571.7	578.7	560.1	607.6
Accumulation	-140.7	-15.5	35.6	73.4	103.1	89.5

Source: Karbownik, *op. cit.*

Table 6.15
Liabilities and Receivables, Hard Coal Industry
(Zl trillion)

Year	Liabilities	Receivables	Balance of liabilities and receivables	zloty/US $ exchange rate (avg. year-end)
1989	1.0	1.3	0.3	6 500
1990	9.7	2.1	-7.6	9 500
1991	14.6	6.5	-8.1	10 957
1992	29.9	8.7	-21.2	15 167
1993	51.6	13.3	-32.3	21 143

Table 6.16
Subsidies and Financial Results
(Zl billion)

Year	Subsidies	Financial result
1989	3 317	343
1990	9 313	416
1991	5 075	−3 535
1992	698	−12 582
1993	–	−15 007

The Polish Government has taken the view that there should be no full write-off of these debts – perhaps rightly, as pressure to reduce the debt should be an additional impetus in the drive to lower costs, and since privatisation of the industry is not foreseen in the near future, there appears to be no immediate need to make the industry more attractive to investors.

The financial restructuring planned for 1994-95 is to include action on debt reduction aimed at increasing financial liquidity within the industry and improving its earning capacity. The measures include:

- agreement proceedings with suppliers of goods and services;

- legal debt settlement proceedings with suppliers of goods and services;

- non-conventional procedures with respect to the state budget, local budgets and central funds;

- ancillary instruments – compensation of liabilities and debts.

The Government's financial support for the programme in 1994 was expected to comprise:

- guarantees for the coal companies of repayment of bank credits, up to Zl 4.5 trillion;

- a subsidy linked to the liquidation of mines, Zl 2.7 trillion;

- a subsidy related to mining damage, Zl 207 billion;

- subsidies for investments, Zl 550 billion.

In addition, the coal companies and mines will be relieved of activities relating to housing management. The industry currently owns 160 000 apartments with a book value of Zl 11 trillion.

Table 6.17
Financial Statements, Hard Coal Industry

	1991		1992		1993	
Output (Mt)	140		132		130	
Exchange rate (Zl/US$)	10 560		13 650		18 150	
	Zl billion	US$ million	Zl billion	US$ million	Zl billion	US$ million
Sales *	47 730	4 520	53 340	3 908	76 440	4 212
Cost of sales	− 46 130	− 4 368	− 60 820	− 4 456	− 80 880	− 4 456
Extraordinary cost items	−1 810	−171	−3 000	−220	−5 220	−288
Result before government levies	−210	−20	−10 480	−768	−9 660	−532
Taxes and dividends	−3 330	−315	−2 100	−154	−5 270	−290
Result after government levies	−3 540	−335	−12 580	−922	−14 930	−823

* Includes marginal quantities of goods and services other than hard coal.

Source of Tables 6.15, 6.16 and 6.17: Piekorz, *op. cit.*

RESTRUCTURING PROGRAMME FOR HARD COAL INDUSTRY

Restructuring of the hard coal mining industry has been on the agenda since 1990 but was effectively initiated only during 1992-93. Until March 1993, no essential decisions had been made to start changing the sector. The acceptance by the Economic Committee of the Council of Ministers in March 1993 of the hard coal mining restructuring programme was a step towards its implementation, but financial resources were inadequate. In mid-July 1993, the programme to prevent coal mine bankruptcy (Stage I), considered essential to encourage real changes in the sector, was initiated.

The restructuring programme has three over-arching objectives: i) bring the coal mining sector back to profitability; ii) maintain the competitiveness of Polish coal on world markets; iii) determine how much is needed for investment in mines and coal preparation plants, and find the necessary funds.

The programme has three stages: Stage I, 1993, Stage II, 1994-95, and Stage III, 1996-2000.

Stage I was aimed at halting the accumulation of losses, creating conditions for profitable operations and protecting the mines against bankruptcy. The fundamental Stage I restructuring tasks included changing the structure of the hard coal mining organisation, adjusting production to market needs, maintaining the necessary flow of exports, reducing employment and increasing productivity, moving prices towards a level covering production costs, starting financial restructuring and preparing business plans for the coal companies. In terms of these tasks, Stage I can be judged a success.

Stage II aimed to bring the coal mines to overall profitability in 1994 and maintain this status in 1995 by further adjusting production levels to domestic and export needs, maintaining the competitiveness of Polish coal on world markets, financing wage increases by boosting productivity, clearing the debts of the industry and obtaining financial resources for investment in replacement and modernisation of machinery.

The mine closure programme for 1994-95 is to be a key element in achieving these goals. Among the fundamental assumptions behind the Stage II programme are:

- no directed subsidies will be given for coal production;

- financial responsibility for closing permanently unprofitable mines is taken by the state;

- in the first quarter of 1994, the coal companies were to conclude long term agreements with the main domestic and export customers;

- coal price liberalisation is to be maintained on the home market provided that prices are below import parity levels for main users, on the basis of concluded agreements;

- there will be no privatisation of the industry in this period, apart from surplus mine surface departments or assets.

It is also assumed that during this stage, in 1995, the mining industry organisation will evolve from individual coal companies into a holding industry structure. Stage II has been approved by the Sejm.

Stage III aims at ensuring that the coal companies maintain minimum profitability despite deteriorating geological and mining conditions and a real increase in wages.

ASSESSMENTS AND RECOMMENDATIONS

Assessments

The Polish hard coal industry is a substantial producer, with large physical reserves, reasonable costs of production and some useful capital stock. It is a major asset to the Polish economy and has good prospects if the necessary restructuring can be assured.

The economics of the industry and its immediate environment are affected by several factors:

- there is a large difference between import and export parities, which gives considerable geographical protection to the producers and represents a possibility for the exercise of domestic market power;

- there is substantial overcapacity and a tail of high cost production;

- if high cost production were to be curtailed, output could easily be made up from more productive mines;

- there are important social constraints on the rate at which production can be rationalised;

- the financial value of a miner in alternative employment under present conditions is low.

Given these factors, the objectives should be to promote the development of an efficient industry selling at prices that permit it to cover its costs, including its environmental costs, and to finance rational investment. Some of the characteristics of the industry identified in this chapter make the objectives more difficult to achieve than might otherwise be the case. In particular, it is difficult to balance the twin needs of rationalising production and stabilising prices, and some trade-off will be necessary.

Recommendations

Prices and costs

The present prices of US$ 30-32 per tonne appear reasonable and are within the import-export parity range of US$ 20-40. If the industry were able to rationalise production and reduce costs, these prices might well be sufficient to ensure its long term viability. However, even these price levels may not cover real production costs, which are almost certainly greater than recorded costs. Prices may thus have to rise further.

There is tension between this supposition and the fact that present price levels are difficult to reconcile with the overcapacity of the industry in a market environment; effective competition among mines should drive prices down to export parity, or possibly even lower. For the moment, a considerable degree of market organisation prevents this. Much evidence exists for this organised market structure. There are good reasons for keeping prices at a reasonable and stable level, although this degree of market organisation conflicts with other objectives, especially the rationalisation of production.

There is no guarantee that present prices are stable, that they will not break down under the twin strains of competition and the need to cover costs. The need to reduce costs, the other part of the equation, is therefore paramount. Although estimates of how far costs may fall are subject to a large degree of uncertainty, there is no doubt that swift, substantial cost reductions offer a way of maintaining competitiveness and encouraging competition.

- **The Polish Government should consider stabilising prices by encouraging long term contracts (of the order of five years) with power stations for a substantial, but declining, part of the supply of coal, within the framework of the industrial and commercial structure to be adopted for the electricity supply industry. The remainder could be subject to competition. This would stabilise the overall price level while allowing the progressive introduction of competition and commercial incentives for restructuring.**

Rationalisation of production

There does not appear to be any actor in the Polish coal industry with a strong motive to rationalise production. From the point of view of the individual mineworkers, the incentives to leave the industry are weak. From the point of view of the state, there is at present no alternative employment for miners, and it makes little overall economic difference if the miner is adding zero value inside or outside the mine. From the point of view of company managers, the amount of labour they can shed is constrained by the informal agreement regarding employment. Moreover, because the sector is not competitive but functions as an organised market, the costs of overmanning can be passed on.

Fostering effective competition would provide economic incentives at company level to reduce costs. The social constraints would still apply, but they would be countered by commercial motivations to act, which now are weak, if they exist at all. It is striking that Weglozbyt, a company operating in the same depressed region as the coal mines and subject to the same social constraints, has reduced its staff by 50 per cent. It is unlikely to be pure chance that Weglozbyt operates in an extremely competitive environment, whereas the coal companies do not.

Effective competition could have a serious effect on prices and this dilemma reflects a fundamental conflict between the objectives of keeping prices at an acceptable level and reducing costs through competition. There is a distinct policy choice between a competitive structure that will benefit consumers and a more organised market that will assist in the financial consolidation of the industry but impede efficiency. The Government appears to have concluded that restructuring should take priority over competition.

- **The priority on consolidation is understandable, but it should be considered temporary, and competition should be encouraged with increasing vigour as restructuring progresses.**

Company structure

There are indications of differences in character and behaviour between the coal concerns grouping several mines and the holding structure adopted by the Katowice Holding Company. These differences appear not to be rooted in legal differences; both are joint stock companies, wholly owned by the state, and in neither case have the mines maintained their legal identity.

The essential difference is in the allocation of revenue. In the case of the mining companies, revenue is distributed among the mines to cover their costs, giving no incentive to reduce costs at mine level. In the case of Katowice, revenue is distributed according to the value of the coal produced by the individual mines, inducing mines to reduce their costs and allowing for competition among mines.

It is too early to be sure, but there seems to be some evidence that the creation of incentives and the delegation of production decisions to mine level at Katowice have worked better than the incentives at play in the coal companies to motivate management to negotiate the reduction of labour with the unions effectively.

One practical way of reconciling the conflict between cost reduction and market stabilisation may be to organise the market at company level but try to create incentives for rationalisation within the company.

- **The Government should examine the internal efficiency of the two models, and – if the**

evidence seems to support such a move – consider internal reorganisation of the management and accounting of the coal companies along the model of Katowice Holding Company.

Management of companies

The technical management of the coal companies appears, from this brief review, to be good. There is, however, a homogenous character to senior managers, most of whom have similar backgrounds, worked as mine managers and developed their careers in an environment of central planning. Although one of the roles of the supervisory boards of the companies is to provide a wider range of expertise, in practice much the same cultural homogeneity exists.

- **The Government, as owner of the companies, should consider appointing some senior managers with different backgrounds in, for example, economics, finance and accounting. Also, the appointments to the supervisory boards should be made more imaginatively. The Government should consider seeking support from bilateral agencies for training of middle management in the economics of coal investment, production and marketing.**

Costs of closure

There are calculations suggesting that the costs of closing mines could be offset within two to three years by the benefits of lower production costs. The closure costs, in this instance, are the technical and environmental costs of closure plus modest redundancy payments. The benefits are the production costs from the closed mines less the costs of increasing production from the remaining mines. We are not in a position to verify these calculations, but they appear plausible and consistent with our discussions with those in the industry.

The social costs of redundancy are real and concentrated, but relief of those social costs through unproductive employment is only achieved by higher prices to consumers and the loss of competitiveness and jobs in industry. If the returns from closure are as high as appears, then part of those benefits could be redirected into job creation in the mining regions and into improved terms of redundancy.

Several western European countries have considerable experience of job development in mining areas, and bilateral co-operation on this matter might be available.

- **The Government needs to make a careful analysis of the economics of mine closure with a view to speeding the rationalisation of the industry. It is encouraging that the terms of reference for a PHARE project on job development, closure economics and environmental management have been agreed.**

Exports

Coal is Poland's main source of foreign exchange and a most important export. Poland has three main coal export markets: neighbouring countries accessible by land freight, Baltic and Scandinavian countries accessible by small and medium-sized ships, and the rest of the world.

In the first case Poland enjoys a geographic rent whose distribution is a result of negotiations and reflects to a considerable extent the market power of the negotiators. In the second case, Poland also enjoys some advantages in that it can supply the Baltic/Scandinavian market on small ships economically without transshipment. This market was scarcely contested by direct supply during the period of the independent mines. In the third case, Poland has no special advantage, but enjoys long-standing relationships with many important buyers.

The markets in contiguous countries are unlikely to grow rapidly. Provided that coal production in these countries also falls as subsidies are phased out, there may still be increases in their imports from Poland. However, significant growth in the volume of Poland's coal exports is likely to depend on the country re-establishing its position in world trade through seaborne exports. At present, the economics of such exports appear to be poor from a commercial perspective. The FOB price at the mine can be as low as US$ 17 a tonne. Marginal production costs including labour costs appear to exceed this level.

From a welfare perspective, there are justifications for export sales even at a commercial loss, but there are also several difficulties. Two problems are that the commercial incentives for restructuring are overshadowed, with delays of the process as a likely result, and that profits – and the industry's possibilities for financing new, productive investments – are lower than they otherwise might have been.

- **Growth in the volume of exports in a context of sustained commercial viability depends strongly on the industry reducing its marginal costs. The development of exports in a commercially rational fashion is a strong argument for more rapid rationalisation of production. The markets for exports should be examined thoroughly to identify all potential areas for growth, including those that may arise as a result of the closure of unprofitable mines in western Europe.**

Final observation

Almost all of our observations stem from the fundamental need to make a balance between cutting costs through competition and maintaining an orderly market. Preference has been given to the latter objective, and this is understandable, but the former is important and effort must be made progressively to introduce commercial incentives through competition, without destabilising the market.

CHAPTER 7

ELECTRICITY AND DISTRICT HEATING

ELECTRICITY

Poland relies to an extreme extent on hard coal and lignite for power generation. About 98 per cent of the country's electricity is produced from solid fuels. There is a pressing need to rehabilitate and upgrade the power plants, which are relatively old (average age 18 years). In the past, power plants were constructed without any effort to limit emissions of sulphur and nitrogen dioxide, with severe pollution problems as a result. Emissions of particulates were also high. In the modernisation of the sector, improving generators' environmental performance has a high priority. Western European standards for existing plants are scheduled to come into effect in 1998. There is no immediate need for new capacity, but rehabilitation, modernisation and bringing the industry up to international environmental standards will require substantial investments. For strategic security of supply reasons as well as for economic reasons, Polish authorities aim to integrate the Polish electricity system into western Europe's UCPTE network.

Industry Overview

The Polish electricity industry has been in a process of restructuring since 1989. In the previous, centrally planned system, large projects, such as a new power plant, were decided on and funded centrally by the Power and Brown Coal Board. The reorganisation of the electricity industry has resulted in three layers of companies – dedicated to generation, transmission and distribution – and, within each layer, companies that are or will be organised as financially independent joint stock companies. The first company to be created was the transmission company, the Polish Power Grid Company. Later, the distribution companies were reorganised as joint stock companies. On the generation side, so far only the combined heat and power plants have been reorganised. It is the intention to transform the generation enterprises into joint stock companies as well, but the organisational structure has so far not been decided on. Individually, the generation companies will lack financial strength to undertake needed investments. A grouping of generators under holding companies is therefore envisaged. The transformation to joint stock companies can pave the way for privatisation and much needed foreign investment.

The CHP plants supplying heat to local district heating systems are to be taken over by local authorities. The large generation plants, or system plants, may be privatised, but probably only later. PPGC is likely to remain state owned for the foreseeable future; at least, the Government will continue to hold the majority of the shares.

The power industry no longer receives public subsidies, but prices to final consumers are fixed by the Ministry of Finance. Prices now cover about half of the full costs – including depreciation costs – of supplying electricity. After "shock therapy" in early 1990, when electricity and other energy prices were increased substantially, price increases over the last few years have by and large been in line with inflation. The Government's pricing policy, here as in other industries dictated by social considerations rather than by financial needs, could jeopardise the reform of the entire industry. The financial position of the electric companies is weak, and could be further undermined unless prices are increased substantially in real terms. Low electricity prices and uncertainty about future prices also discourage foreign participation.

PPGC has proposed a reorganisation of the market for electricity. It envisages a system of contracts between generators and the transmission company, to guarantee revenue for companies needing significant investments. In the medium to long term, the intention is to open the market gradually for competition among generators. Later, the generators would be allowed to compete for direct supplies to the distribution companies. The local supply monopolies of the distributors will be retained for low voltage consumers.

Demand

With recession and changes in the structure of the economy, total final electricity consumption declined by almost 18 per cent from 1989 to 1992. Industrial electricity use fell by almost 30 per cent, whereas residential demand stayed about the same. Other sectors' consumption dropped by around 10 per cent. In 1993, total final electricity use rose by 1 per cent. Fairly strong increases in industrial and service sector demand more than compensated for continued declines in the residential sector and agriculture.

Electricity demand will probably continue to increase in response to economic growth, structural change and electricity efficiency developments. This last variable will depend strongly on electricity price developments, as will Polish households' evaluation of electricity as an option for heating and cooking. The levels of construction and of retrofitting buildings will also be factors, and the pace at which electric appliances are introduced in households and businesses will be a significant determinant. In 1991 fewer than 30 per cent of Polish households had freezers, and fewer than 50 per cent had electric clothes washing machines. Office buildings are generally poorly lit, and computers, printers and fax machines are relatively few and far between.

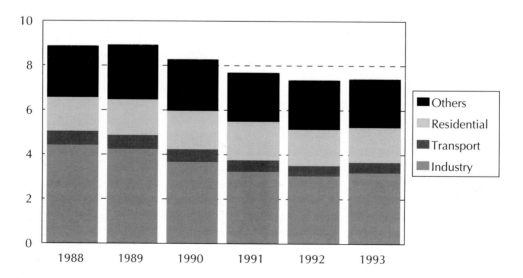

Figure 7.1
Total Final Consumption of Electricity, 1988-93
(Mtoe)

Sources: CIE, IEA Secretariat

In 1992, PPGC developed a series of electricity consumption scenarios, two of which are shown in Figure 7.2.

The low scenario, in which GDP grows by an average of 2.3 per cent a year from 1991 to 2010, has demand in 2010 exceeding its 1990 level by 51 per cent, and its lower 1993 level by 59 per cent. Electricity use per unit of GDP is about the same in 2010 as in 1988. In the high scenario, built around economic growth of 4.2 per cent a year, demand in 2010 exceeds the 1990 level by 82 per cent and the 1993 level by 91 per cent. This scenario puts the electricity intensity of the economy about 14 per cent lower in 2010 than in 1988.

Supply

Solid fuels have been the main input to power generation throughout the history of the Polish electricity industry. At the end of the Second World War, 93 per cent of the country's installed generating capacity was solid fuel plants (see Table 7.1 and Figure 7.3). In 1992, non-solid fuels accounted for only about 1.5 per cent of total

power generation. Some 55 per cent of Poland's electricity is based on hard coal and 42 per cent on lignite. Abundant reserves have made solid fuels a key factor in Poland's economic development in general and that of the electricity industry in particular. Moreover, as in other centrally planned economies, the emphasis was on using indigenous energy resources as much as possible.

The country has no hydro resources of importance, more than two-thirds of it being flat terrain; 75 per cent of the installed hydro capacity of 2 000 MW is pumped storage. Even so, in view of the predominance of solid fuels, these pumped storage plants are important for load balancing. They are constructed mainly to meet the 24 hour fluctuations in demand that cannot be met by the relatively inflexible solid fuel plants. The largest pumped storage plant, Zarnowiec, has installed capacity of 680 MW. The genuine hydropower plants, most of which are run-of-river plants in the north and west, are small and old.

Natural gas contributes virtually nothing to Poland's electricity supply. As the country possesses limited gas reserves, increases in demand have to be met mainly from imports. In the past, limited import possibilities resulted in gas being reserved for industrial uses. The use of

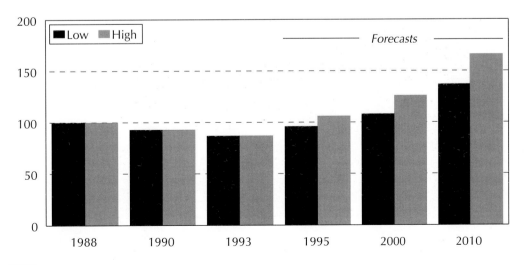

Figure 7.2
Developments in Electricity Demand, 1988-2010
(Index, 1988 = 100)

Source: PPGC

oil in power generation has also been of marginal importance. In the early 1970s, one major power plant was built to burn heavy fuel oil, but as a result of international oil price increases, it was mothballed. A nuclear power programme was planned, and construction of a Soviet type light water reactor plant with total capacity of 880 MW was started in the early 1980s. However, public opposition to nuclear power, triggered by the Chernobyl accident, and the fact that it had been apparent since the early 1980s that there was no imminent need for new generation capacity, led the Government to abandon the project in 1991, when the plant was 40-50 per cent completed. The present Government has not ruled out the nuclear option for some later stage.

According to a recent study[1], power generation from lignite should remain at its current level or perhaps decline slightly. Continued growth in electricity demand should be met initially by increased use of coal, but later in the 1990s by natural gas as well. The latter fuel should be used for peaking purposes and – primarily for environmental reasons – in some CHP plants.

Table 7.1
Capacity and Generation in Public Power Plants, 1993

Installed capacity (MW)	29 438
Lignite plants	9 103
Hard coal plants	18 328
Gross electricity generation (TWh)	125.3
from lignite	52.4
from hard coal	68.8

Sources: CIE.

Figure 7.3
Fuel Shares in Power Generation, 1992
(TWh)

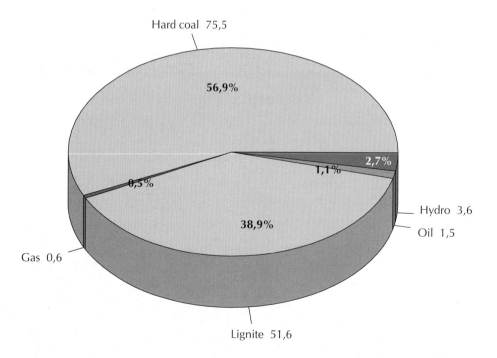

Hard coal 75,5
56,9%
2,7%
1,1%
0,5%
Hydro 3,6
Oil 1,5
38,9%
Gas 0,6
Lignite 51,6

Sources: CIE, IEA Secretariat

1. "Least Cost Investment Study for the Polish Power Sector", PPGC and Verbund-Plan GmbH, Vienna, 1994.

In PPGC's high growth scenario, natural gas starts contributing to power generation in the second half of the 1990s; in the low growth scenario it is phased in later (see Figure 7.4). In the former scenario, the use of lignite for power generation declines only moderately after 2000, implying a need for new lignite production capacity from around 2010. The latter scenario offers no such prospects for the mining industry; with low electricity demand growth, lignite use could be supplied from mines already in operation.

The uncertainties surrounding future rates of growth in electricity demand, and the extent to

Figure 7.4
Fuel Mix in System Power Plants and CHP Plants, 1992-2010
(PJ)

High Scenario

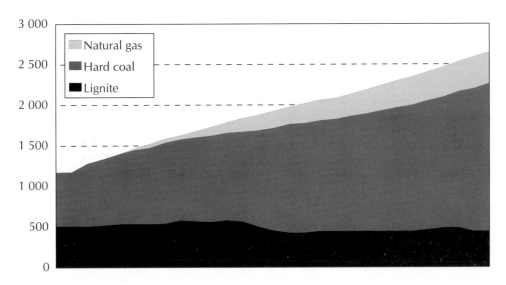

Low Scenario

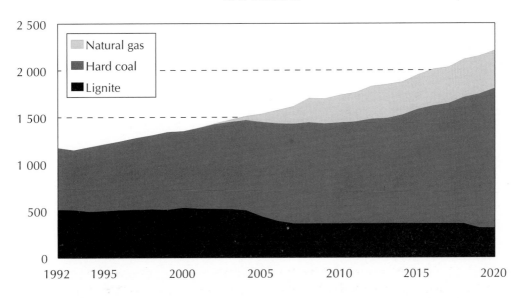

which coal will be called upon as swing fuel, give rise to difficult policy and planning problems for the power and hard coal sectors. There is an urgent need for more reliable electricity demand and generation forecasting in general, and for revisions of scenarios and plans that still reflect conditions in the Polish economy in the late 1980s and thus may be severely outdated.

In both PPGC scenarios, the demand for natural gas for central power generation and in CHP plants reaches more than 10 bcm a year. Such a development would clearly necessitate improved security of gas supplies.

As a result of declines in demand, the ratio between total installed capacity and maximum demand on the system increased from 1.31 in 1985 to 1.44 in 1993 (see Table 7.2). This rough indicator points to increasing overcapacity.

Table 7.2
Installed Capacity and Electricity Demand
(MW)

	1985	1990	1993
Total installed capacity	30 107	31 952	32 750
Yearly maximum demand	22 832	23 392	22 749

Sources: CIE.

The comfortable relationship between capacity and demand conceals a growing, largely inherited, number of financial and technical problems in the electricity industry.

In the 1970s, facing increasing demand for electricity, Polish authorities embarked upon a programme of rapid capacity addition. An average of 1 150 MW of new capacity was commissioned each year – twice as much as the average for the 1960s. In the 1980s, capacity additions fell back to about the level of the 1960s. In the early 1990s, plant construction was reduced further; there are now no plans for new power plants.

In the 1970s, capacity additions kept pace with demand increases; there was little room for

retirement of old and outdated plants. In the 1980s, while capacity additions were reduced to accommodate lower demand growth, tightening constraints on the Polish economy inhibited the replacement of old capacity. Moreover, the centrally planned economies gave low priority to maintenance and upgrading. Expenses came to reflect the central planning system's "production philosophy" and emphasis on tangible investments; individual power plant managers were given neither incentives nor funds for plant and equipment upkeep. Consequently, the Polish electricity supply system was deteriorating.

The power plants built in the 1970s comprised several 200 MW units on a given site. Earlier, the typical unit size had been 120 MW, or sometimes even smaller. Only in the late 1970s and early 1980s were some 500 MW units constructed. All power plant elements, including boilers, turbines and generators, were produced in Poland by state owned mechanical engineering companies, each producing a different element. Standardisation made it possible to achieve economies of scale in plant design and construction, and relatively high reliability in operation. However, unit sizes were probably too small to obtain the full benefits of economies of scale in operation. The concept also meant that plant standards lagged behind developments in combustion and control technology, as well as environmental control.

The uneven pace of capacity construction over the last 30 years and limited retirement of old capacity have given the Polish power industry an age problem that is getting increasingly serious. More than half the current capacity was built in the 1970s. About 60 per cent of the total is more than 15 years old and 40 per cent is more than 20 years old. The problem has been exacerbated by insufficient expenditure on maintenance and modernisation.

PPGC has estimated that of the total installed capacity of 32.7 GW, more than 20 GW needs rehabilitation and about 2.8 GW should be retired from production before 2005 (see Table 7.3).

Most of the capacity to be retired before 2000 was constructed in the 1960s or before. Most of the rehabilitation deemed necessary before

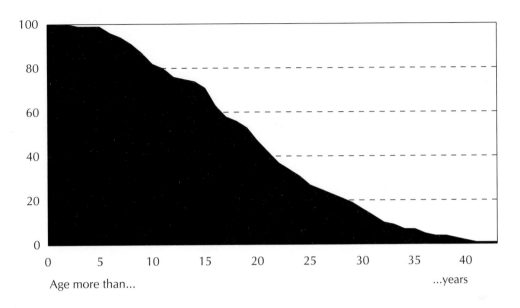

Figure 7.5
Age Distribution of Public Thermal Power Plant Boilers, 1993
(%)

Age more than...   ...years

Source: CIE

2000 concerns power plants built in the 1970s. The 200 MW units constructed then were originally intended to have an operating time of 100 000 hours. Many have exceeded this limit. Their useful lifetime could be extended. Rehabilitation costs, including environmental protection costs, are estimated to range between US$ 50 and US$ 350 per kW of capacity. As there are also plans to extend the transmission and distribution systems, the Polish electricity supply industry's total investment needs for the rest of the 1990s are estimated to be of the order of US$ 8 billion.

Poland has a relatively high share of CHP units in the electricity system. They supply local district heating networks with heat. In the public power system, 11 per cent of the electricity generated in thermal power plants comes from CHP plants, nearly all of them fuelled with hard coal. Of the total thermal electricity generation capacity of 27 400 MW, co-generation units account for almost a fifth, or 5 200 MW. These units have a thermal capacity of about 12 000 MW. A number of CHP plants also operate heat-only boilers that are used to meet peaks in heating demand. The CHP plants account for about 76 per cent of total heat production in urban areas with more than 40 000 inhabitants. The share of CHP in total power generation could probably be increased from its current level of about 18 per cent. Some new CHP plants would probably be fired with natural gas, as they would be in or near urban areas where new environmental regulations will favour the use of gas.

Table 7.3
**Planned Rehabilitation
and Retirement
of Capacity, 1994-2005**
(MW)

	Modernisation	Retirement
1994-2000	14 547	1 193
2001-2005	6 200	1 580

Source: PPGC

Transmission Grid and International Connections

The Polish transmission grid, owned and operated by PPGC, consists of 12 400 km of 400 kV and 220 kV lines, plus a relatively short 750 kV link to Ukraine (see Table 7.4).

Table 7.4
High Voltage Lines, 1992

Voltage (kV)	Length (km)
750	114
400	4 168
220	8 215

Source: PPGC

The first high voltage transmission circuits were 110 kV. Later, transmission grids were constructed as 220 kV lines, and more recently the emphasis has been on reinforcing the system by constructing 400 kV lines.

Poland is part of the integrated eastern European network, the IPS-CDO, composed of the former CMEA countries, and its international interconnections reflect this. AC connections are particularly strong with the Czech Republic and Ukraine. The major international interconnections are:

Czech Republic:
> two 400 kV lines from Wielopole to Albrechtivce and Nosowice;
> two 220 kV lines from Bujakow and Kopamina to Liskovec;
> one 110 kV line from Boguszow to Porici
> (total transfer capacity of about 1 200 MVA).

Germany:
> three 400 kV and two 220 kV lines
> (total transfer capacity of about 2 000 MVA).

Ukraine:
> one 750 kV line between Ukraine's Khmelnitska nuclear station and Rzeszow;
> one 220 kV line between Zamosc and Dobrtotvorska
> (total transfer capacity of about 1 300 MVA).

In addition there is a connection between north-eastern Poland and Belarus, which formerly was used to supply an enclave in the Polish system. This enclave is now integrated in the Polish system.

Integration of the Polish grid with the UCTPE system is a strategic objective of PPGC. On the initiative of PPGC the transmission companies of Poland, Hungary, the Czech Republic and Slovakia formed in 1992 a regional co-operation group called CENTREL. Its primary objective is to prepare for integration with UCPTE. PPGC sees such integration as a means of improving security of supply and allowing a higher quality of electricity supply.

One system improvement to be obtained from integration is a reduction in frequency fluctuations. The relatively large fluctuations in the eastern system are due mainly to insufficient primary regulation capability in Russia, Ukraine and Belarus. In the longer term, integration could also promote expansion of trade in electricity between Poland and western European countries.

The CENTREL members and electric utilities in the west have signed an agreement on steps to be taken before integration with UCPTE. Some investments will have to be made to ensure that regulation capabilities – in particular primary regulation – are adequate, that generation capacities can be dispatched efficiently and that near-border stations have sufficient capacity to handle cross-border flows. There is also a need for extensions of the Polish 400 kV grid to improve the capability for managing internal flows.

UCPTE supports the principle of integration, and its managing board has accepted this agreement as a basis for proceeding with preparations for integration. In September 1993 the four CENTREL utilities and VEAG, the transmission company of the new German Länder, undertook a test of their capability to comply with UCPTE requirements. They were disconnected from the eastern system and their generation systems were run as one integrated system. For almost 48 hours the utilities proved their capability of maintaining the frequency variations within the band required by UCPTE. Since the beginning of 1994, the CENTREL utilities have complied with the parameters required by UCPTE.

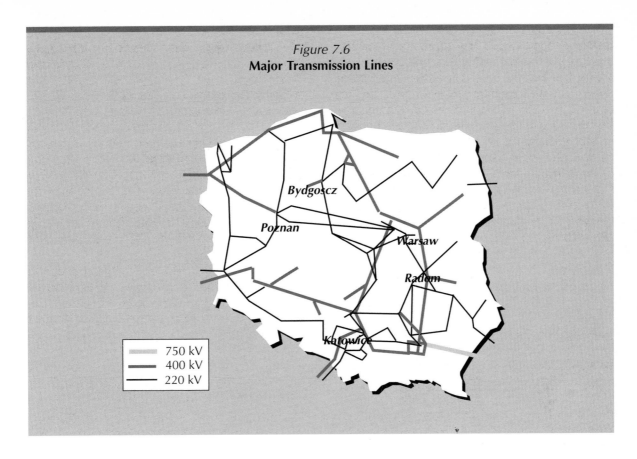

Figure 7.6
Major Transmission Lines

- 750 kV
- 400 kV
- 220 kV

Table 7.5
Lignite Production and Generation Capacity by Mine, 1993

	Lignite production (1 000 tonnes)	Gross electricity capacity (MW)	Commissioning dates
Total	71 900	8 703	
Belchatow	37 500	4 320	1982-88
Turow	15 500	2 000	1963-71
Patnow	9 500	1 200	1967-69
Adamow	4 400	600	1964-66
Konin	5 000	583	1958-64

Not included is 400 MW of mothballed oil-fired capacity at Patnow.

Source: MoIT

Lignite

Lignite is produced on a large scale in Poland in five mines delivering practically all of their production to adjacent power plants. By far the largest of the mines is Belchatow, which feeds a power plant complex with generation capacity of 4 320 MW (see Table 7.5). Very little co-generation takes place at the lignite plants, which are sited close to lignite resources rather than heat demand centres. All of the lignite production is from opencast mines. Five mining complexes are organised in three groups, with the Patnow, Adamow and Konin mines forming one group.

109

There are plans to increase production at Patnow by converting two 200 MW oil fired units to burn lignite. The units were commissioned in 1973 and 1974, but because of the increase in oil prices they were never used.

In the Polish Energy Programme of 1992, the MoIT estimates that production from the existing lignite mines will have declined by some 20 per cent by 2005 as the mines begin to be depleted. There are, however, possibilities for developing new mines close to the power plants supplied from the existing mines. A new mine, Szeczercow, which is close to the Belchatow complex, is under consideration.

Belchatow is not only the largest mine, but also the most recent and probably the most efficient. Its excavation and transportation equipment is in reasonably good condition. The other mines need investment in equipment. All the lignite mines are overstaffed. Total employment is 27 600, a figure that could probably be reduced substantially without any major investments in new equipment.

Operating costs for lignite production are estimated at US$ 0.75-0.90/GJ depending on the geological structure of the mine and the quality of the lignite. There are no reliable estimates of the real capital costs involved in lignite mining. As in other parts of the energy sector, the book value of equipment does not reflect its actual economic value. An indication of the level of capital costs may be deduced from a rehabilitation plan drawn up for the Turow mine: it estimated that investments of US$ 825 million (at 1991 prices) in new excavators, conveyors and auxiliary equipment was needed to maintain production. At a production rate of 16 Mt a year, this corresponds roughly to capital costs for a modernised mine of US$ 0.55/GJ, assuming a lignite heat content of 9 448 MJ/tonne, an equipment lifetime of 15 years and 5 per cent real rate of interest on dollar loans. If operating costs are added, at the current level of staffing, full economic costs of this production reach US$ 1.30-1.45/GJ. The corresponding hard coal price is US$ 28.50-32 per tonne. Accordingly, lignite produced from existing mines is competitive with coal for power generation at the prevailing coal price of US$ 32/tonne. The MoIT has calculated that the full costs of lignite from the proposed new Szczercow mine would be as high as US$ 68/tce, however, rendering it far

from competitive at current Polish or international coal prices[2]. Such costs would not even justify continued mining to feed an otherwise redundant lignite power plant. Electricity from lignite plants is priced according to the costs of generating electricity with hard coal.

In short, existing lignite mines can supply fuel for power plants at costs competitive with generation from hard coal, and over the years operating costs could be brought down by reducing the workforce. Production from new mines, on the other hand, appears to be clearly uneconomic. In the medium to long term, lignite production is therefore likely to decrease.

According to the reorganisation plans for the electricity industry, the lignite mines will be owned by three companies that will also own the associated power plants. Such vertical integration is appropriate. There is no other market for the lignite. As costs for transporting lignite would be prohibitive, the electricity plants and the mines are technically and economically interdependent.

Environmental Issues[3]

As Table 7.6 shows, the electricity industry is a major contributor to air pollutant emissions in Poland.

The share of the electricity industry in total air emissions is relatively high in Poland because of the predominance of coal and lignite in generation and the scarcity of pollution abatement equipment. Emissions from power generation have declined since 1987, but because of declines in electricity demand resulting from the economic recession rather than improvements in plants' environmental performance. Flue gas desulphurisation (FGD) and low-NO_x technology are only now being introduced. Particulate precipitators are common on larger plants.

Under environmental regulations adopted in 1990, new emission standards for existing plants are to come into force in 1998. For new coal and lignite fired plants, FGD is obligatory. All plants will need low-NO_x burners and improved dust

---

2. "Energy Policy of Poland and the Draft Programme to the Year 2010", MoIT, Warsaw, 1992.
3. See Chapter 11 for further details.

Table 7.6
Total Emissions of SO$_2$, NO$_x$ and Particulates, with Share from Electricity, 1987 and 1992

	SO$_2$		NO$_x$		Particulates	
	Total (1 000 tonnes)	Share from power generation (%)	Total (1 000 tonnes)	Share from power generation (%)	Total (1 000 tonnes)	Share from power generation (%)
1987	4 200	48.8	1 530	26.8	3 400	25.6
1992	2 820	46.4	1 130	32.7	1 580	26.6

Source: MoIT

removal. The new emission limits are in line with the EU standards. Proposed new ambient air quality standards will add to the requirements for emission reduction, depending on local circumstances. Uncertainty about interpretation of the new ambient standards, the future dispatching of individual power plants and availability of investment funds makes it difficult for the generation companies to plan environmental investments. The financial implications of the new standards for the electricity industry are therefore uncertain. However, estimates indicate that investments of the order of US$ 5 billion may be needed.

A first series of FGD installations is being carried out or the units have been ordered. On the largest lignite plant, Belchatow, composed of twelve 360 MW units, four units are being equipped with FGD in a project financed by the Dutch electricity generators' association, SEP. On the hard coal plants, six 200 MW units are being equipped with FGD and plans call for eight other 200 MW units to get FGD, in addition to 480 MW of smaller generating units. Low-NO$_x$ burners are to be installed in conjunction with the rehabilitation programme.

Pricing Policy

Before 1990, electricity prices bore no relation to supply costs, and the sales revenue of the industry had no influence on investments or other decisions affecting expenditures. Prices were kept low, particularly for households.

Electricity prices, like gas and heat prices, are determined by the Ministry of Finance. It is the stated intention of the Government to raise electricity prices to cover the economic costs of the electricity system, and a policy of periodic reviews and price changes has been in place since early 1990. Prices are still far below full costs, however, because of social and political considerations. These include a fear that industry would not be able to compete and expand, and thus that production and employment growth rates would suffer, under a cost covering price regime. There is also a widespread feeling that households' energy expenses – particularly those of low income households – are burdensome enough as it is. According to GUS, households spend an average of 9.3 per cent of their disposable incomes on energy, whereas western European households spend between 3.5 and 4.5 per cent.

Electricity prices were increased sharply at the beginning of 1990. For households, they went up fourfold and for industry they rose three and a half times (see Figure 7.7). The effects of this shock therapy were quickly eroded, however, as inflation, then very high, brought real prices of electricity back towards their pre-1990 levels. In early 1991, the real price for households was again increased sharply to the level obtained at the start of the reform process, but there was only a modest increase in the price for industrial users. Since early 1991, electricity prices for both industry and households have only kept up with the general inflation rate.

There is consequently a long way to go before electricity prices approach economic costs. The World Bank has estimated that Polish industry in

1993 paid prices corresponding to 58 per cent of supply costs, and that household users paid 47 per cent. An increase to the level of estimated full economic costs – which would entail a doubling of prices from today's levels – would bring them close to levels in France, Italy and the United Kingdom (see Figure 7.8). The ratio between the prices for households and for industry is still lower than is typical for western European countries, suggesting cross-subsidisation of household consumption. The amount of cross-subsidisation has been reduced significantly,

Figure 7.7
Real Electricity Price Developments, 1990-early 1994
(Index, December 1989 = 100)

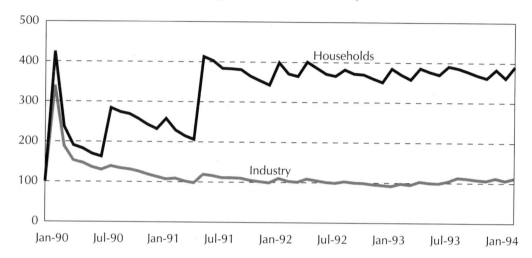

Note: Real prices are current prices in zlotys deflated with the consumer price index.

Sources: World Bank, OECD

Figure 7.8
Electricity Prices in Poland and Selected IEA Countries, 1993
(US$/MWh)

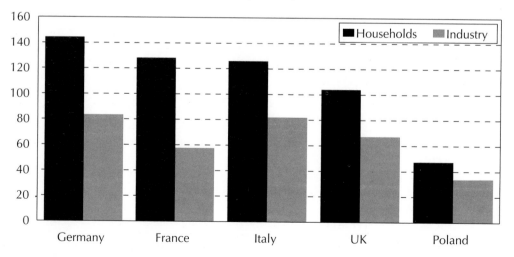

Sources: MoIT, IEA Secreteriat

however. Households used to pay only about 20 per cent of the price charged to industry. They now pay about 40 per cent more than industrial users.

One reason electricity prices are lower in Poland than in western Europe is Poland's lower coal prices. However, this explains only a small part of the difference. To illustrate, if the price of coal for Polish generators were to increase by US$ 10 a tonne, it would add only US$ 4-5/MWh to generating costs, leaving a substantial difference between Polish and western European prices.

Underpricing starves the electricity companies of cash to finance investment programmes, and is an impediment to attracting foreign investors. In view of the massive and urgent needs for investments in rehabilitation and pollution abatement, this issue is of crucial importance.

There is general agreement between public authorities involved – most notably the Ministry of Finance and the MoIT – on the necessity for further real electricity price increases. The Ministry of Finance has agreed to bring prices to their full economic levels over a period of five to six years. According to a plan drawn up by the Ministry, future price increases are to exceed the forecast inflation rate by 50 per cent. However, as inflation is very difficult to predict, the outcome with respect to the real price of electricity is highly uncertain. In spite of the general agreement on the ultimate goal of pricing policy, there remains an obvious risk that the pricing of electricity will continue to be subordinated to general economic and social policy considerations. An alternative method, to price electricity in line with costs and to compensate low income households directly through cash payments, has so far not been realistically considered. There is a political preference for indirect and hidden subsidies, rather than burdening the state budget with direct cash compensation.

The electric companies' earnings in recent years have been squeezed between coal price increases higher than inflation and electricity price increases only in line with inflation. Table 7.7 illustrates this squeeze from 1992 to 1993.

As consumer prices increased by 37.3 per cent in 1993, average electricity prices declined by 1.6 per cent in real terms. At the same time coal prices increased about 10 per cent in real terms.

Despite underpricing, the electricity industry's financial statements indicate that it is doing very well. The electricity supply industry as a whole reported a nominal rate of return on invested capital of almost 25 per cent for the first three quarters of 1993, and companies were in a positive tax position. These financial results, however, are distorted because most asset values were fixed in 1990-92 and have since been eroded by inflation; when assets are undervalued, so is depreciation. Accounting for inflation, a real rate of return of, say, 10 per cent would have required a rate of return on invested capital in 1993 of about 45 per cent instead of the actual 25 per cent.

It is difficult to establish the precise extent of the undervaluation of assets. The MoIT estimates asset values at between five and ten times their recorded values. The book value of the generation companies' assets is, roughly calculated, about US$ 70 per kilowatt of installed capacity. The costs of building a new coal-fired power plant in the west are about US$ 1 500 per kilowatt of installed capacity. Even when adjusted for the high age and insufficient maintenance of Polish power plants, these figures indicate that assets may be even more undervalued than the MoIT acknowledges.

The financial problems of the industry stem from this undervaluation of assets as well as from the low level of prices. Both problems need to be resolved. An increase in electricity prices to their economic levels without a revaluation of assets would generate profits liable to taxation. Parts of the funds needed for modernisation would thus be taxed away. The Treasury's fear of losing tax revenue is probably the main reason no revaluation has been undertaken.

Table 7.7
Average Prices of Coal and Electricity, 1992 and 1993

	1992	1993	% change
Average ex-mine price of coal for power generation (Zl 1 000/tonne)	266	405	52.3
Average price of electricity (Zl 1 000/MWh)	536	724	35.1

Source: MoIT

Restructuring Programme

Under the system in place before 1990, investments were planned and funded on two levels. Large projects, such as the building of a new power plant, were decided on and funded centrally by the Power and Brown Coal Board. Smaller projects were planned at the enterprise level and funded out of the enterprises' budgets. Although the electricity industry was planned and developed as a national asset, the Power and Brown Coal Board did not function like the nationalised industries in western Europe from a financial point of view. Each enterprise kept track of its revenues and expenses and paid its taxes and a dividend to the Ministry of Finance. However, all major decisions were taken centrally, and the individual enterprises in fact generated insufficient cash to fund their investment needs. Hence managerial responsibilities were in practice limited to the technical operation of the plants. Furthermore, the financial system in force meant that accounts did not reflect real costs, and that costs and revenues were not linked to separate activities in a transparent way.

Since the liquidation in 1990 of the Power and Brown Coal Board, the Polish power industry has consisted of three functional and organisational layers of companies:

- 28 generation companies responsible for the lignite plants, hard coal plants, hydro production and CHP plants;

- 33 local distribution companies that buy power from the grid and sell it to the final consumers in their areas, maintain the distribution networks in their areas and operate some smaller CHP and heat-only boilers;

- PPGC, which dispatches the major power plants, manages the high voltage grid and buys power from the generators for resale to the local distribution companies.

The industry also includes three lignite mining companies. A number of auxiliary service companies, civil engineering companies and R&D enterprises that were part of the industry until 1990 have been turned into independent companies.

One of the first steps in the reform process has been to commercialise the parts of the electricity industry. The state owned enterprises in all three layers will be transformed into joint stock companies with the state as the sole stockholder. The purpose of the transformation is to create a basis for managerial and financial independence, cost transparency and, ultimately, improvements in economic efficiency. The first enterprise to be transformed was PPGC. Later the CHP enterprises and distribution companies were re-established as joint stock companies. The Government intends to commercialise the hard coal generation plants and lignite plants as well.

The transformations are complicated by the fact that they imply transfers of ownership of assets between enterprises. For example, it took a full year for PPGC to complete its takeover of the transmission grids formerly owned by the distribution companies.

The state Treasury is the shareholder of the commercialised companies. The MoIT supervises them on behalf of the Treasury. When the hard coal generation plants and the lignite plants are commercialised, the shares in these companies too will be held by the Treasury, while the function of owner will be taken by the MoIT.

The organisational structure of the electricity industry has been a subject of debate both within the industry and within the Government, and several questions remain to be settled. Discussions have focused on, among other things, the levels of concentration in power generation and distribution. For distribution, a conclusion has been reached. At the outset of the restructuring process, the aim was to merge the 33 local distribution companies into 12 to 15 companies. Local opposition and protests from trade unions led to a decision to leave the number of distributors unchanged.

The most controversial part of the reorganisation concerns the hard coal and lignite generating plants and the lignite mines. The most recent proposal, floated in the spring of 1994, implied a relatively high degree of concentration in the generation sector (see box).

The 1994 plan met with strong resistance from the generation companies and employees. Its publication triggered a strike by workers in the lignite mines. The miners fear that commercialisation and reorganisation would endanger employment security. Managers fear that the state through the holding companies will

Figure 7.9
Proposed Ownership Structure of Hard Coal Generation Companies

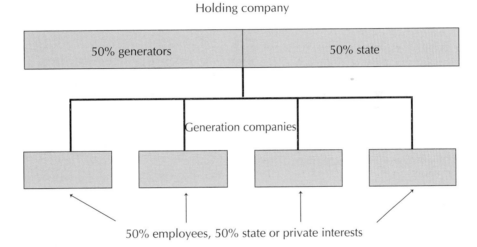

Holding company

| 50% generators | 50% state |

Generation companies

50% employees, 50% state or private interests

continue to rein in the companies' decision making powers even where the latter are partly or fully privatised.

According to the proposal, the holding companies will administer the financial flows and thus have a decisive influence on investments. Individual generation companies will be financially too weak to undertake needed investments and shoulder the concomitant financial burdens. This situation will be of particular gravity in the short to medium term, given the pressing investment needs and the fact that financial constraints necessitate realistic priorities.

The proposed structure of five groups of generation companies is a compromise between, on the one hand, the need to centralise financial resources and decision making, and, on the other, the advantages of decentralisation. The World Bank has advocated creating more than five groups of companies. A larger number is seen as a prerequisite for opening the wholesale electricity market to competition.

Trading Arrangements and Competition

PPGC has launched a three phase plan to create a set of market based electricity trading arrangements. In the first phase, a system will be put in place that is intended to guarantee investors' revenues and allow time for uneconomic generators to adapt. In the later phases, the wholesale market will gradually be opened to competition among generators. The three phases are outlined below.

Phase I (1994-97): limited competition

Public generators

- All units enter into either four year initial contracts, or long term contracts, with PPGC, covering all of the capacity of the units in the first year and between 20 and 100 per cent of their capacity – varying by unit – in the rest of Phase I.

- Long term contracts are agreed only for generators needing significant investments.

- Generators compete for annual capacity contracts with PPGC in years two to four.

Local generators

- All local generating companies may sell directly to distributors at avoided cost.

The initial contracts with PPGC will secure the generators' revenues, thus providing a basis for foreign investments in generation and for rehabilitation and environmental upgrading. PPGC will sell to distribution companies at a bulk supply tariff plus separate, transparent charges for the use of the transmission network. These charges will be published and controlled. According to the draft energy law, the Energy Regulatory Authority will monitor and enforce the transmission charge system.

In this phase, competitive forces will be at play in the negotiations between generators and PPGC over the short term contracts. Such contracts will, however, play a relatively limited role in total electricity supplies. The main purpose of opening to limited competition is to allow generators to learn the mechanisms of an electricity market. There will be no competition in dispatching or supply in this phase. PPGC will dispatch the individual plants according to their energy costs and supply the electricity needs of the distribution companies on a bulk supply tariff. Distributors will retain their local supply monopolies almost unimpeded.

Local generators, mainly CHP plants, will be allowed to sell electricity directly to the distribution companies. The price of such sales should be the distributors' avoided cost, i.e. the price at which they can purchase from PPGC. The economic advantages of co-generation of electricity and heat will be allocated to heat consumers. (Under the current pricing regime, the advantages go to electricity consumers.)

Prices to final consumers will be determined by the bulk supply tariff plus transmission charges and the costs of the individual distribution companies. Prices will reflect differences between distributors' cost levels, though the differences between neighbouring companies' prices should not exceed 10 per cent, and differences across all distribution areas should not exceed 20 per cent. The authorities do not want consumers contesting large price differences. However, the proposed limits are not economically based. The proposal seems to be a consequence of the wish to retain a relatively large number of distribution companies, which increases the risk of local cost and price differences. For the system to work, a compensation mechanism between distribution companies would be needed.

An underlying assumption in PPGC's proposal is that the overall electricity price level will approach the economic costs of supplying power during Phase I and that the price path can be guaranteed by the Government's making a firm political commitment. Otherwise it will not be feasible for PPGC to fulfil the revenue guarantees in its contracts with the generators.

Phase II (1998-2008): competition in supply and dispatch

The major changes envisaged in this phase are the introduction of competition among the generators for short term contracts with PPGC and the introduction of a pool mechanism creating competition in the dispatching of power plants.

The major new elements will be:

- Generators without long term contracts compete to sign short to medium term contracts with PPGC.

- All new contracts are contracts for differences (see below).

- Long term contracts are reserved for generators needing significant investments.

- All generators offer a bid price to PPGC and generation units are dispatched according to the bid prices (= the pool)

- Large high voltage consumers can choose to purchase at the bulk supply tariff or from distributors.

Depending on generators' investment needs in this phase, the competitive short or medium term contracts will account for most of the market. In addition, dispatching will be based on competitive price bidding in the pool and all power plants will be paid the pool price. Supplies under contract, however, will refer to "differences": under the contracts, PPGC will pay the generator the difference if the contract price is higher than the pool price, and the generator will pay PPGC the difference if the pool price is higher than the contract price. This system is designed to ensure generators their revenues and PPGC the price for its energy purchases.

Phase III (from 2008)

In the final phase, generators and distribution companies (and large consumers having access to high voltage grids) will contract directly with one another, and the role of PPGC will be reduced to administering the grid and the power pool. There will be third party access to the grid, but the supply monopolies of the distribution companies for consumers on the low voltage grid will be maintained.

This proposed new market organisation has been under discussion for some time, but it has not been possible to obtain agreement within the Government or between the Government and the electricity industry. It is therefore uncertain whether, how and when any changes will be made. The plan as it stands represents a number of compromises. For one thing, the process would be very gradual. In Phase I and part of Phase II, financial constraints and large investment needs are seen as necessitating central allocation of resources. The transmission company, PPGC, would thus retain a significant measure of influence on the generation companies. Furthermore, the likelihood that the proposed measures will achieve the stated ultimate purpose of the reform – competition in the wholesale market for electricity – appears debatable. The envisaged structure of the generation companies may turn out to be less than fully compatible with this aim. And the current plans call for only two groups of hard coal generation companies, which appears insufficient to create competition.

Recommendations

- **Important progress was made in 1990 in aligning electricity prices with economic costs. Prices are, however, still about 50 per cent lower than supply costs, and price increases in recent years have only kept up with inflation. The Government should decide on a programme of real price increases to make prices cover costs within a relatively short span of years.**

- **A decision on the organisation of the electricity industry is pending. The Government should accelerate the process and together with the PPGC lay down a firm plan for the organisation of the market. Companies and individual investors cannot be expected to decide on large investments without feeling confident about the future stability of the rules of the game.**

- **Updated electricity demand and generation forecasts are urgently needed for both the electricity industry and the hard coal sector – which, according to projections published in 1992, is supposed to function as swing fuel supplier to the electricity industry in the years ahead.**

- **The Polish Government should consider postponing the introduction of new environmental standards for power generation. The Government has decided on 1998 for the introduction of EU standards for existing power plants. This tight time frame will add · to the funding and other problems the industry will be facing in trying to fulfil its rehabilitation and modernisation related investment plans.**

- **Integration of the Polish grid with the western European co-operative organisation UCTPE is under preparation. The Government should encourage this work, which points towards improvements in Poland's security of electricity supplies and will create a basis for growth in electricity trade and exchanges with the west.**

DISTRICT HEATING

General Issues

District heating plays an important part on the Polish energy scene. The district heating systems are important consumers of energy, predominantly coal, and important suppliers of heat to households. About 70 per cent of Poland's urban households are serviced by district heating networks, and 53 per cent of the country's total residential heating needs are covered by district heating. By enabling households to stop burning coal themselves, the extension of district heating systems has helped improve local air quality. However, the systems are themselves major emitters of sulphur and NO_x.

District heating was the only part of the energy sector with a decentralised structure before 1989. There were about 50 district heating enterprises, most of them state enterprises under the supervision of the voivodships. Some of these enterprises owned and operated several distinct district heating systems.

Up to the end of 1989, government policies limited the enterprises' earnings and capacity for self-financing, primarily by controlling heat tariffs. In exchange, major investments were financed by the state through local governments; the enterprises were responsible only for network replacement investments. This system linked investment decisions to the availability of budget funds rather than to the technical and economic requirements of the district heating grids. It did not support optimisation of network planning.

The following are the major issues to be solved for the district heating industry:

• There is a massive need for renovation and efficiency improvements in heat production and in the grid system, which suffer from a legacy of insufficient maintenance.

• A reorganisation of the sector is well under way, holding out promise for more rational investment and maintenance decisions. On the regulatory level, however, many ministries and local authorities have a say in the district heating enterprises' operations. Rationalisation of the regulatory regime and clarification of responsibilities and tasks are needed.

• Pricing policies over the last few years have substantially reduced the gap between the costs of supplying heat and the prices charged to consumers. However, system-wide efficiency improvements will gain speed only when metering and consumption-dependent invoicing are introduced.

• Although the development of centralised district heating was an improvement over individual building coal stove heating from an environmental perspective, the district heating industry is a substantial contributor to Poland's environmental problems, especially urban air pollution. The district heating enterprises use coal as their main fuel and are responsible for 11 per cent of the country's emissions of sulphur, 10 per cent of particulate emissions and 8 per cent of NO_x emissions. District heating involves a large number of small, low stack boilers and has a disproportionate impact on local air quality in urban areas.

Regulation and Organisational Structure

On a general level, the district heating industry is supervised by the Ministry of Physical Planning and Construction, but industrial and utility plants supplying heat to district heating networks are supervised by the MoIT. For local planning purposes, the individual district heating enterprises report to municipalities. Some plants report to voivodships.

The draft energy law stipulates that the Ministry of Physical Planning and Construction will retain its role as general supervisor of the industry. Its role will be to set standards for consumer services and conditions for operation of the district heating systems. The Ministry will also be involved, together with the municipalities and voivodships, in the planning and optimisation of the district heating systems. The energy law makes heat planning obligatory for the local authorities. The voivodships will be responsible for co-ordinating heat planning within their areas, and will ensure that heat planning conforms with the Government's energy policies and legislation in general. Plans will be based on heat demand forecasts and will detail the heat supply sources, giving preference to CHP plants and waste heat from industry. Each district heating enterprise will need a licence to operate.

Heat tariffs, now controlled by the Ministry of Finance, will become the responsibility of the voivodships. The Energy Regulatory Authority will have no right to interfere in individual tariff setting, but is to be consulted in the elaboration of nationwide guidelines for heat tariffs. The final

Table 7.8
Organisational Change in District Heating Industry
(number of companies)

	January 1988	January 1992	March 1993
Total	51	291	473
Voivodship enterprises	34	11	5
Regional enterprises	10		
Municipal enterprises	6	92	91
Budgetary municipal units		91	171
Municipal enterprises with other activities		60	51
Enterprises run by unions of municipalities		5	6
Publicly owned joint stock companies		27	100
Enterprises owned by housing cooperatives	1	4	27
Private enterprises		1	22

Source: CIE

responsibility for the guidelines rests with the Ministry of Physical Planning and Construction and the Ministry of Finance.

The district heating companies have been undergoing organisational restructuring since 1990. The 50 or so enterprises have been split into independent companies according to the areas covered. Unlike the electricity grid, the district heating systems are not physically integrated, and the organisational restructuring aims at creating companies responsible for one physically integrated network each. The network may cover one or several municipalities, with the companies differing widely in terms of size and supply pattern. There is also much variety with respect to how the companies are set up legally (see Table 7.8).

The largest enterprises supplying heat to major cities have been organised as joint stock companies, whereas many of those covering smaller urban areas have been organised as municipal utilities. Most are separated from the municipalities as utilities having their own resources and budgets (in Table 7.8 these are called "budgetary municipal units").

The reorganisation at the local level has sometimes been carried out with scant concern

for its legal and economic consequences. The energy law should remedy this situation, but because it has been delayed, much of the reorganisation will have taken place before a national framework has been put in place. As a result, the structure of the enterprises could need adjustment later. There is a risk of creating companies that are financially too weak to undertake the investments necessary to become more efficient and repair the failures of the past. In addition, especially among the smaller of these newly created enterprises, the necessary managerial, technical and organisational abilities may be lacking.

Structure of Heat Supply

The Polish district heating systems use a variety of heat sources. Table 7.9 provides an overview of the structure of the heating capacity.

Major sources of supply are CHP plants and the public power industry, which deliver heat from co-generation and heat-only boilers. District heating enterprises operate about 2 800 boilers, many of them relatively small and old. They supply heat mainly to systems outside the major

Table 7.9
Heat Supply Capacity, 1993
(MW)

	Thermal capacity
Public power and CHP plants	23 202
Heat plants owned by public power industry	3 666
Autoproducers' CHP and heat plants	4 400
Heat plants operated by district heating enterprises	14 800

Source: CIE

urban areas. The efficiency of heat production in the public power and CHP plants is considered satisfactory. The central heat-only boilers, however, are outdated and technically in poor condition. Their average thermal efficiency is about 66 per cent. Local small boilers are the worst technically, with estimated thermal efficiency of less than 50 per cent.

In 1993 about 45 per cent of Poland's total heat supply originated from CHP plants. The district heating enterprises do not own any of these units themselves. The share of co-generation in total electricity generation is about 10 per cent, which leaves room for increasing the contribution of co-generated heat in the total heat supply substantially. One option would be to construct gas-fired CHP units supplying local district heating systems. An increased share of co-generation would bring benefits in the form of total energy efficiency increases, air emission reductions and end-user price reductions for heat.

Technical Problems

Technical deficiencies in Polish district heating systems result in low energy efficiency and high maintenance costs. Consumers are connected to the network via various types of substations, including heat exchangers and mixing pumps; some industrial users are directly connected.

Substations and receiving stations are generally of poor quality and there is a lack of automatic control systems. Measurement of delivered heat is practically non-existent. Consumers have different heating needs; the system usually leads to overheating in some buildings and an excessively high return temperature of the water.

One of the most urgent problems is pipe corrosion, both internal and external. This leads to a high number of failures and to interruptions in supplies. Repairs are complicated by damage to sectioning valves – low water quality causes corrosion and leaks – or by the absence of valves. Network analysis has shown that water losses are about four times higher in Poland than in western Europe because of condensing losses at the production plants, leaks caused by pipe corrosion and leaks in components and installations. High water losses result in poor water quality; the make-up water is insufficiently treated and often not fully demineralised or deoxygenated. High oxygen content results in corrosion, which in turn leads to water losses in a vicious circle of decreasing water quality. Some systems need make-up water in quantities that exceed the capacity of the water treatment plants, and untreated water is used to keep up water pressure. The return water is generally filtered by coarse strainers incapable of removing small particles and sludge. In combination with the insufficient treatment of the make-up water, this results in the total amount of particles increasing over time. The particles and sludge create clogging problems in systems being modernised with regulatory valves. Similar problems in housing complexes make thermostatic valve regulation of water flows susceptible to break-downs.

Due to the absence of metering equipment, heat losses are not recorded properly. They have been estimated theoretically at between 10 and 45 per cent. They could be lowered by replacing inadequately insulated pipes with modern polystyrene insulated pipes as used in the west.

Pricing Policy and Costs

Heat prices in Poland are currently controlled at a level below the economic costs of providing heat. The Ministry of Finance fixes a maximum heat price quarterly. Applicable nationwide, it takes no account of variations in local costs of supplying heat. Before economic reform began, heat prices were extremely low. Real heat prices were increased sharply in 1990 and 1991, but much more moderately in 1992 and 1993.

The difference between costs and the heat price is covered by subsidies. The state subsidises housing co-operatives, which form the bulk of the market, and municipalities pay the subsidies for other consumers. At the end of 1991, subsidies covered 78 per cent of the total costs of heat supplies. This share had been reduced by the beginning of 1994 to about 27 per cent, and the Ministry of Finance planned to increase the nominal heat price by almost 70 per cent during 1994, in which case most district heating systems would no longer need subsidies. The adaptation of prices to economic costs is much more advanced for district heating than for electricity or gas.

District heating system costs vary considerably depending on location, type and efficiency of heat supply, and size, density and efficiency of the network. These differences are reflected in the prices charged by the individual enterprises. In the first three quarters of 1993, heat prices before subsidies averaged Zl 100 800/GJ (US$ 6.3/GJ) but actual prices were in a wide range either side of the average (see Figures 7.11 and 7.12). Some of the most expensive district heating enterprises are relatively small utilities, mainly using costly and inefficient small heat-only boilers. Heat from larger heat-only boilers and from CHP plants has a higher share in the total heat supply. The large heat-only boilers and CHP plants have higher efficiency and lower costs than the small heat-only boilers (see Table 7.10).

Table 7.10
Price of Heat Supply by Type of Plant, 1993
(Zl 1 000/GJ)

Public power and CHP plants	78.8
Heat plants owned by public power plants	91.4
Other heat plants	114.1

Source: CIE

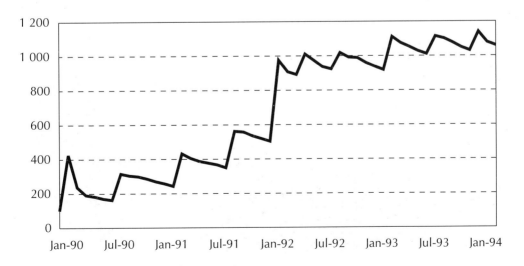

Figure 7.10
Real Heat Price Developments, 1990-early 1994
(Index, December 1989=100)

Note: Real prices are current prices in zlotys deflated with the consumer price index.
Sources: World Bank, OECD

The price range is so wide because of a limited number of small, high cost enterprises. Figure 7.12 shows the variation in average sales-weighted prices, from the least expensive 10 per cent to the most expensive 10 per cent of total heat sales. The average price of the most expensive tenth is about 40 per cent higher than the average price for the whole market. The maximum price fixed by the Ministry of Finance is valid nationwide and the subsidies vary accordingly among district heating enterprises. Removal of subsidies would result in the variations in the costs of supplying heat being fully reflected in consumer prices.

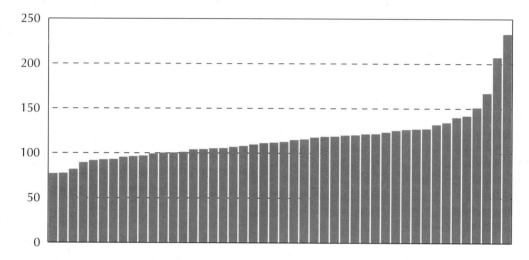

Figure 7.11
Distribution of Heat Prices by Voivodship, 1993
(Zl 1 000/GJ)

Source: CIE

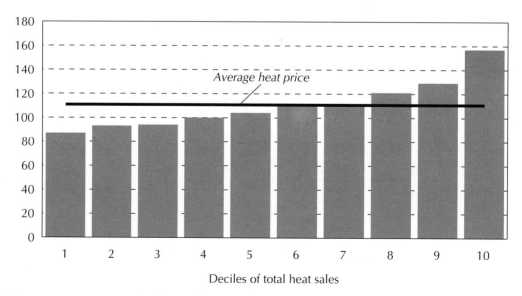

Figure 7.12
Average Heat Prices per 10% of Heat Sales, 1993
(Zl 1 000/GJ)

Deciles of total heat sales

Source: CIE

The wide variation in costs and end-user prices is considered a political problem in Poland. When state subsidies are terminated, municipalities in areas where prices are higher than average may come under increased pressure to increase their subsidy payments. Because of high unemployment rates and the general financial problems of large segments of the Polish population, an estimated 20 to 30 per cent of households have not been paying rent, including charges for heat and hot water.

Building more local gas-fired CHP plants, or taking other steps to reduce the number of inefficient, small heat-only boilers, would tend to reduce the price differentials. But many of the small enterprises that are supplied mainly from such boilers are in a precarious financial situation and could have problems financing new CHP plants.

Increasing heat prices to cover economic costs will be only the first step towards more efficient use of heat in households. In the most widespread tariff system, heat consumers are essentially charged according to the living space of their apartments. This flat rate system is a consequence of the absence of metering of individual households' heat consumption. In addition, radiator and valve systems often do not allow individual consumers to regulate the heat according to their needs. For heat prices to provide incentives to use heat more efficiently, metering equipment and more sophisticated valve systems will have to be installed.

Recommendations

- **The Government should continue to raise the regulated heat price to the level of economic costs of providing heat, with the aim of abolishing all public price subsidies.**

- **The share of co-generation in heat production is lower in Poland than in western Europe. Increasing the share might lead to higher average efficiency of heat production, less air pollution and lower heat prices.**

- **In reorganising the district heating industry, the Government should provide for enterprises to be licensed according to a model used nationwide and consistent across the regions.**

- **The budgets and accounts of district heating enterprises owned by municipalities should be separated from those of other local activities.**

- **The Government should work out a clear division of responsibilities among the various public authorities involved in the district heating industry.**

- **Training should be provided for the staff and management of the smallest district heating enterprises. There is a need for training in the use of modern technology, in organisation and management and in issues related to tariffs.**

ANNEX TO CHAPTER 7

Table 7.11
Principal Power Plants

Station	Installed electrical capacity (MW)		Main fuels (see Notes)	First year of operation
	Total	Subtotal		
Belchatow	4 320	12×300	BC, FO	1982 (first unit)... 1988 (last)
Kozienice	2 600	8×200 2×500	HC, FO, N.G.	1972...1975 1979...1979
Turow	2 000	10×200	BC, FO	1963...1971
Dolna Odra	1 600	8×200	HC, FO	1974...1977

Station	Installed electrical capacity (MW)		Main fuels (see Notes)	First year of operation
	Total	Subtotal		
Patnow	1 600	8×200	BC, FO	1967...1974
Polaniek	1 600	8×200	HC, FO	1979...1984
Ryonik	1 600	8×200	HC, FO	1972...1978
Jaworzno III	1 200	6×200	HC, FO	1977...1978
Lazisza	1 040	2×120 4×200	HC, FO	1967 1970...1972
Lagisza	840	7×120	HC, FO	1963...1970
Siersza	740	2×30 4×120	HC, FO	1962 1969...1970
Adamov	600	5×120.	BC, FO	1965...1966
Olstroleka B	600	3×200	HC, FO	1972
Konin I, II	583	1×28 3×55 3×50 2×120	BC, FO	1964 1958...1959 1961 1964
Skawina	550	3×50 4×100	HC, FO	1957...1961 1958...1960
Stalowa Wola	385	1×35 1×10 2×120 1×60 1×40	HC, FO	1954 1957 1965...1966 1982 1985
Jaworzno II	350	7×50	HC, FO	1953...1962
Blachownia	281	4×55 1×28.5 1×32.5	HC, FO	1957...1958 1968 1968
Halembra	200	4×50	HC, FO	1962...1963
Jaworzno I	146	1×20 1×8.8 3×35	HC, FO	1938 1952 1952...1958
Pomorzany	120	2×60	HC, FO	1960
Miechowice	110	2×55	HC	1953
Warszawa-Siekierki (CHP)	622			
Krakow-Leg (CHP)	460			
Wroclaw (CHP)	267			
Warszawa-Zeran (CHP)	250			
Lodz III (CHP)	198.5			
Gdansk II (CHP)	187.5			
Lodz II (CHP)	179.3			
Bialystock II (CHP)	173			
Bydgoszcz II (CHP)	169			
Poznan-Karolin (CHP)	155			
Czechnica (CHP)	110			

Station	Installed electrical capacity (MW)		Main fuels (see Notes)	First year of operation
	Total	Subtotal		
Gdynia III (CHP)	110			
Lodz IV (CHP)	110			
Zabrze (CHP)	106			
Bielsko-Biala (CHP)	100			
Chorzow (CHP)	100			
Ostroleka A (CHP)	94			
Bedzin (CHP)	55			
Szczecin (CHP)	48			
Szombierki (CHP)	43.8			
Lodz I (CHP)	36			
Warszawa-Powisle (CHP)	33			
Gdansk-Olowianka (CHP)	23			
Gdynia II (CHP)	23			
Bydgoszcz III (CHP)	21.4			
Gdynia I (CHP)	20			
Poznan-Garbary (CHP)	20			
Bydgoszcz I (CHP)	14			
Zielona Góra (CHP)	10.5			
Cieszyn (CHP)	-			
Czestochowa (CHP)	-			
Zar	500		Hydro p.s.	
Wloclawek	160.2		Hydro	
Zydowo	150		Hydro p.s.	
Solina	136		Hydro	
Dychow	79.5		Hydro p.s.	
Zarnowiec	68		Hydro p.s.	
Roznow	50.9		Hydro	
Koronowo	26		Hydro	
Tresna	21		Hydro	
Debe	20		Hydro	
Porabka	12.6		Hydro	

Notes: C = Coal unspecified, HC = hard coal, BC = brown coal, L = lignite, FO = fuel oil, NG = natural gas, Hydro p.s. = hydro pumped storage.

Source: IEA, "Electricity in European Countries in Transition", Paris 1994

CHAPTER 8

GAS

Gas plays a relatively small part in Poland's energy balance: in 1993 its share of TPES was a little over 8 per cent, compared with an OECD Europe average of 18.1 per cent. Furthermore, Poland's 1993 consumption of 9.7 bcm was considerably down from the late 1980s; in 1989 Poland used 12.7 bcm of natural gas and 3.1 bcm of coke oven gas.

Gas also has a narrower range of uses in Poland than is typical in OECD countries: primarily industrial processes and residential cooking. Residential heating, the largest single use in many OECD Europe countries, is relatively uncommon in Poland – only around 12 per cent of houses connected to the grid use gas for heating – and gas is not yet used for power generation.

Gas will play a more important role in Poland's energy balance if the plans of the Government and the Polish Oil and Gas Company are realised. There will be advantages for Poland in terms of diversification away from the very heavy dependence on coal, in environmental terms, in convenience for customers and potentially in terms of energy security if this issue is effectively addressed.

If present plans are carried out, significant physical interconnections will be in place and Poland's gas sector could be similar to that of western European countries by early next century.

But the realisation of these plans is by no means guaranteed and will present Poland with some difficult challenges.

INDUSTRY OVERVIEW

POGC is one of the last fully integrated monopoly hydrocarbon enterprises in Europe. It is responsible for the complete natural gas chain from exploration though development and production to transmission, storage and distribution both to industrial and residential customers. The company also handles upstream oil activities. It comprises 23 separate affiliates operating with their own budgets:

- two geophysical entities;

- four oil and gas exploration and drilling entities;

- three oil and gas production entities;

- six units operating regional transmission and distribution networks supplying gas and providing services to residential and industrial gas users;

- three construction units;

- three ancillary units;

Figure 8.1
POGC Headquarters Organisation

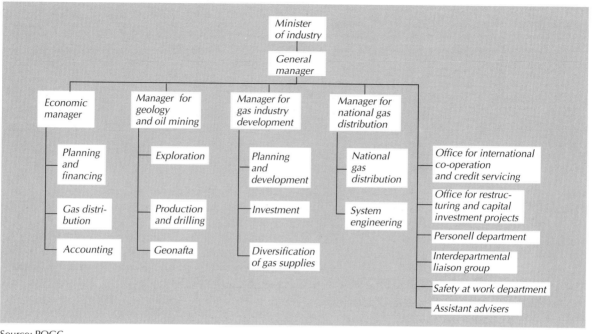

Source: POGC

Figure 8.2
Gas Consumption, 1980-93
(bcm)

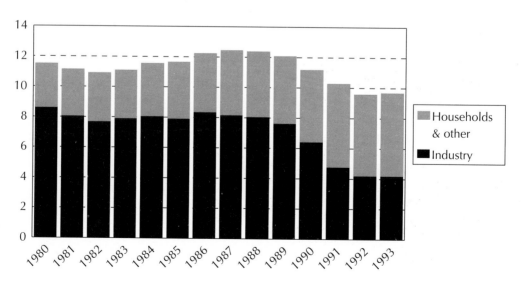

Source: POGC

- one designing and engineering office;

- POGC proper, including the National Dispatching Centre for the domestic gas network.

DEMAND

Figure 8.2 shows developments in gas demand since 1980. Although demand has fallen in recent years, two different trends underlie this decline: i) a substantial fall in demand from industry, which previously accounted for nearly two-thirds of total demand; and ii) relative stability in the residential/ commercial market, now the largest demand sector. Industrial demand is concentrated in a few energy-intensive branches, with fertilizer production and the glass and iron industries accounting for around two-thirds of this sector's gas consumption. There are around 2 300 industrial users. Figure 8.3 shows a breakdown of industrial demand since 1980. There has been a particularly sharp fall in metallurgical industry use.

Polish data do not allow disaggregation of demand in the buildings sector, but it is believed to consist mainly of residential demand. The number of connections is growing by around 200 000 per year, or by more than 3 per cent. Figure 8.4 shows the number of households connected to the grid. Of POGC's 6.23 million household customers in 1993, only around 730 000, or 11.7 per cent, used gas for space heating because of the prevalence of district heating systems and former requirements of formal approval for gas heating. This 11.7 per cent is nonetheless over twice the 5.4 per cent share of households using gas for space heating in 1988. This increase and the willingness of consumers to pay for new connections suggest that there is some pent-up demand for gas in the residential sector.

Another promising market is district heating, now almost entirely coal-fired. For environmental reasons and convenience, many municipalities are likely to wish to convert to gas. This has happened – to cite just one example – in a number of cases in the new Länder of Germany.

These factors suggest that strong growth in gas demand is likely in some sectors. In others the outlook is less certain. Figures 8.5 shows two POGC consumption forecasts up to 2010, based on different scenarios for economic growth. In addition to increases in the buildings sector, the

Figure 8.3
Fuel Gas Consumption in Industry, 1980-93
(bcm)

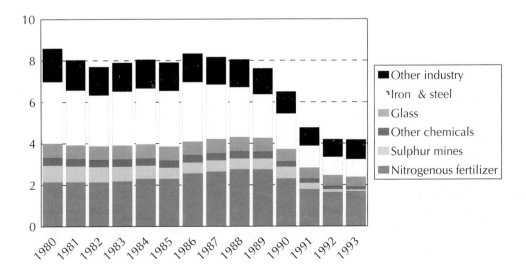

Source: POGC

forecasts show substantial growth in industrial demand, from 4.2 bcm now to 6.7-8.3 bcm in 2000 and 9-10 bcm in 2010. While it may seem optimistic to expect industrial demand to more than double, the forecasts for industry in 2010 are only a little higher than the level in the second half of the 1980s, so the rate of growth is by no means inconceivable.

Similar uncertainty surrounds power generation demand. The POGC projections show it rising from nothing today to as much as 25-30 per cent of gas demand in 2010. Put another way, the electricity industry's gas demand in about 15 years could exceed total current gas demand. POGC assumes gas will be used for baseload power generation because it expects shortages

Figure 8.4
Number of Households Covered by Gas Grid, 1970-93
(millions)

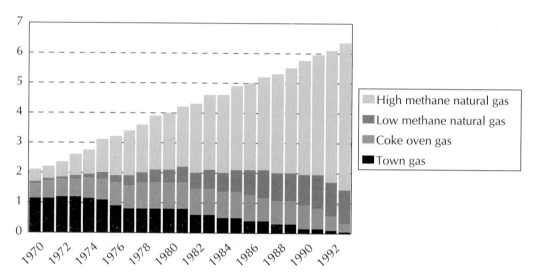

Source: POGC

Figure 8.5
Gas Consumption, 1994-2010
(bcm)

Low Scenario

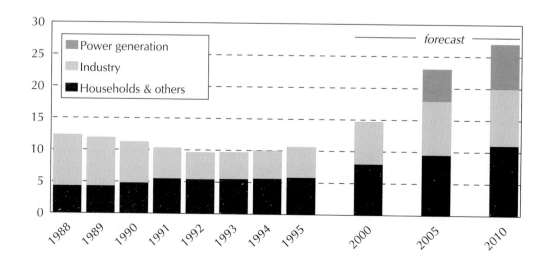

130

High Scenario

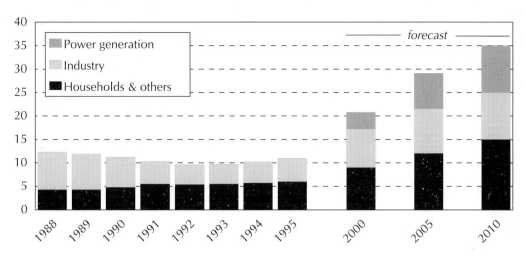

Source: POGC

of other fuels for generation. Again, this projected share seems fairly optimistic. It is true that Poland's coal-dominated electricity generating sector would benefit from some diversification, and the liberalisation of investment planning in generation should encourage alternative approaches. However, gas is unlikely to be able to compete easily with larger coal and especially lignite-fired plants for baseload. Many Polish commentators expect the use of gas to be limited to middle order and peaking plant and CHP stations for the foreseeable future, in which case it is unlikely that the highest demand forecasts will be realised. Demand developments for generation as well as in industry will to a large extent depend on how strictly Poland's rigorous new environmental rules are applied.

POGC's projection of demand in 2010 around 27-35 bcm, with 7-10 bcm in power generation, may understate the uncertainties that western forecasters try to take into account, typically by showing wider ranges and/or more conservative central projections. For instance, a projection by a Sofregaz-led consortium for the European Commission shows Poland using 20-41 bcm in 2010, with 25 bcm as the central projection. The low case assumes virtually no gas-fired power generation, the central case about 5 bcm, the high case about 10 bcm. A forecast by the consulting firm of Purvin and Gertz also projects demand of around 25 bcm, with a little over 5 bcm of power generation use.

Accurate long term forecasting of demand for gas is taking on greater importance as Poland proceeds with reform: first, because future import contracts are likely to be less flexible (see below) and to require firmer commitments than its present agreements, e.g. via take or pay provisions; and second, because as prices reach economic levels and controls are removed, the pent-up demand for gas will peter out. In the future gas may not simply sell itself, as it were; it will have to be sold in competition with other fuels. Planning for a given level of sales will not be the same as achieving it.

SUPPLIES

Current supplies are about 40 per cent indigenous and 60 per cent imports from Russia. The level of imports has fallen along with demand, but has remained in the range of 50-75 per cent of supply in recent years. Imports will have to increase if projected demand is to be met.

Production and Exploration

Production

Four types of gas are produced in Poland:

- indigenous high methane natural gas, i) from conventional deposits in the Carpathian region of south-east Poland, ii) in the form of methane extracted from coal mines and iii) produced from low methane natural gas (see below) by removing the nitrogen;

- low methane natural gas from 48 fields in western Poland, with a high nitrogen content and correspondingly low calorific value, about two-thirds that of the high methane gas;

- coke oven gas, distributed in parts of Silesia, with a calorific value about half that of high methane natural gas;

- manufactured (town) gas from coal gasification.

In addition, some districts use an LPG-air mixture for local distribution.

In 1993, Poland produced 4 bcm of natural gas: 1.8 bcm of high methane gas, 0.3 bcm of coal-bed methane and 1.9 bcm (in high methane equivalent terms) of low methane gas. Coke oven gas (0.6 bcm in 1993, equivalent to 0.3 bcm of high methane gas) and town gas are being replaced by natural gas. Coke oven gas is due to be phased out by 1996; on present assumptions town gas will be largely superseded by 1997.

Assuming that current and future exploration efforts are successful, indigenous production of natural gas is projected to increase moderately, to 5.4 bcm, by 2000 before falling back to 4.9 bcm by 2010.

Exploration

POGC is the sole producer of low and high methane natural gas, and has a monopoly of imports, transmission, storage and distribution. It enjoyed a formal monopoly of oil and gas exploration and production until 1991, when licensing was opened to domestic and foreign companies. Two licensing rounds have since been held; their terms were considered by foreign companies to have created a fair opportunity to compete, and several, including Exxon, Shell, British Gas and Amoco, participated. POGC did not participate in these rounds as such, although the company was granted licences in the most promising of the areas in question, where some exploration has already been undertaken. For future rounds it is expected that international companies will get around two-thirds of the licences and POGC the rest. However, as POGC has many other investment priorities and a shortage of investment funds, the company may be unsure

about its ability to take on extra commitments, especially at a time of significant retrenchment and restructuring, described later in this chapter.

Although price controls on gas distributed in Poland still exist and licence holders are obliged to offer the right of first refusal to the Government for the purchase of any gas discovered, it is not felt that these factors have discouraged exploration. The Government undertakes to offer export parity prices, and any gas it does not purchase can be exported.

Nevertheless, Poland is not regarded as a highly attractive prospect by international companies. There seem to be two main reasons:

- Prospects of available acreage: A recent estimate of onshore resources puts them at 158 bcm – much lower than pre-reform assumptions, though offshore resources and coal-bed methane would add to this figure. Poland is fairly well explored, and relatively little territory is available for licensing, given POGC's ownership of most of the prospective acreage. The arguments for targeting licensing rounds at foreign companies rather than POGC point to the need for POGC to release more acreage. Such a move would enable new exploration approaches, technology and finance to be brought to bear to help define and develop the potential of Polish territory. Otherwise Poland may find it difficult even to maintain present levels of production, much less increase output as projected.

- Tax regime: Many foreign companies believe that tax exemptions of various sorts, particularly for imported equipment, are necessary to make exploration viable. In 1994 the US company Amoco apparently came close to giving up a licence granted in October 1992, covering some 2.7 million acres near Warsaw and Lublin, because of dissatisfaction with the tax treatment. Other companies have also found problems in agreeing a tax regime. Changes announced in August 1994 are likely to go some way towards solving the problem.

Coal-Bed Methane

A resource that may become important for Poland is coal-bed methane. Although production costs are relatively high and the full economic potential of this form of gas remains to be assessed, Poland undoubtedly has large reserves of coal-bed methane of high quality. In Upper Silesia, 25 hard coal deposits together contain an estimated 47 bcm of extractable methane, and eight other deposits are believed to contain a similar amount. Some estimates of the country's total coal-bed methane resources go as high as 1 trillion cubic metres. POGC believes that the quality as a general rule is high enough for the gas to be injected straight into the transmission system.

The hard coal mines plan to increase the ratio of coal-bed methane recovered to total volumes released, and to make efficient use of what they recover. It is estimated that 230 million cubic metres out of a total of almost 900 million cubic metres was captured in 1992, implying a recovery ratio of about 25 per cent, and that about 170 million cubic metres out of the 230 million captured was used, mainly in local boilers, for a utilisation ratio of about 75 per cent. The gas can be used in nearby power plants, a practice that is catching on in districts with gas-rich mines and is being encouraged by the Higher Mining Authority. Measurements done near the Belchatow lignite

mine confirm emissions of methane also from lignite deposits.

The coal-bed methane issue has generated considerable foreign interest. The US company McKenzie has set up a joint venture with a Polish coal mining company, and several other international and Polish oil and gas companies have obtained concessions and started exploration and development to help delineate and recover this resource, especially in the Silesian coalfield region. Two examples are Amoco, which recently embarked on a three year exploration programme; and Metanel, a Polish company, which is undertaking a significant drilling programme.

The scale of Poland's future coal-bed methane production remain very uncertain, but output of 1-1.5 bcm a year by 2000 and perhaps twice that by 2010 seems feasible. This level of production would make a useful contribution to Poland's gas balance but would not redress it completely. Higher levels of production of coal-bed methane, significantly reducing import dependence, cannot be ruled out, but equally cannot at this stage be assumed with any confidence.

Figure 8.6
Supply Cost Estimates for Gas Delivered to Warsaw
(US$ per 1 000 cubic metres)

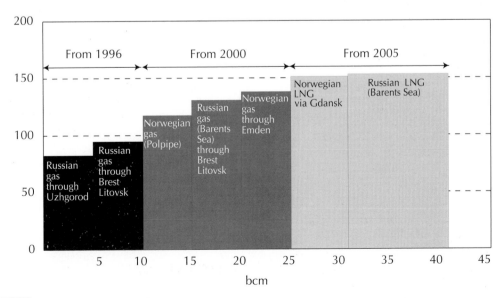

Source: POGC

Imports

The projected growth in gas demand points to a need for substantial increases in imports, to 10-15 bcm in 2000 and conceivably to 20-30 bcm in 2010. Poland would then be dependent on imports for up to 85 per cent of its gas supplies. POGC is naturally interested in diversifying its sources of supply and has looked at a number of options. For the period up to 2010, two potential suppliers – Algeria, which could supply LNG, and Iran – are considered too expensive and the lead times would be too long. This means there are effectively only two broad options:

- North Sea gas from the UK or Norwegian sectors, by dedicated pipeline or through the main European system;

- Russian gas through the existing network or a proposed new transit pipeline.

The first option has been discussed in various forms, of which the most concrete was the so-called Polpipe project. In its original form, this would have taken gas from the Britannia field on the UK continental shelf across Denmark and via the Baltic states to Poland, avoiding the complications of transit through the main European network. However, other options for the Britannia field – e.g. landing in Britain, where beach prices are currently higher than in Europe – were also considered. The means of financing a dedicated pipe for Poland, even with the participation of other central European countries, are unclear. At the time of writing, gas from the Britannia field seems unlikely to be landed in Britain. Other options for supplying North Sea gas to Poland, such as deliveries from the Norwegian sector, are also being discussed, but specific projects have not been identified.

The likely main source of imports in the future, as now, is therefore Russia. The present arrangements date from CMEA days. Supplies are provided to Poland via the Brotherhood pipeline from the Orenburg field (2.8 bcm in 1993) and the Yamburg field (2.5 bcm) in payment for services supplied during the construction of pipelines for these fields. The Orenburg arrangement runs from 1974 to 1998, the Yamburg agreement from 1989 to 2008.

THE EUROPOL GAS PROJECT

The Europol Gas Company has been set up to contract for the Polish segment of a new gas pipeline transmitting Russian gas to Poland and onwards to western Europe. The pipeline would enter Poland from Belarus and follow a more or less straight route across Poland to the German border near Frankfurt an der Oder. Europol Gas's task would be to design, construct and manage the pipeline; it is not responsible for the gas supplies as such. The gas in the pipeline would belong to the Russian company Gazprom. The long term function of the pipeline would be to deliver gas from the Yamal peninsula to central and western Europe, but until that area is developed other Russian gas would be transmitted.

The main owners of the company are POGC (48 per cent) and Gazprom (48 per cent). The remaining 4 per cent is owned by a company named Gas Trading Limited, whose shareholders include Gazprom, POGC, Polish import and export companies (including Weglokoks) and the German company Wintershall. About 60 per cent of Gas Trading Limited is held by Polish interests, which therefore own just over 50 per cent of Europol Gas.

The eventual aim is to build 665 km of pipeline (2 x 56 inches) with five compressor stations of 50-100 MW each, capable of carrying some 67 bcm a year. Poland would have an option for 14 bcm. Over the whole project, investment costs – estimated at US$ 2.5 billion – would be shared 85-15 by Gazprom and POGC, reflecting their shares of the gas transported.

At this stage, however, it is by no means clear when or even whether the pipeline will reach the final state: this will depend mainly on factors outside Poland's control, such as demand in west European markets and Gazprom's ability to raise finance.

A first phase, mainly designed to meet Polish requirements, is at an advanced stage of planning. The construction of 102 km of pipeline from Gorzyca on the Polish-German border to Lwowek west of Poznan was scheduled to start in April 1995. This project, whose cost is estimated at US$ 135 million, would be financed mainly by POGC and allow transportation of about 500 million cubic metres a year.

It would be misleading to call these agreements contracts as such. The former practice was to trade within the framework of economic co-operation plans and agreements and negotiate exact volumes and prices annually. While this gave considerable flexibility, for instance in adjusting to demand changes, it also gave – and gives – little security to either side, whether on volume or on price. Since the collapse of the CMEA arrangements, import prices have moved to European levels, roughly speaking, but formal long term supply contracts remain to be negotiated. Although there have been short term disruptions in transit through Ukraine, there are no immediate problems related to Poland's import capacity or Russia's supply situation in ensuring that the required level of imports is deliverable. The longer term expansion plans of POGC, however, will require new contractual arrangements, which most likely will require firm commitments on POGC's part, of the sort typical in European gas supply contracts (e.g. take or pay agreements).

If the Europolgaz project (see box) develops to the extent forecast – which is by no means assured – Poland will have the capacity to import around 20 bcm a year from Russia, and would no doubt

need to undertake broadly matching levels of commitment. This would make the economics of securing supplies from any other source questionable. Yet if the project goes ahead it is likely to be an economic source of supply for Poland: if gas from this source proves competitive in German and other western European markets, it ought to be even more competitive further up the pipeline in Poland. Figure 8.6 shows one estimate of relative costs. Poland may have to face some hard decisions in terms of the trade-off between diversifying sources of supply and minimising costs.

TRANSMISSION, DISTRIBUTION AND STORAGE

Transmission and Distribution

Figure 8.7 shows a map of the Polish gas transmission system. The main system is for the transmission of high methane gas. Smaller systems transmit low methane gas or coke oven

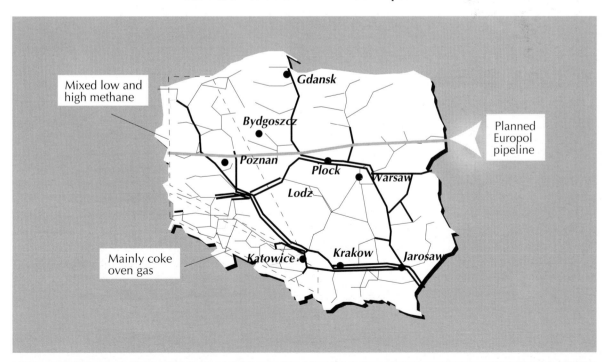

Figure 8.7
Gas Transmission and Distribution Pipelines

gas but are being adapted for high methane gas – the norm in OECD Europe. There are 16 400 km of transmission lines. Pressure is maintained by means of 27 compressor stations with total capacity of 102 MW. A further five stations on gas fields have a total capacity of 15 MW. Relatively low working pressure in the transmission pipelines – 55 bar – is an impediment to upgrading. Two small interconnections with the German system have recently been built. In the north, at Swinoujscie, some gas is exported to Germany. Volumes are small, less than 20 million cubic metres a year, but the capacity of the link allows for growth to 60 million cubic metres a year. In the south, at Zgorzelec, the intention is to enable imports of 1-1.5 bcm a year of natural gas to replace the coke oven gas now used in this part of the country, though current exchanges here are also less than 20 million cubic metres a year.

The main natural gas import capacity is in central Poland, where Russian gas is received through a lateral to the Northern Lights pipeline system, and in the south-east, where Russian gas is received via Ukraine through the Brotherhood line. Recently imports have run at just over 5 bcm a year, but there is capacity to increase them to almost 10 bcm a year, of which 60 per cent would go to central Poland and 40 per cent to the south-east.

Capacity expansion projects are ambitious. POGC plans to build some 16 000 km of transmission lines by 2010, in addition to the Europol Gas project.

Around 68 000 km of distribution lines serve 2 800 localities and more than 6 million customers – slightly over half the households in Poland. Figure 8.8 shows the growth of the transmission and distribution infrastructure in recent years. The pace of expansion has held up well despite economic recession and recent consumer price increases. The system has grown by over a third since 1990, and some 200 000 new customers are connected each year. POGC plans to construct between 45 000 and 60 000 km of distribution pipelines by 2010.

One reason for the rapid growth to date – which, as Figure 8.8 shows, has been especially marked at distribution system level – is the unusual method of financing new developments. The normal practice in Poland is for new consumers – municipal or communal organisations or even individuals – to finance infrastructure development via up-front payments for connection or through regional development grants. Ownership of the new infrastructure and responsibility for its maintenance passes to POGC. This form of financing is effective given the present constraints on investment, as the

Figure 8.8
Length of Pipeline System, 1975-93
(1 000 km)

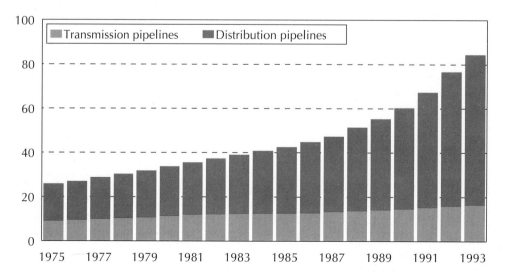

Source: POGC

growth in the distribution system indicates. But it also entails some difficulties – it has, for instance, led to a somewhat haphazard development of the distribution system, it does not ensure that developments in transmission and storage match those in distribution and that the overall infrastructure is balanced and sound, it may well cease to be acceptable to consumers as prices rise to economic levels and it can lead to cross-subsidies between different "vintages" of customers. While some level of customer contribution to new connections is part of many countries' approach to expansion of the distribution system, it would be desirable for the level of connection charges to be set on a transparent economic basis so that it is clear how far the basic gas price covers the cost of infrastructure maintenance and development, and connection charges are levied only for the extra costs imposed on the system by a particular customer connection.

Storage

Poland's four underground storage facilities have a total working capacity of 620 million cubic metres and a combined withdrawal capacity of 6.5 million cubic metres per day. All are in depleted natural gas fields in the south east. This is operational rather than strategic storage, designed to cope with seasonal demand variations. Poland has a more favourable load factor than some western European countries because of its high industrial load (which is not weather sensitive) and relatively low residential heating sales. The ratio of winter peak demand to summer demand is around 2.5:1, compared with 4:1 or more in some western European countries. Even so, storage is inadequate to ensure that peak winter demand is covered – residential sector demand is about 20 million cubic metres a day higher at winter peak than in summer. Short term supply disruptions in gas arriving via Ukraine have therefore led to supply shortages, and in some cases major industrial users have been cut off.

The projected growth in Polish demand, including significant growth in residential demand if gas-fired residential heating becomes as widespread as expected, will inevitably lead to a deterioration in the load factor of demand. Gas-fired power generation could further exacerbate this trend if, as some expect, gas will be used first for middle order and peaking plant. It is therefore urgent for Poland to construct new gas storage and to look at other ways of matching supply and peak demand, e.g. flexibility in purchase contracts and the use of interruptible contracts. All these options entail some cost, but that is an unavoidable part of ensuring a secure gas supply, even leaving aside wider political uncertainties over supply.

The options should be assessed and compared to establish the least cost mix. To make this judgement it is all the more urgent that prices are set on an economic basis:

- First, so that proper price signals can be passed to consumers, enabling them to assess the value of security of supply. Formally interruptible contracts have been proposed, but the relatively low level of general prices and the fact that security cannot in any event be guaranteed have made them unattractive.

- Second, to help finance the necessary investments. POGC plans to develop 800 million cubic metres of salt cavity storage – one facility is already under construction – with finance from the World Bank and other sources. Poland has many depleted natural gas fields, and POGC plans to build 4.5-5.5 bcm of storage, with withdrawal capacity of 80-100 million cubic metres a day, by 2010. This would mean expanding existing capacity tenfold. The French company Sofregaz is helping POGC assess the volume of storage required. Whatever the level, a significant expansion will be needed and will depend on adequate financing.

This comment applies generally to infrastructure investment. POGC has produced two financing forecasts based on its two demand scenarios (Table 8.1). Both would require very substantial

Table 8.1
Investment Needs for Gas, 1994-2010
(Zl billion)

	Low Demand Scenario	High Demand Scenario
Upstream	40 800	40 800
Transmission	25 998	35 418
Storage	23 870	25 790
Distribution	53 931	70 118
Total	144 599	172 126

Source: POGC

investment, including significant investment in storage. Total investment over the next 15 years would be some US$ 7-8 billion.

SECURITY OF SUPPLY

As is apparent from the description above, Poland has some difficult issues to resolve in relation to the security of its gas supplies. The country depends heavily on imports and this dependence will increase. Furthermore, at present it has only one external supplier for its imports, accounting for around 60 per cent of supplies. Dependence on imports is not of itself a security problem, but IEA countries normally seek to diversify their imports so that no single source accounts for more than about 30 per cent of supplies. Where this is not practicable – for example in Austria, which, like Poland, is on the pipeline route from Russia – flexibility is sought in other ways, for instance by using storage (Austria has three times as much as Poland despite lower consumption, with firm plans for expansion) and interruptible supplies. Poland has little flexibility in its system, with inadequate storage, no interruptible supplies and limited interconnection capacity apart from the main supply route, the Brotherhood line.

This problem has been recognised in principle. Some useful progress has been made, including the development of interconnections with Germany and the construction of some additional storage. There are plans to improve security further. But it is essential for these plans to be properly costed, for an optimum mix of measures to be identified and for a framework to be in place that will allow them to be implemented. The draft energy law provides in Article 11 for electricity generators to be required to maintain fuel stocks, but appears to have no equivalent provision for gas; nor is it clear how the stocking requirement would apply to gas-fired power generation or what level of storage, interruptibility, etc., should be aimed for in gas supply.

The Polish authorities appear to be putting a lot of faith in the transit pipeline proposal, the argument being that the existence of major customers further down the pipeline will reduce the risk of disruption to Poland's supplies. That argument has some

validity, and a further interconnection with Germany – already part of Poland's strategy – will in any event increase the flexibility of Poland's gas supply system. However, as the case of Austria shows, this would not normally be considered a sufficient solution to the problem of gas security.

The Polish authorities list other means of increasing gas security as well: intensified gas exploration, development of storage capacity (especially in depleted gas fields), increased coal-bed methane production and diversification of import sources. It is not clear whether these will prove adequate, or what the right mix would be:

- Gas exploration and coal-bed methane production are unlikely to change the overall supply picture substantially, as has been noted. In any event recent problems with potential foreign investors suggest that even modest expansion plans may prove difficult to carry out.

- Storage certainly needs to be developed but this will be expensive, and it will require a major effort even to keep pace with projected growth in demand and deteriorating load factors, let alone achieve significant security improvements.

- Diversification is worth pursuing but would have to be costed carefully. It is unlikely, for geographic and economic reasons, that a new external supplier or suppliers would take a sufficiently large share of the market to affect Russia's dominance.

If gas supplies cannot be made available at an acceptable level of security, one significant purpose in diversifying Poland's energy balance towards this fuel will not be achieved. The Polish Government needs to clarify its policy on security of gas supply and ensure that POGC has the necessary means, including financial resources, to implement that policy.

PRICES AND TAXES

POGC figures indicate that Poland's indigenous gas is a little cheaper than imports[1]. Future liberalisation of the sector, economic logic and the terms of production licences should all help

---

1. The World Bank questions these figures, holding that if certain anomalies in POGC's accounting system were removed, indigenous gas would appear to be slightly *more* expensive than imports.

ensure that prices are related to those at which gas could be exported (after taking account of transport costs). Import prices are broadly at European market levels – around US$ 95 per 1 000 cubic metres at the time of writing – and related to fuel oil prices.

Table 8.2 and Figures 8.9 and 8.10 show recent developments in consumer prices for gas in Poland, movements in purchase costs of imported

gas and some comparative data from western Europe. In dollar terms import prices have risen very substantially, over sixfold, since 1990. Consumer prices have also moved up very fast, slightly outstripping the rise in import prices. In national currency terms the increases have been even steeper.

Gas price increases have been very substantial – faster, for instance, than those for household electricity. The Government is to be congratulated for its firm stand in moving towards economic price levels.

At present, however, consumer prices have yet to match economic levels. Prices are set by the Ministry of Finance, which has to balance the need to cover costs with the social problems price increases entail. Prices now broadly cover operating costs but do not produce funds for replacement of capital or system expansion. Following an increase in the first quarter of 1994, tariffs were:

Residential customers: Zl 3 257 per cubic metre
Industrial customers: Zl 1 772 per cubic metre.

After a further increase in September 1994, prices are now about 10 per cent higher.

Table 8.2
Gas Price Index
(December 1989 = 100)

	Households	Industry
January 1990	500	350
January 1991	1 783	574
January 1992	8 003	767
January 1993	10 914	909
January 1994	12 948	1 126
June 1994	15 952	1 362
September 1994	17 547	1 498

Source: World Bank

Figure 8.9
High Methane Natural Gas Tariffs for Households
(US$ per cubic metre)

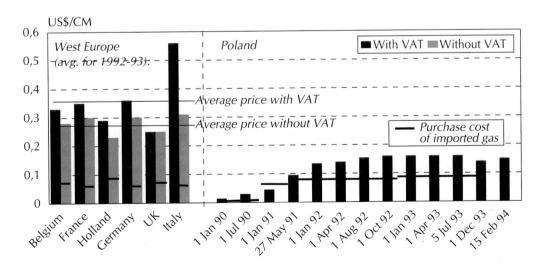

Note: Gas consumption for room and water heating and cooking

Source: POGC

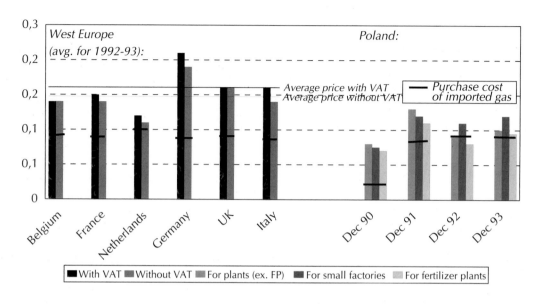

Figure 8.10
High Methane Natural Gas Tariffs for Industry
(US$ per cubic metre)

Source: POGC

Added to these tariffs are fixed charges varying with peak demand (measured by the capacity of the supply meter). Overall, at a rate of Zl 22 000 to the US dollar, the prices following the September 1994 increases were roughly equivalent to:

Residential: US$ 0.16-0.18 per cubic metre
(US$ 160-180 per 1 000 cubic metres)

Industrial: US$ 0.11-0.13 per cubic metre
(US$ 110-130 per 1 000 cubic metres).

Compared to the import price of US$ 95 per 1 000 cubic metres, prices now are not completely out of line with costs, but they are still below a fully cost reflective level or a western European equivalent level, as shown below:

Industrial: US$ 0.14-0.16 per cubic metre
Residential: US$ 0.25-0.40 per cubic metre.

On this basis, prices are somewhere between 50 per cent (residential) and 80 per cent (industrial) of their proper levels. Bearing in mind the evidence of unmet demand, the investment requirements of the industry and the low level of dependence on gas for heating (which reduces the social problems that high prices would otherwise entail), correct pricing must be a high priority. The

Government should ensure that the commendable momentum of its gas price reforms is maintained and that consumer prices for gas reach an economic basis as soon as possible.

Availability of metering does not seem to be a major problem with gas – about six out of seven consumers, including all industrial consumers and residential heating customers, have gas meters. As in many other parts of the energy sector, however, non-payment, particularly by industrial customers, is a significant problem. The Government needs to face up to this issue and allow POGC to cut off customers who do not pay their bills. Gas imports have to be paid for, and they represent a real financial burden to the Polish economy. If firms cannot pay an economic price for this gas, their output may not be economic. Transitional problems, including employment problems, need to be dealt with, but relieving firms of the discipline of paying for their inputs is not helpful for the viability of the Polish economy or for the gas industry. Non-payment transfers the cost from the customer (who ought to bear it) to others (who ought not to be saddled with the cost and may be even less able to afford it).

Gas is liable for VAT at the rate of 7 per cent.

REGULATION

The draft energy law sets up a potentially effective framework for regulation of gas transmission, distribution and supply. The draft law (November 1994 version) provides, for instance, for:

- access to energy grids (Article 5);

- licensing of energy suppliers by an independent Energy Regulatory Authority, which would also set quality standards, conditions for access to the grid, etc. (Article 26);

- unbundling of accounts (Article 48);

- principles for price setting, including coverage of suppliers' costs, protection of consumers' interests and discrimination between consumer groups solely on cost grounds (Article 49);

- approval of suppliers' tariffs by the ERA if provided for in the licence.

These arrangements should in principle help create a clear and accountable regulatory framework and a separation of the roles of government as setter of the policy framework, administrative regulator and owner. Yet this framework has been qualified both within the draft law and by prior decisions. Within the law:

- the President of the ERA holds office at the pleasure of the Prime Minister, has no security of tenure and can apparently be removed without stated reasons (Article 24);

- the Minister of Industry and Trade is to establish detailed terms of tariff setting for gas, although the ERA must be consulted (Article 50);

- other ministry tasks, such as laying down "detailed conditions of operation and planning of the development of energy and fuel supply" (Article 14) and "specific terms for development planning and investment financing, connection of users to the grid ..., operation of grid and equipment", etc. (Article 9), appear to override and overlap both with ERA functions and tasks that the industry ought to perform itself.

Furthermore, in a number of areas the Government is making long term decisions that might properly fall within the purview of the regulator, for instance on pricing. The formula for electricity pricing is discussed in Chapter 7. For gas, a similar desire to compromise between the need to move to higher, cost reflective prices to make money available for investment, on the one hand, and social concerns on the other, has led to a different approach. Plans call for prices to increase by some 30 per cent in real terms from the beginning of 1994 to the end of 1997.

The need to phase in price increases and provide for a transitional period is understandable; the United Kingdom had a similar programme in the early 1980s calling for annual 10 per cent real increases. It is further recognised that the Polish Government has to make some difficult decisions. Nevertheless the Government should give careful consideration to two important points:

- The need to determine an end point for the transition period so that within a reasonable number of years, prices will clearly reach their proper economic levels and normal regulatory oversight can occur. A 30 per cent increase may not be enough. If help for low income consumers is needed, it can be provided more effectively than by wholesale price distortions – through targeted welfare payments to those groups, for instance.

- The need for the ERA to be seen to be independent and have sufficient authority and legal power to make and enforce its own decisions. If these conditions are not satisfied, the ERA could become an unnecessary extra layer of bureaucracy. Responsibility for decisions would be blurred, the temptation for the Government to interfere in the commercial operation of the industry would be increased and the possibility of encouraging outside capital investment, or of the industry raising its own finance from internal resources, would be jeopardised.

RESTRUCTURING/PRIVATISATION PLANS

As can be seen from the description in the beginning of this chapter, POGC needs substantial restructuring to adapt to a free market economy. The company is large and unwieldy, embraces too many different sorts of activity, allows internal cross-subsidisation of unprofitable activities, fails to distinguish clearly between monopoly activities requiring regulation and activities that should be exposed to competitive markets, and leaves responsibilities blurred, particularly between government and company.

Realising this need, and heeding advise from the Anti-Monopoly Office, the Government adopted a restructuring plan with the following objectives:

- separation of core and ancillary activities;

- transparency of accounting between upstream and downstream activities;

- improved cost control;

- precise division of authority and responsibility between the individual units within POGC.

The plan is to be carried out in stages:

i) in the first stage, for which the original deadline was April 1994, technical support facilities – equipment and vehicle repair works, design functions, etc. – were to be commercialised and partly privatised, i.e. set up as separate companies with a POGC shareholding of less than 50 per cent;

ii) by April 1995 the upstream exploration companies were to be subject to the same reform;

iii) the next stage (no deadline yet) would amount to separating out the upstream production companies;

iv) the downstream gas business would be unbundled into a transmission company and distribution companies.

Figure 8.11 shows the proposed structure and timetable.

The decision to maintain POGC shareholdings in the companies to be spun off in stage i) is defended by POGC and government spokesmen as needed to provide for continued supervision of companies administering credits from the World Bank and the European Bank for Reconstruction and Development. Also, they note, a scarcity of outside investors may make continued POGC participation necessary as an interim solution.

Reform is certainly needed, and the original objectives of the restructuring as well as the implementation priorities – first hiving off ancillary activities, then creating a clear distinction between

Figure 8.11
Organisational Restructuring of POGC

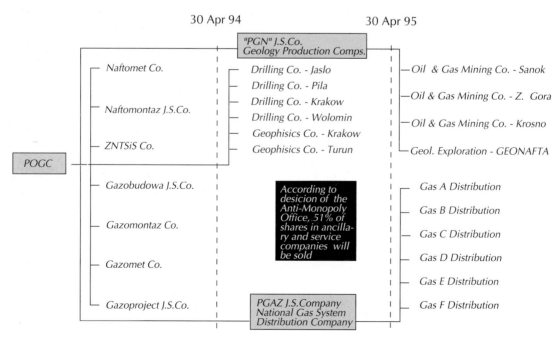

Source: POGC

142

upstream and downstream – are commendable. The Government should consider taking the process further, particularly with respect to the possibility of full privatisation or separation from POGC of upstream and ancillary activities. This is a longer term aim, presupposing that the companies are rationalised so as to be attractive to investors. However, the quicker it can be realised, the better. POGC's continued shareholding, even of a minority of shares, would give it effective control of the companies and make it difficult for them to operate genuinely at arm's length, so undermining the objectives of improved accountability and autonomy. Furthermore the co-ordinating role envisaged for the head office of POGC, which will include responsibility for "the implementation of energy policy ... concerning domestic hydrocarbon resources" and "guaranteeing the interests of the state in this energy subsector", suggests a continued blurring of the roles of government and state company. The Government needs to make a clear distinction between its role in setting the energy policy framework and the commercial operation of companies, including state owned companies, within this framework.

In any case, the implementation of the plan has fallen seriously behind schedule, and the Government now appears to be backtracking on its original intentions rather than expanding on them. The April 1994 deadline was not met; consideration is still being given to the desirability of spinning off ancillary activities before corporatising the whole company. Recently, alternative approaches not involving separating out the exploration and, in time, the production arms of the company have been discussed.

This inertia is disturbing in view of Poland's ambitious plans for the expansion of its gas system. To proceed gradually ("by evolution", according to present proposals) towards the "creation of opportunities for attraction of capital (domestic and foreign)" may be to risk jeopardising the possibility of realising those expansion plans by removing the possibility of attracting outside finance at an early stage.

CONCLUSIONS AND RECOMMENDATIONS

The Polish Government and POGC have ambitious plans for the expansion of gas use in Poland, which are to be commended. Such a strategy holds promise of significant benefits in terms of energy diversification and environmental protection. Much progress has already been made towards the reforms necessary to achieve this objective. However, much remains to be done. Many pieces are not yet firmly in place, including a stable and clear pricing and regulatory regime, a fully commercialised corporate structure for POGC, a firm basis for planning future supply and demand in a market context and a clear framework for security of supply. These points need to be addressed without delay if Poland is to realise its objectives for the gas sector.

- **The Polish Government should move forward as quickly as possible to secure a stable framework of pricing and regulation. POGC needs such a framework to be able to undertake sufficiently rigorous planning and reduce the uncertainties in its present forecasts.**

- **The Government should adhere to its original plans to restructure, corporatise and privatise POGC, preferably faster than originally envisaged. The present size of the company, the scope of its activities and the lack of transparency in its decision making and accounting may become increasingly serious impediments to efficiency improvements.**

- **The Government should consider ordering more release of acreage by POGC. The acreage now available appears insufficient to attract the level of foreign investment called for by the Government's domestic gas production projections.**

- **The Government should furthermore develop a transparent tax regime providing a stable framework and incentives for investment in exploration and production, as well as securing an appropriate share for the Polish people in any profits from the exploitation of Polish natural resources.**

- **Regarding the financing of additions to the distribution pipeline network, it would be desirable for the level of connection charges to be set on a transparent economic basis so that it is clear how far the basic gas price covers the cost of infrastructure maintenance and development.**

- The Government needs to clarify its policy on security of gas supply and ensure that POGC has the means, including financial resources, to implement that policy.

- While Poland should continue to pursue the option of supplies from the North Sea or elsewhere, it needs to recognise the possibility that it will have only one main external supplier for the foreseeable future and build additional flexibility into its system accordingly.

- The Government should give priority to constructing new gas storage and at the same time look at other ways of matching supply and peak demand. All options should be compared to establish the least cost mix. This can only be done when prices are set on an economic basis.

CHAPTER 9

OIL

GENERAL ISSUES

Governments have important roles to play with respect to the oil sector. Governments presiding over domestic oil reserves have to establish a framework for the exploration and development of these reserves. They may also involve themselves more directly by setting up one or more state companies alongside the private companies in the industry. Because a high proportion of the world's proven oil reserves is concentrated in an area where stability can be a problem, all governments should oversee the building up and maintenance of strategic oil stocks. They should also tax the oil industry, and make sure that it operates in accordance with national and international laws and standards.

Compared with the network based energy subsectors, however, the oil sector usually presents governments with fewer and simpler problems regarding how to allocate functions between the state and the private sector and how to regulate the latter's activities. As the natural monopoly problem is absent from the oil supply chain, oil industry regulation does not need to be particularly heavy. There are international markets in crude oil and refined products in which import prices are set. Furthermore there are no technical or other reasons to assume that state interference in oil importing, refining, distribution or retailing will help make oil products available to users as cost-efficiently and cheaply as possible.

The Polish Government's dilemmas regarding the oil sector should be even simpler than the norm because the sector is relatively small. Poland is an insignificant oil producer, and oil accounts for only about 15 per cent of TPES. Yet the oil sector has presented successive Polish governments with problems.

Important decisions have been made. The country's security of oil supplies has been improved. Oil product prices have been increased, and certain products are now sold for what the market will pay for them. Some of the enterprises making up the Polish oil industry have been transformed from purely state organisations to Treasury owned joint stock companies. On the retailing level there is real competition. But the Government is still heavily involved in oil product pricing and for more than three years has been pondering alternative master plans for restructuring and privatising the industry.

This hesitation may have a lot to do with the large revenues that the oil industry is expected to generate for its owners. Most forecasters expect fairly rapid growth in the Polish oil product market, if for no other reason than its current smallness. Decisions on liberalising this market may thus have significant revenue consequences for the state.

Management as well as worker resistance to change may have contributed to the delays. Both sides know what they have, but not what structural reforms and privatisation might bring. The main state owned companies in the industry currently enjoy some protection from private domestic and foreign competition. They are supposed to use this temporary protection to modernise themselves, and to some extent they are doing so. However, the protective measures may have muted the urgency of the need for reform. There may also be expectations in the industry that competition will be kept at arm's length for longer than promised. As for the workers' interests, structural reforms and privatisation will clearly imply a shedding of jobs. Everybody admits to overstaffing. In the long term, the reforms may result in new jobs – but people live, in Poland as everywhere else, in the short term.

These concerns notwithstanding, the Polish Government has committed itself, vis à vis international organisations, to gradually dismantling its protective arrangements, and the date from which the oil industry will have to fend for itself is drawing close. The sector may have only the time needed to get ready for international competition.

INDUSTRY OVERVIEW

Poland is almost totally dependent on imported crude oil. The country receives a mixture of Russian Urals and North Sea, Iranian and Middle Eastern crudes. In socialist times, Ciech – the state owned oil and chemicals trading company, operating on behalf of the Ministry of Foreign Trade and under the guidance of the central plan – accounted for all of Poland's crude imports. In 1992 Ciech lost its monopoly status and started to function as an intermediary between the refineries and foreign crude suppliers. It continues to account for a significant share of Poland's crude imports, but its position is under increasing pressure, as the refineries at Plock and Gdansk have started to deal directly with their suppliers.

Russian crude is imported on the Druzhba pipeline system, the Polish part of which is managed by Przedsiebiorstwo Eksploatacji Rurociagow Naftowych, a state owned company. Non-Russian crudes are imported via Poland's ports on the Baltic Sea, the most important of which is Gdansk, where tankers unload to a PERN pipeline running to the Plock refinery or to a pipeline to the nearby Gdansk refinery.

Poland's own production of crude oil and other liquids accounts for only about 1 per cent of total supplies. Onshore, the state owned Polish Oil and Gas Company, which is basically a natural gas organisation, produces some NGL and condensate. Offshore, another state owned company, Petrobaltic, produces a little crude on a trial basis. The POGC volumes are transported to refineries by rail and Petrobaltic's crude goes by ship.

The refineries sell most of their products to Centrala Produktow Naftowych, a state organisation, which used to be the sole provider of oil products to the Polish market but now faces competition in both wholesaling and retailing. Products are transported on PERN owned product pipelines or by rail – i.e. by DEC, a CPN owned rail tanker rental company that co-operates with PKP, the Polish railway – to CPN owned storage facilities. CPN runs almost 200 oil product depots around Poland, supplying mainly its own service station network but also private retailers and large industrial, agricultural or service sector end-users.

The refineries also sell to:

- an increasing number of private wholesalers, which pick up products at the refineries and transport them by rail or truck to their own depots;

- a few private retailers located so close to the refineries that they can make ends meet buying directly from them, truckload by truckload;

- large end-users;

- their own still embryonic but growing service station networks.

The private wholesalers sell to the private retailers that have mushroomed since CPN lost its monopoly position. The group of private retailers includes some foreign oil companies but is made up mainly of small, independent Polish operators.

As Poland's refineries do not have the capacity to supply all of Poland's oil product needs, the country imports considerable quantities, mainly gasoline and gasoline components, and mainly via its Baltic Sea ports. There are a quite a few operators in this business – Ciech still accounts for a fair share of total imports, but is losing out, especially in the area of motor fuel imports, to the refineries, CPN, private Polish wholesalers and foreign oil companies.

Imported products and components are mainly loaded onto rail tankers and sent to the refineries, to CPN's depots and to private wholesalers' depots. The refineries and CPN have facilities for blending

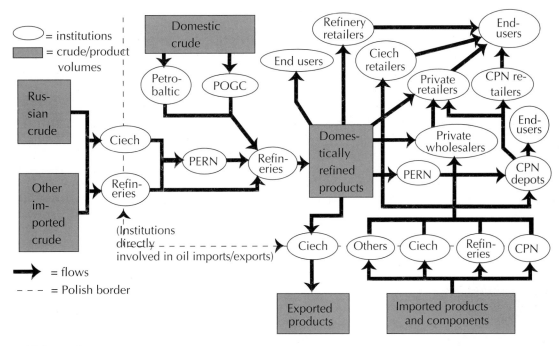

Figure 9.1
Polish Oil Sector: Institutions, Flows

Source: IEA Secretariat

imported and domestic products, as must be done to make supplies meet today's product quality standards. Imports not used for blending are sold by CPN and private wholesalers and retailers directly to motorists and other end-users.

Poland exports some residual fuel oil. Ciech is in charge of this business, which is necessitated by the relatively low level of sophistication of the Polish refineries; there is not enough capacity to convert residuals to lighter products that would be easy to market domestically. If planned investments in the refinery sector take place, these exports will decline during the 1990s. If funding problems materialise, and if there is little or no growth in Poland's own residual fuel oil consumption, they may remain on today's level. In any case, Ciech will probably face increasing competition from the refineries in this area.

DEMAND

Poland uses little oil for the size of its population and total energy consumption. The oil share in TPES has increased unevenly since the early

1970s, but in 1993 it was still only about 15 per cent, compared with 43 per cent in OECD Europe. The main reasons for this difference are the modest size of Poland's road transport sector and the dominance of coal in all other fuel consumption sectors.

Consumption Developments until 1990

Poland's oil product consumption, including refinery fuel use but excluding international bunkers, peaked in 1979 at 16.2 Mt. Three years of economic decline brought consumption down to about 14.1 Mt in 1982. Economic growth resumed in 1983, but by 1989 GDP was only 3 per cent higher in real terms than in 1979, and oil consumption stagnated in 1987 at slightly less than 16 Mt a year.

Important structural features of Poland's oil consumption, as the 1980s drew near their end, were that:

- there were no oil-fired public electricity plants;

Figure 9.2
Oil Requirements as Share of TPES, 1971-93
(%)

Sources: CIE, IEA Secretariat

Table 9.1
Oil Consumption by Product, 1983-93
(Mt)

	1983	1986	1989	1990	1991	1992	1993
NGL	171	169	267	138	144	159	171
Naphtha			973	933	773	780	850
Motor Gasoline	3 558	3 687	3 349	3 087	3 646	3 802	3 908
Jet Fuel/Other Kerosene			507	225	250	238	343
Gas Diesel	5 517	6 175	5 716	4 957	4 601	4 739	4 904
Residual Fuel	3 197	3 133	2 776	2 374	2 084	1 881	2 004
Other Products	1 813	2 064	1 789	1 052	879	1 001	899
Refinery Fuel	480	486	535	426	398	433	783
Total	**14 736**	**15 714**	**15 912**	**13 192**	**12 775**	**13 033**	**13 862**

Note: Excluding bunkers.

Sources: CIE, IEA Secretariat

- industry accounted for only 9 per cent of total final oil product consumption;

- the combined share of "other sectors'" – agriculture, households and services – was only about 10 per cent;

- because so little oil was used in industry and "other sectors", transport accounted for nearly 60 per cent of total consumption;

- non-energy oil use was about 21 per cent of total use.

In OECD Europe, 20 per cent of total final oil consumption was accounted for by industry, 52 per cent by transport, 22 per cent by "other sectors" and 6 per cent by non-energy use. The figures testify to the position of coal in Poland's industry and power sector, to the low level of penetration of gas oil into the household sector and to the underdeveloped state of services.

Consumption Developments since 1990

The launching of the economic transformation programme resulted in a 17 per cent drop in oil product consumption from 1989 to 1990. GDP fell by 11.6 per cent, implying that the oil intensity of the Polish economy declined by about 6 per cent during the first year of economic shock therapy. Industry suffered larger setbacks than services, especially the more oil-intensive branches.

In 1991, economic activity dropped by 7 per cent and oil consumption by 3 per cent; the oil intensity of the economy consequently rebounded by about 5 per cent. Industrial production and oil consumption in industry continued to fall, but for industry as a whole the oil consumption decline rate slowed from 27.5 per cent in 1990 to 12.5 per cent in 1991. And the use of oil for transport, which had dropped by 16 per cent in 1990, increased by 4.7 per cent in 1991.

Total oil consumption declined marginally from the first half of 1991 to the corresponding period of 1992, but since the third quarter of 1992 it has increased consistently on a year-on-year basis, driven mainly by rises in the transport sector.

Industrial oil consumption apparently bottomed out in 1992-93. However, industry has become more marginalised as an oil consumer – in 1993 it accounted for only about 6 per cent of total consumption.The iron and steel producers, suffering tremendously from a loss of markets and from a hardening of credit policies, saw their oil use fall by three-fourths and their share of total industrial oil consumption decline from 27 to 13 per cent from 1989 to 1993. The cement and other non-metallic minerals subsector used slightly more than half as much oil in 1993 as in 1989.

"Other sectors", including a number of rapidly expanding, mainly private service industries, have increased their oil consumption since economic reforms were introduced, and accounted in 1993

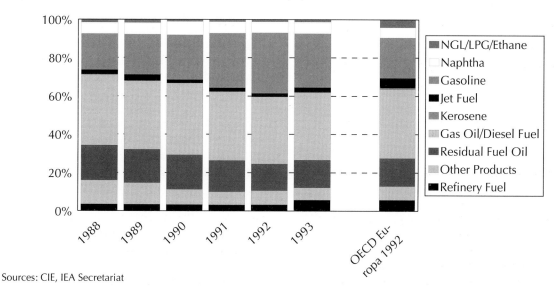

Figure 9.3
Structure of Domestic Oil Product Use, Poland and OECD Europe
(%)

Sources: CIE, IEA Secretariat

for 14 per cent of total oil use. Non-energy oil consumption declined in both absolute and relative terms through 1991, but increased moderately over the following two years.

The changes in the sectoral structure of Poland's oil consumption have led to changes in the product structure. Consumption of gasoline dipped in 1990, but jumped by 18 per cent in 1991, 17 per cent in 1992 and 3 per cent in 1993. The share of gasoline in total oil consumption increased by 8 percentage points from 1989 to 1993, to about 30 per cent. Consumption of gas oil/diesel fuel declined at about the same rate as total oil use, whereas consumption of residual fuel declined slightly faster.

The Poles had already started to redirect their demand for oil products from heavier to lighter fuels in the early to mid-1980s, and this process has gained speed as a consequence of economic reforms. At present, Poland's oil product consumption, compared with that of OECD Europe, is characterised by smaller shares of refinery fuel, heavy and light fuel oil, aviation fuel and the products at the light end of the barrel, but a considerably bigger share of gasoline.

The Warsaw region and south-western Poland, including the Katowice, Wroclaw, Poznan and Lodz regions, account for the bulk of the country's oil product consumption.

Consumption Outlook

Poland's oil consumption will almost certainly continue to increase in the years ahead. Demand growth rates will depend on how fast the Polish economy picks up, on structural change and other factors of relevance to overall energy demand (see Chapter 3), on international oil price developments and on some factors more or less specific to the oil product markets, e.g. Polish policies on passenger car imports, motor fuel taxation, road construction and transport in the widest sense. International car and truck fuel efficiency developments will also play a role.

Industrial oil consumption may not pick up quickly. The iron and steel industry and the other heavy industries that account for the bulk of the sector's heavy fuel oil consumption are still in crisis – in 1993, as in 1992, the metallurgy subsector's output amounted to 60 per cent of 1989 production – and their restructuring and privatisation raise a number of problems. In the construction subsector, which accounts for almost half of industry's light fuel oil consumption, output increased by 13 per cent in 1993, yet its oil use apparently declined.

Households and services use relatively little oil. Some observers think households and companies will start burning light fuel oil instead of coal, which is troublesome to use and polluting, and which will lose its economic attraction as fuel price relations change and personal incomes take off. Much will depend on how far and how fast the Government manages to implement its gas network expansion plans.

As road transport accounts for more than 60 per cent of total final oil consumption and the share is increasing, car and truck driving and the factors determining volumes of road vehicle use merit special attention in the context of developing oil demand forecasts for Poland.

Poland's passenger car fleet increased by an average of 7.2 per cent a year from 1985 to 1989[1], and despite the declines in GDP and personal income that resulted from the implementation of the Balcerowic plan, the growth rate increased to 8.6 per cent in 1990 and 16.2 per cent in 1991. The zloty's depreciation against OECD countries' currencies and certain changes in the Government's customs and tax policies dampened the Poles' enthusiasm for buying (mainly imported) cars, and the growth rate declined to 6.4 per cent in 1992 and about 4 per cent in 1993.

The car fleet will probably never again increase as fast as it did in 1991, not even in the context of a rapidly expanding economy and a liberal import regime. A huge pent-up demand for private cars was released in 1990-91 when the Government liberalised import rules. However, it appears equally unlikely that the growth rate will decline towards OECD levels, at least in the short to medium term and under

---

1. International Road Federation, World Road Statistics, various editions.

moderately optimistic assumptions on the Polish economy. In 1993 Poland had only 18 cars per 100 inhabitants. The corresponding figure for France was 42.

Other factors that will affect car fuel developments are the average fuel efficiency of cars in use and the average driving distance of Polish motorists. There will be a movement towards more efficient cars within each engine size bracket, but at the same time there will probably be a movement from small cars towards bigger, stronger, faster and more fuel consuming vehicles, as has been seen in the OECD countries. Regarding driving distance, there is every reason to expect increases as the Polish road network is improved (in 1993 the Government approved a plan to construct 2 000 km of motorway over 15 years), motor fuels become more available and lifestyles change.

About 95 per cent of Poland's passenger cars are gasoline powered. The proportion of diesel powered cars may increase somewhat depending on the Government's fuel price policies.

Poland's truck fleet increased by close to 7 per cent in 1990, about 10 per cent a year in 1991-92 and an estimated 1.5 per cent in 1993. Most of the country's 1.28 million trucks (as of the end of 1993) are heavy, i.e. over 3.5 tonnes. They accounted for the bulk of the 2.8 Mt of diesel consumed in 1993 in the road transport sector. As road transportation accounts for a much smaller share of total goods transport in Poland than in OECD Europe, a certain shift from rail to road is to be expected. This trend will come on top of a general trend towards increased total goods transport as economies stabilise in Poland, the other former CMEA countries and presumably, in time, the former Soviet republics.

In a policy document dated November 1992, the Ministry of Trade and Industry suggests alternative energy consumption scenarios according to which total final oil consumption will be 2-10 per cent higher in 1995 than in 1990, 9-23 per cent higher in 2000 than in 1990 and 33-71 per cent higher in 2010 than in 1990.

CRUDE OIL SUPPLY

Domestic Production

By the end of the 19th century, Poland was among the world's major crude oil producers. A large number of shallow wells had been sunk into anticlines in the Carpathian Mountains in southern Poland. Output peaked in 1909 at 41 000 barrels a day. However, by 1938 production had slipped to about 10 000 barrels a day, and systematic exploration efforts since the late 1940s have not restored the Polish oil industry to its former glory; in 1993 production amounted to less than 0.2 million tonnes – about 3 800 barrels a day – corresponding to 1.5 per cent of Poland's crude oil use. Onshore, mainly in the Carpathian forelands, POGC has in recent years produced 0.16-0.18 Mt a year of NGL and condensate as by-products of its high methane natural gas production. Offshore, Petrobaltic – originally a joint venture between the governments of Poland, the Soviet Union and eastern Germany, since 1992 a fully Polish state owned enterprise – is carrying out test production from one of a series of small oilfields discovered on the eastern part of the Polish continental shelf.

No large oil field has been discovered. Average field reserves have been only 0.5 Mt and flow rates have tended to be low.

POGC has for some time been drilling beyond the usual maximum depth of 3 000 metres with the purpose of testing the potential of some deep Carpathian structures. Moreover, Poland has held two licensing rounds for oil and gas exploration concessions, and some foreign companies have shown interest[2]. These developments notwithstanding, nobody expects Poland to emerge as a significant oil producer. Hopes of discovering much more crude oil onshore are not high. The country's gas production is expected to increase by about 40 per cent during the second half of the 1990s before starting to decline after the turn of the century. If NGL and condensate output grows in tandem, onshore production might peak at 0.22-0.25 Mt a year. There are no official forecasts for Poland's offshore crude oil production, but the

---

2. See Chapter 8 for details.

known fields are small – reserves in the one where production has started are thought to be about 3 Mt, and potential production is estimated at 8 000 barrels a day – and although such estimates tend to slide upwards on closer inspection of the field and especially as production gets going, it would be very optimistic indeed to see domestic production making much of a dent in Poland's oil import dependence.

Crude Oil Imports

Import developments, sources, organisation

Until 1989, Poland imported crude and products almost exclusively from the Soviet Union. Since then, the institutions involved in oil imports have diversified their business to the extent that Poland in 1993 got 56 per cent of its imported crude from the North Sea, Iran and the Middle East.

Poland has diversified its oil imports as a consequence of:

- the breakup of the CMEA trading area, which led to increases in the prices that Russia charged eastern European countries for its crude;

- the structural problems of the Russian oil industry, which have led to fluctuations in supplies of Russian oil and made Polish authorities acutely aware of their security of supply problem;

- changes in Poland's oil consumption structure, with a lightening of the barrel and a tightening of product quality standards that together have favoured imports of lighter, lower sulphur crudes than Russian Urals.

In socialist Poland, Ciech managed crude oil imports as well as foreign trade in refined products and a number of other chemicals. The central planning process generated estimates of Poland's oil product and crude needs during the forthcoming planning period. Ciech then contracted for supplies, mainly from Russia, of the necessary volumes. Today the refineries make their own crude import decisions on the basis of their assessments of available market forecasts. Ciech, now a joint stock company owned by the Treasury (51 per cent) and the Polish petrochemical industry, including the Plock and Gdansk refineries (49 per cent), has retained a significant share of Poland's crude imports, operating as an intermediary between the refineries and their foreign suppliers. This share is declining, however; suspecting that they can do without Ciech's services, the refineries have started to buy directly from the suppliers. In 1992 Ciech accounted for

Table 9.2
Crude Oil Imports by Supplier Country, 1985-93
(Mt)

	1985	1989	1990	1991	1992	1993
Total	**13.7**	**14.7**	**13.1**	**11.5**	**12.8**	**13.6**
Russia	12.2	12.9	10.8	6.3	5.0	6.0
UK	-	-	0.5	0.5	2.8	2.7
Norway	-	0.1	0.4	1.0	1.3	1.5
Iran	0.5	0.4	0.9	2.8	2.8	2.4
Iraq	-	1.3	0.5	-	-	-
Saudi Arabia	-	-	-	0.7	0.3	-
Libya	1.0	-	-	-	-	-
Others	-	-	-	0.2	0.6	1.0

Source: CIE

152

93 per cent of Poland's crude oil imports; in 1993 its share was about 78 per cent. The refineries apparently do not accept Ciech's assertion that there is a need for a central import organisation and that Ciech because of its size and market expertise usually gets deals so much better than what the refineries can get for themselves that the difference more than covers Ciech's fees.

Import modes and infrastructure

Poland imports Russian crude oil on the Druzhba (Friendship) pipeline system, which runs from the Volga-Urals area – where it links up with pipelines carrying Siberian oil – through western Russia and Belarus to Poland. (A southern branch runs from Mozyr in Belarus through Ukraine to the Slovak Republic.)

The Polish part of the Druzhba system consists of two parallel pipelines with a length of 650 km. Construction of the first pipeline started in 1960, and deliveries commenced in 1964. The second line was put into operation in 1972/73. Both cross the Belarusian-Polish border north of Brest, run to Plock, continue westward and cross the Polish-German border about 70 km north-east of Berlin. Further downstream is the refinery at Schwedt in Germany.

Poland imports non-Russian crude oil on tankers unloading mainly at Gdansk. Restrictions on the use of the Great Belt – the straits between the Danish islands of Sjaelland and Fyn, functioning as the "gate" to the Baltic Sea – put a limit of about 150 000 dwt on the size of the tankers that can go to the Polish Baltic cities. Gdansk's Northern Harbour terminal can handle about 8 Mt of crude oil and products a year now, but an oil jetty that will double its capacity is under construction. From the port there are crude oil pipelines to the Gdansk refinery and to nearby storage facilities operated by PERN to handle short term imbalances between deliveries and refinery needs. From these facilities crude oil is sent on the Pomeranian pipeline to other storage facilities near Plock, where Russian and non-Russian crudes are blended to suit the Plock refinery's needs of the day.

The Pomeranian pipeline, between Gdansk and Plock, was put into operation in 1975. It was built

Figure 9.4
Crude Oil and Refined Product Pipelines

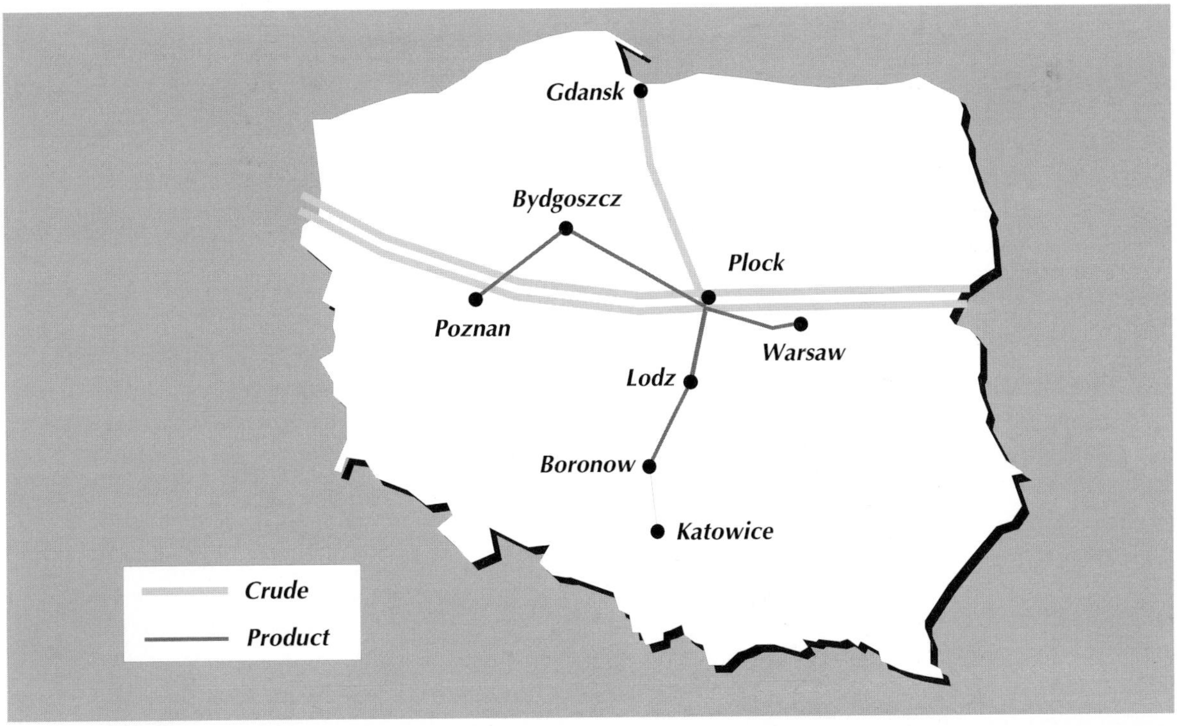

153

Table 9.3
Crude Oil Pipeline Systems on Polish Territory

	System	Pipeline 1	Pipeline 2
Length of pipelines (km)	Druzhba eastern part:	234	234
	Druzhba western part:	416	416
	Plebanka Tank Farm-Plock refinery:	14	14
	Pomeranian:	237	
Diameter of pipelines (mm)	Druzhba eastern part:	630	820
	Druzhba western part:	529	820
	Plebanka Tank Farm-Plock refinery:	529	610
	Pomeranian:	820	
Number of pump stations	Druzhba eastern part:	3	
	Druzhba western part:	4	
	Plebanka Tank Farm-Plock refinery:	1	
	Pomeranian:	2	
Throughput capacity (Mt/year)	Druzhba eastern part:	37	
	Druzhba western part:	27	
	Pomeranian:	21	

Source: PERN

to supply Russian crude to the Gdansk refinery, but since the 1980s its main function has been to carry non-Russian crudes to the Plock refinery. To increase Poland's independence of Russian oil, an additional discharging head was built in 1992 and a second pump station in 1993. There are plans to expand the capacity of the system further by building a third discharging head and a third pumping station.

PERN officials estimate that during the first half of 1994, the capacity utilisation of the Druzhba pipeline system on Polish territory was about 60 per cent, while the Pomeranian pipeline could have carried twice as much crude as it did.

PERN's three crude oil tank farms – one at Adamow on the Druzhba pipeline, one at Gdansk and one at Plebanka near Plock – have capacities of 348 000 cubic metres, 600 000 cubic metres and 850 000 cubic metres, respectively. PERN intends to expand and upgrade the Plebanka and Gdansk facilities. These plans are to some extent linked to an agreement signed in December 1993 on using the port of Gdansk for crude shipments to the Schwedt refinery in Germany. Crude oil will be sent on the Pomeranian pipeline to Plock, and from there on the Druzhba pipelines to Schwedt. According to PERN spokesmen, there is also a possibility that Elf will want to import non-Russian crude via Gdansk for the Leuna refinery.

REFINING

Overview

Poland's seven refineries have a combined crude oil distillation capacity of about 17 Mt per year. The two biggest, at Plock and Gdansk, have capacities of 12.6 Mt a year and about 3 Mt a year, respectively. The Plock refinery is reportedly able to use only part of its distillation capacity, as its upgrading capacity is reached at crude throughput levels of 9-10 Mt a year. Five small refineries in southern Poland account for the remaining 1.5 Mt a year of distillation capacity.

The Polish refining industry reached its present capacity in the mid 1970s. The 1980s brought a stagnation in domestic refined product demand and hence little need for additional capacity. Since the late 1980s, however, changes in the structure of demand and in product quality standards have rendered the industry increasingly unable to accommodate Polish consumers' demand for lighter products in general and motor fuels in particular. Plock and Gdansk produce more middle distillate and less gasoline than typical western European refineries, reflecting a lack of reforming capacity. In recent years they have invested in new equipment as well as storage capacity and loading and transportation infrastructure.

The Polish refineries' output amounted to about 13.9 Mt in 1993 after having developed along a U-curve since economic reforms were introduced. Changes in import rules and customs rates in 1990 and 1992 generated swings in the demand for domestically refined products.

In 1993 the Plock and Gdansk refineries were transformed from state enterprises into joint stock companies operating under commercial law,

although with the Treasury as sole shareholder. The five smaller refineries were at the time of writing still state enterprises.

Plock Refinery

The decision to build a refinery and petrochemical complex on the route of the Druzhba pipeline at Plock, about 100 km north-west of Warsaw, was made in 1959. Petrochemia Plock, the state enterprise established for the occasion, carried out the decision during the early 1960s. The refinery was extended, and the first petrochemical plants were built, in 1969-74. After having invested heavily in the Gierek period, however, Petrochemia Plock spent little during the 1980s. Investments started to pick up in 1989, and took off in 1992 when the refinery ploughed back some Zl 1.1 trillion – more than US$ 100 million at the time – i.e. about 50 per cent of its net profit. In 1993 investments amounted to Zl 2.15 trillion (US$ 137 million).

The Plock refinery no longer depends on Russia and the Druzhba pipeline system for its crude supplies. In 1992 it started to receive crude on the Pomeranian pipeline from Gdansk, and today

Table 9.4
Refinery Output, 1988-93
(1 000 tonnes)

	1988	1989	1990	1991	1992	1993
Total	**14 816**	**14 997**	**12 640**	**11 565**	**12 603**	**13 902**
Refinery gas	278	251	179	239	295	293
LPG/Ethane	249	280	141	142	158	170
Naphtha	1 073	1 085	985	773	780	850
Motor gasoline	2 651	2 763	2 193	2 172	2 933	3 172
Jet fuel	174	192	201	135	128	229
Kerosene	4	3	1	4	7	12
Gas oil/diesel fuel	5 174	4 845	3 963	3 675	4 401	4 955
Residual fuel oil	3 252	3 686	3 631	3 480	2 982	3 341
Other products	1 961	1 892	1 346	945	919	880

Sources: CIE, IEA Secretariat

Plock gets about half of its feedstock from the United Kingdom, Iran and Middle Eastern countries, and the rest from Russia. Blending North Sea and Russian crudes reduces the need for desulphurisation. However, as transportation costs are lower for crude imported on the Druzhba system rather than by tanker, Petrochemia Plock has no plans to reduce the share of Russian supplies further.

By early 1994 the Plock refinery consisted of:

- four crude oil distillation units with total capacity of 12.6 Mt a year;

- five catalytic reforming plants producing high octane components for motor fuels, with total capacity of about 2 Mt a year;

- two fluidal catalytic cracking (FCC) plants processing vacuum distillates into gasoline fractions and diesel oils, with total capacity of 2.3 Mt a year;

- three diesel oil hydro-desulphurisation plants used for removing sulphur from diesel oils, with total capacity of 1.8 Mt a year.

In addition there are a lubricating oil complex, an alkylation plant producing high octane components for gasoline, an aromatics complex, an asphalt oxidation plant and various other process units.

Although Petrochemia Plock is by far Poland's most complex refinery, it is not very sophisticated by western European standards. The capacity of its FCC plants implies a much lower conversion ratio than the averages for, say, UK or German refineries.

The Plock refinery is establishing its own network of wholesalers, applying a franchise concept, and it is constructing a truck loading terminal so as to be able to supply wholesalers and retailers directly. The terminal, which was commissioned at the beginning of 1994, will when fully operating have a capacity of 2.5 Mt a year. Moreover, the refinery is building up its own fleet of tank trucks; by mid-1994 it had 15 trucks at its disposal and there were plans to acquire another 15. These investments are intended to reduce the Plock refinery's dependence on CPN and enable it to tap into CPN's wholesaling revenues.

The petrochemical plants at Plock include a Claus sulphur recovery unit producing liquid sulphur, with capacity of 50 000 tonnes per year, two steam crackers producing ethylene and propylene (360 000 tonnes a year), a phenol plant (45 000 tonnes a year), two ethylene oxide and glycol plants (100 000 tonnes a year), a butadiene plant, a benzene plant, an MTBE plant, two polyethylene plants and two polypropylene plants. The petrochemical part of the complex is inseparably linked to the refinery part. There are no alternative feedstock suppliers.

Plock reportedly produces more than half the plastics used in Poland. The company exports polyethylene, but the ratio of exports to domestic sales – slightly less than half of production is exported now – is decreasing. The domestic market for petrochemical products is expected to increase rapidly; plastics consumption per capita is much lower in Poland than in OECD Europe. Company spokesmen consider their petrochemical facilities too small to be internationally competitive, but think that by increasing their polyethylene and polypropylene production capacity and by becoming more energy efficient, they will be able to defend their share of the domestic market.

Petrochemia Plock's revenue during July-December 1993, i.e. its first half year as a joint stock company, amounted to Zl 26.6 trillion or US$ 1.33 billion at an exchange rate of Zl 20 088/US$. The company's gross profit before taxes and mandatory write-offs was reportedly Zl 3.2 trillion, and net profit was Zl 1.7 trillion. Revenue and net profit in nominal terms were apparently up 13 and 30 per cent, respectively, from January-June 1993, but changes in accounting practices following the transformation of the company from state enterprise to joint stock company make comparisons difficult.

The company reports revenue on the basis of invoices issued; there are no comments on non-payment problems. The level of reported depreciation costs – equivalent to only a little more than 3 per cent of the reported value of fixed assets – puts another question mark on the accuracy of the net profit figure as an indicator of the company's financial strength.

Petrochemia Plock's president has stated that the complex needs to invest up to US$ 1.5 billion between 1994 and 1997 to become internationally competitive. Unless the Government contributes funds, which is not in the cards, or the refinery is privatised, this target will not be reached; the company's plans for 1994 and 1995 indicate an investment level of about US$ 150 million a year.

These funds are to be used to improve energy efficiency, to reduce emissions of SO_x, CO and VOCs, and to expand its motor fuels and ethylene production capacity. Investment projects include:

- revamping the crude distillation units;

- expanding the FCC capacity;

- constructing a visbreaker with capacity of 1 Mt a year;

- revamping the gasoline blending facilities;

- building an isomerisation unit for blending high quality unleaded gasoline;

- revamping the petrochemical complex's olefin production capacity;

- building new polyethylene and polypropylene plants;

- installing facilities to reduce SO_x emissions.

With 8 300 employees, Petrochemia Plock is overstaffed. Management is aware of this problem and its consequences for costs and competitiveness. The workforce was reduced by 200 in 1993, but only through retirements; there were no layoffs. Options are limited by the fact that unemployment is a serious problem in the Plock area. At the same time, Petrochemia Plock, like other formerly state-run companies, lacks people with marketing and other capitalist economy skills.

To overcome these imbalances, streamline the company's operations and cut costs, the Plock management plans a series of restructuring and reorganisation measures. Various divisions and departments are to be converted to independent companies, with some 51 per cent of the shares held by their employees and the remaining shares held by Petrochemia Plock. The newly independent companies will continue receiving orders from Plock, but after a period of learning how to operate on their own in a market environment, they will be expected to start broadening their base of customers. The company's design office, engineering department and road transportation department are first in line to be spun off.

There is much scepticism among Plock's employees about the proposed structure. Workers fear that fending for themselves will mean reduced job security. Paradoxically, Petrochemia Plock's better financial results since its transformation to a joint stock company seem to have increased workers' unwillingness to leave the parent company. At the request of the local Solidarity trade union branch, the design office will be run as a separate business on a trial basis for three months before the arrangement is finalised.

Gdansk Refinery

Rafineria Gdanska, which started operations in 1976, now has a crude oil distillation capacity of about 3 Mt per year. Recently this capacity has been almost fully utilised – in 1993 throughput was 2.82 Mt. The refinery intends to double its capacity, but cannot fund the necessary investments on its own; its management is therefore keenly awaiting the Government's decision on a privatisation strategy for the oil industry.

The refinery's sales in 1993 amounted to 3.34 Mt. Sales exceed crude distillation as the refinery imports products and components that it is not equipped to make itself, and blends them with its own output to produce fuels that meet today's performance and environmental standards. Sales of almost all products have increased significantly over the last couple of years.

Rafineria Gdanska gets all its crude supplies from countries other than Russia, and receives them by sea. In 1993 its feedstock was made up of Iranian Light (70.4 per cent), Brent (27.6 per cent) and Polish crude produced from the test field off the Baltic coast (1.6 per cent). The refinery, which has a crude oil storage capacity of 460 000 cubic metres, has become a shareholder in the company that runs the Port of Gdansk's Northern Harbour terminal so as to help ensure uninterrupted crude and component supplies.

Finished products leave the refinery in rail tanker wagons (56 per cent in 1993), in trucks (32 per cent) and – after having been transported back to the Northern Harbour terminal in a short pipeline – in ships (12 per cent).

The Gdansk complex is a mixed hydroskimming-lube oil refinery. Its main process units are in two production trains, one handling output of motor fuels, the other supplying lubricants, fuel oils, waxes and other heavy products. The main units in the first train include an atmospheric distillation tower, a naphtha hydro-desulphurisation unit, a catalytic reformer with capacity of 0.45 Mt a year, a kerosene sweetening unit, a gas oil hydro-desulphurisation unit, an LPG splitter, various fuel blending units, a hydrogen sulphide recovery unit and a Claus plant. The main units in the second train include a vacuum distillation unit with capacity of 1.5 Mt a year, a furfural extraction unit, a propane de-asphalting unit, dewaxing facilities, hydro-finishing facilities and a bitumen blowing unit.

According to the company's annual report, Rafineria Gdanska's sales in 1993 amounted to Zl 19.8 trillion (US$ 1.16 billion at an exchange rate of Zl 17 064/US$). Profit before tax was reported at Zl 1.29 trillion and net profit at Zl 720 billion.

Total investments in upgrading and building facilities amounted to Zl billion 319 in 1991, Zl 324 billion in 1992 and Zl 415 billion in 1993 (US$ 30 million, US$ 23.4 million and US$ 24.3 million at each year's market rate). The refinery's managing director estimates the company's total capital needs at about US$ 1 billion.

Rafineria Gdanska's annual report for 1993 highlights the following projects:

- Construction and assembly work on a new catalytic reformer was started. This unit, which will enable the refinery to increase its production of gasoline (at the expense of heavier products) and replace the current reformer, will be ready for start-up during the spring of 1995.

- A modern nitrogen manufacturing plant was put in operation.

- The company's heat and power plant was equipped with a new boiler.

- The refinery's network of service stations in the Gdansk area was increased to seven.

The company has taken steps to improve its environmental track record. For instance, by making its operations somewhat more energy efficient, using lower sulphur refinery fuels and

introducing a vapour recovery unit in the gasoline loading gantry, it reduced its SO_2 emissions by 12 per cent and its NO_2 emissions by 7 per cent from 1991 to 1993.

The refinery has begun a restructuring programme with the intention of preparing itself to operate in a market environment and becoming more attractive to foreign investors. Accounting principles have been revised, the management structure has been changed – the marketing, economic and market analysis, quality control and public relations functions have been upgraded – and the staff has been slimmed down to 1 850.

Other Refineries

The five smaller refineries in southern Poland are at Jedlicze, Jaslo, Gorlice, Czechowice and Trzebina. Their combined distillation capacity is about 1.5 Mt a year. All were built before the Second World War – two have been in operation since before the turn of the century – and all are primitive by today's standards. None is served by pipeline; they receive their feedstock, and dispose of their products, by rail. They were built mainly to process domestic crude, and they still get between a third and a half of their feedstock from POGC. The rest comes from the Plock refinery and from neighbouring countries.

The small refineries produce a wide range of products, but relatively more lubricants and heavy products than the big refineries. Some of them have established themselves in niche markets; for instance, the Jedlicze refinery has specialised in recycling used lubricants.

Poland's southern refineries are a headache for the authorities; they probably cannot be made profitable, and they appear too small and unsophisticated to be savable by any reasonable infusion of capital. At the same time they are cornerstone enterprises in their areas, which suffer from high unemployment as it is. Suggestions as to what to do with them include deepening their specialisations in certain products, then making them "satellites" of the big refineries, or turning them into wholesale depots.

Plans for New Refinery in Southern Poland

Poland's oil refining capacity is expected to fall increasingly short of its oil product consumption. In the MoIT's scenarios from late 1992, liquid fuel consumption in 2010 exceeds today's crude oil distillation capacity by up to 5.5 Mt a year. The gap, which will have to be filled by product imports, may in fact become bigger, as incremental demand will be mainly for light products, which Poland's refineries already produce at near capacity.

Discussions on whether to increase capacity at the existing refineries or to build a major new refinery have been going on for years. The latter proposal, in its latest form, would involve building a refinery with distillation capacity of about 6 Mt a year and equipment to produce 60 per cent gasoline in southern Poland, at Kedzierzyn-Kozle on the Oder River. There is already a chemical plant at this location, implying possibilities for synergy. The refinery would be in an area (about 100 km in diameter) where one-third of Poland's domestic oil consumption takes place and where demand is increasing faster than anywhere else in the country. It is claimed, assuming a crude oil pipeline were to be run south from Plock to this area, that the economics of the project look good. In the short run an undersupply of motor fuels in the Czech Republic and product quality problems on the Russian side of the border would keep competition from these countries in check; in the longer run transportation cost differences would represent a sufficient level of protection for a Polish refinery in the area.

In late 1994 a consortium of some 20 Polish companies was established to move the project forward. Perhaps driven by uncertainty about the intentions of the Plock and Gdansk refineries, CPN has joined this group, which is to create a joint stock company to build the refinery. However, the question of how to secure financing for the project is far from resolved.

Polish authorities appear to have adopted a wait-and-see position. There is little disagreement on the assertion that, ideally, a significant share of Poland's refinery capacity should be located in the south. It is argued, however, that this does not justify expanding the present capacity on the scale, and at the costs, of the plans for a new southern refinery. Investments in the refinery – estimated at US$ 1.5 billion – and a crude

pipeline would draw resources from other projects. Risks would be high, too, as domestic demand developments are uncertain and as the competition from Czech, German and Russian refineries may become stiffer than is now expected. The Government may have taken note of recent information from Elf and Treuhand on the profitability of the Leuna refinery, which at 6-8 per cent is disturbingly low, possibly indicating that the conclusions of the feasibility studies on a new Polish refinery are too optimistic.

If the Gdansk refinery were converted to an export refinery, the domestic market might be able to absorb the output of a third big refinery, but currently there is overcapacity in the Baltic area, making this another high risk option. Instead, the Gdansk refinery is to be expanded to meet Poland's incremental domestic product needs in the short to medium term.

Under the circumstances, it seems likely that no major decision on how to meet Poland's oil product needs in the long term will be made before decisions on how to restructure and privatise the Polish oil industry have been made and implementation of those decisions has started.

OIL PRODUCT IMPORTS

Poland's oil product imports peaked in 1980 at about 3.8 Mtoe. They fell steeply in the early 1980s, bottomed out in 1983 at 2.9 Mtoe and fluctuated during the rest of the 1980s in the 3.2-3.5 Mtoe per year range.

As has been noted, 1990 brought a 17 per cent decline in total final consumption of oil products. The share of imports in Poland's consumption of gasoline increased from 18 per cent in 1989 to 35 per cent in 1990; the share of imports in the country's gas oil/diesel consumption increased from 25 to 30 per cent. The liberalisation of import rules and changes in customs policies introduced by the Mazowiecki Government led to an unforeseen substitution of imported high quality products for domestic output. The refineries saw a 2.4 Mt or 16 per cent decline in throughput. In 1991 the refineries suffered another 1.1 Mt or 8.5 per cent drop in

Table 9.5
Oil Product Imports, 1989-93
(1 000 tonnes)

	1988	1989	1990	1991	1992	1993
Total	**3 087**	**3 196**	**2 764**	**2 564**	**2 027**	**1 286**
Motor gasoline	363	604	1 073	1 327	1 340	643
Aviation gasoline	31	19	7	43	5	8
Jet fuel	196	331	38	78	122	119
Gas oil/diesel fuel	1 326	1 386	1 491	1 090	546	455
Residual fuel oil	1 055	764	101	12	1	-
Other products	116	92	54	14	13	61

Sources: CIE, IEA Secretariat

Figure 9.5
**Motor Fuel Imports as Shares of Motor Fuel Consumption,
and Refinery Crude Oil Processing, 1989-93**

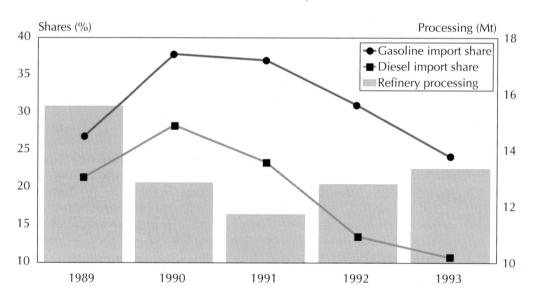

Source: CIE

throughput, and pressures to provide some kind of protection for the domestic refining industry started to build up.

In 1992 various restrictions on oil product imports were put in place: customs tariffs and excise duties were raised and licensing and quota arrangements were introduced. As a result, imports dropped by more than 20 per cent while refinery processing bounced back to its 1990 level. This trend has continued; in 1993 imports declined by another 36 per cent. Taxes (and price ceilings) have worked to re-establish the import of gasoline and diesel as a business reserved, for all practical purposes, for Polish state enterprises. Regardless of their efficiency, private wholesalers and

Figure 9.6

Margins on Imported Motor Fuels, 1993
(Zl/litre)

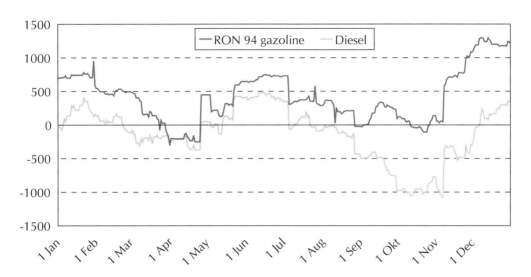

Source: Statoil Poland

retailers have not been able to make a profit buying motor fuels from abroad and reselling them on the Polish market. In periods during 1993, margins on diesel fuel and certain grades of gasoline were negative.

As regards product structure, Poland's oil product imports have changed markedly since the late 1980s. From 1989 to 1993 the gasoline share of total imports increased from 19 to 50 per cent while the diesel share declined from 43 to 35 per cent and the heavy products share dropped to zero. These developments reflect the changes since 1989 in the structure of Poland's oil product consumption and in the composition of the refinery sector's output.

The Poles now consume more gasoline, but less diesel and residual fuel oil, than they did when the reform process started. The refineries processed more crude oil in 1989 than in 1993, but managed to get more gasoline and only slightly less gas oil/diesel fuel out of their feedstock in the latter year than in the former. The incremental production of gasoline fell short, qualitatively as well as quantitatively, of the incremental demand for gasoline, resulting in

increases in gasoline imports. However, the refineries' production of diesel fuel has held up better than domestic consumption, resulting in a halving of diesel imports from 1989 to 1993.

Products come mainly from the Scandinavian countries, Germany and the United Kingdom, but also from the former Soviet republics of Russia, Ukraine, Belarus and Lithuania. As the profitability of importing and reselling products has declined, some formerly important suppliers have become marginal. However, growth in the sales of components to Polish refineries has to some extent compensated for declines in the sales of refined products to wholesalers.

Although Ciech's monopoly on oil product imports has been abolished, the state retains control over import developments. Companies interested in establishing themselves as importers must first obtain a general licence – valid for one year – from the Ministry of Foreign Economic Cooperation. Applicants must show that they are not newcomers to the fuel business, provide information on their financial position and give proof of their irreproachability as taxpayers. They must also document their access to storage facilities. Licensed importers must apply twice a year under a quota system for the amounts of gasoline and gas oil they intend to import during the following period. For 1994, quotas amounting to 1.8 Mt of leaded and unleaded gasoline and 800 000 tonnes of gas oil were allocated. Imports of other products, such as LPG and fuel oil, are not subject to quotas. Importers must also obtain a permit for each contract they sign. This may take time, and makes the business of importing oil products to Poland a cumbersome process.

Polish authorities have apparently become more liberal in their granting of general licences; as of April 1994 a total of 50 companies (including Ciech, CPN and the refineries, which formally are subject to the same rules as the private wholesalers and the foreign oil companies) were allowed to import oil products into Poland. At the same time, however, price and margin developments have rendered private importation of oil products increasingly unprofitable.

According to Poland's agreements with the European Union and GATT, the licence and quota system is to be abolished on 1 March 1997. Polish officials have announced, however, that they will ask the EU for a two year extension to give the industry more time to restructure.

Product Distribution Modes and Infrastructure

Oil products are distributed in several ways. From the Plock refinery, product pipelines owned by PERN run south-east to Mosciska near Warsaw and further on to Emilianow; south to Koluszki close to Lodz and on to Boronow; and north-west to Nowa Wies Wielka near Bydgoszcz and on to Rejowiec close to Poznan.

Most of these lines carry all sorts of products, though the newest segments – the line from Koluszki to Boronow, which was completed in 1993, and the line from Nowa Wies Wielka to Rejowiec, which was opened in early 1994 – are as yet only used for diesel fuel.

PERN does not report the capacities of these pipelines. Other sources[3] estimate the Plock-Warsaw segment and the Koluszki-Boronow segments at 1 Mt a year, the Plock-Nowa Wies Wielka segment at 1.8-2.5 Mt a year and the Plock-Koluszki segment at 1.4-3.6 Mt a year.

There are plans to build a pipeline from Boronow to Katowice. Once these have been carried out, The Poznan and Katowice areas will receive their supplies by pipeline, i.e. in the most cost-efficient way. There are also plans to build a pipeline from Gdansk to the terminal at Bydgoszcz.

At the end of each product pipeline there are storage and in some cases blending facilities owned by CPN. From these facilities products are taken to retailers by rail or truck. Products also go by rail or truck directly from the refineries to depots in areas too far away to be served from the product pipeline terminals.

Rail transportation, which in 1991 amounted to 77 per cent of all oil product transportation in Poland, is carried out by DEC, a state owned and CPN managed company operating more than 12 000 rail tankers, and PKP, the state owned railway company. Road transportation is carried out by CPN, which owns a fleet of about 900 tank trucks, and by the refineries, private wholesalers and private retailers using their own trucks or buying transportation services from a fast growing private transportation industry.

Although DEC is part of what might be called the "CPN group", it also sells rail transportation services to private wholesalers and retailers. It charges CPN less than these other customers, however, on the grounds of the scale of CPN's operations and usage of DEC's facilities.

Products are imported via the Baltic Sea ports, especially Gdansk and Szczecin, then loaded onto rail tankers and transported to the storage facilities of the refineries, CPN and independent wholesalers.

The Plock and Gdansk refineries have invested heavily in distribution facilities, with the intention of positioning themselves vis à vis CPN in the tug of war over influence and profits in the oil sector. In 1993 Petrochemia Plock installed gasoline blending facilities and built its own truck loading terminal, as described above. Rafineria Gdanska embarked on a strategy of downstream integration in 1992 and has acquired its own fleet of railway cisterns as well as trucks to serve its network of gasoline stations in the Gdansk area as well as independent wholesalers and retailers; the refinery now sells about two-thirds of its gasoline output outside the CPN system.

---

3. IGF, Enerfinance.

The transportation of oil products from refineries or import terminals to end-users appears to be taking place under increasingly competitive conditions, leading to higher efficiency, better service and sounder prices.

RETAILING

Until 1990 oil product retailing was carried out exclusively by CPN. The Mazowiecki Government abolished CPN's monopoly status, and in 1990-91 more than 2 000 private service stations were established. The system of customs and taxes at the time provided for relatively high retailing margins and made the business look very attractive to Polish entrepreneurs and foreign oil companies alike. Changes in the rules in 1992 and 1993 brought the profitability of retailing down and the mushrooming of private outlets to a halt. Now Poland has about 3 930 service stations. CPN controls 1 360 of them while other Polish companies and individuals and a handful of foreign companies own about 2 570 stations (not all of them open year-round).

Poland has about 12.5 service stations per 1 000 km^2, and about 0.6 stations per 1 000 registered passenger cars (1993). As these ratios are considerably lower than the averages for the EU countries, even relatively conservative oil product consumption growth scenarios hold promise for the retailing business.

CPN's gasoline and diesel market shares have declined from 100 per cent before 1990 to 72 per cent for gasoline and 43 per cent for diesel in 1993. CPN's total oil product sales declined by more than 50 per cent in four years, from about 12 Mt in 1989 to 5.7 Mt in 1993.

Most of the non-CPN outlets are one or two pump motor fuel stations owned and operated by individual Polish entrepreneurs. Although these outlets constitute two-thirds of all of Poland's service stations, they account for little more than a third of the retail sales of gasoline. Many of them are poorly sited and would not have been established but for the extraordinarily high profits that could be made from retailing in 1990-91. A rationalisation of this part of the business is expected.

Other Polish players in the retailing sector are the Plock and Gdansk refineries and Ciech. The Gdansk refinery owns and operates some ten stations in northern Poland. The Plock refinery, which adopted a retailing strategy at a later stage, runs a single station outside Plock as a pilot unit, with the intention of opening a chain of stations or establishing a network of retailers on a franchise basis later in the 1990s. Ciech is involved in several hotel and service station complexes around Poland. Foreign investments in the Polish retailing business have so far been modest. There is, as has been noted, a great deal of interest in the Polish market. Several foreign oil companies are positioning themselves there, and some – Neste, Esso, Statoil, Conoco, Agip, DIA and Aral – have started operations. So far, however, they are running a total of only 12-15 service stations on a trial basis. Low margins, a limited availability to foreign companies of suitable sites for stations, and uncertainties about the future rules for retailing in general and about what will happen to the CPN network in particular (see section on restructuring, below), are the main reasons companies are holding back.

SECURITY OF SUPPLY

Polish authorities are to be commended for having increased Poland's security of oil supplies markedly in recent years. The Plock refinery gets about 50 per cent of its feedstock from countries other than Russia, the Gdansk refinery has in recent years processed only non-Russian crudes and Poland imports oil products mainly by sea and from the west. The country's combined crude and product imports must thus be characterised as sufficiently diversified. Furthermore, the infrastructure is in place to allow Poland to supply its oil needs, in case of emergency, entirely from non-Russian sources.

However, Poland's crude and products storage situation is far from reassuring. Information on the country's storage capacity and actual crude and product stocks is classified, and thus difficult to obtain. In addition to PERN's three crude oil tank farms at about 1.8 million cubic metres, USAID estimated the refineries' combined product storage capacity in 1990 at 1 million cubic metres, and CPN's and the private wholesalers' product depots may hold as much as 2 million cubic metres. By late 1994, crude and product stocks were estimated at a level corresponding to about 17 days of net imports.

MoIT officials seem to feel that a reasonable target would be to increase stocks to a level equivalent to 30 days of net imports by 2000. There may be a will to build up stocks faster, but the Government holds that in the present situation, characterised by huge investment needs, an overburdened central budget and a scarcity of funds in the oil industry, other ends and activities should be given priority. The Government's target contrasts sharply with IEA membership conditions: as a general rule, IEA Member countries must be able to document the existence of strategic and commercial crude and product stocks equivalent to 90 days of net imports, a level chosen after careful evaluation of various realistic supply cut-off scenarios. For Poland, this level would have corresponded to roughly 3.6 Mt in 1993.

OIL PRODUCT PRICES AND TAXES

Prices

In spite of tenfold increases in gasoline and diesel prices and even bigger jumps in fuel oil prices since the turn of the decade, end-user oil product prices weighted together and expressed as one

index were only marginally higher in real terms at the end of 1993 than at the beginning of 1988. Big nominal price increases in 1989 and the third quarter of 1990 were quickly undermined by inflation, and since early 1991 product prices have risen in parallel, more or less, with the consumer price index.

Comparing oil product price developments in Poland with those in OECD Europe, converting zlotys to the US dollar at the market exchange rate, indicates that prices are still significantly lower in Poland.

Table 9.6
Oil Product Prices in Poland, 1988-93
(as fractions of weighted average product prices in OECD Europe)

	1988	1990	1992	1993
Premium leaded gasoline	0.38	0.33	0.50	0.49
Automotive diesel	0.49	0.39	0.56	0.61
LFO to industry	0.40	0.47	0.68	0.75
HFO to industry	0.69	0.51	0.50	0.55

Sources: CIE, IEA Secretariat

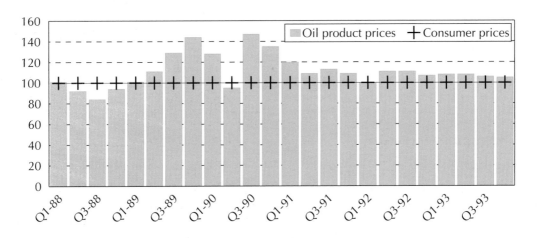

Figure 9.7
Changes in Oil Product Prices Relative to Overall Consumer Prices, 1988-93
(Index, CPI=100)

Source: IEA secretariat

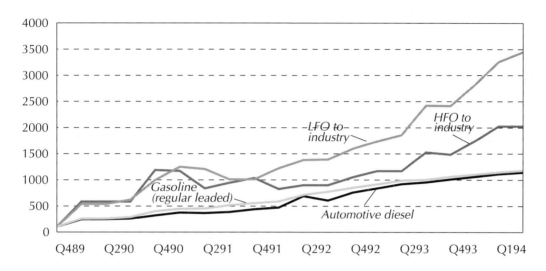

Figure 9.8
Nominal Oil Product Price Changes, end 1989-early 1994
(Index, Q4-89 = 100)

Source: IEA secretariat

Using an estimated purchasing power parity exchange rate yields different results, putting the price of premium leaded gasoline about 5 per cent higher, and the prices of the other products from 20 to 60 per cent higher, in Poland than in OECD Europe in 1993.

Polish officials often point out that although fuels appear cheaper in Poland, in terms of the goods they squeeze out of household or company budgets, they are dearer to Polish consumers than in the OECD. This may be an argument for a gradual approach to price liberalisation, but shielding the economy on these grounds for too long could cement inefficiencies and generate bigger problems for the future.

Oil product retail prices have been only partially deregulated. Fuel oil and various other products consumed mainly by industry are sold at market prices, but the state remains in indirect control of automotive fuel price developments. Three to four times per year the Ministry of Finance adjusts excise taxes and sets new maximum retail prices for gasoline (except 98 octane gasoline, which has to be imported and may be sold for whatever the market will bear) and diesel fuel. For CPN, these maximum prices are binding. Private retailers are formally allowed to charge higher prices, and

occasionally some of them do. But CPN's market leadership is still too strong for its competitors to step far out of line for too long.

Apparently there is no such thing as an objective, transparent price setting formula. The Ministry of Finance has to take into consideration crude and product import price changes, i.e. world oil market and zloty/dollar exchange rate developments. However, the Ministry is also charged with keeping the budget deficit under control, implying an interest in extracting as much revenue as possible from the oil sector in the form of taxes; and, on the other hand, with keeping inflation under control and hence in preventing oil product prices from rising too steeply. Finally, as the Ministry has to be concerned about the oil industry's low international competitiveness, it has an interest in the longer term in leaving the entities whose survival is considered vital with enough money to undertake necessary investments.

The Ministry of Finance makes these trade-offs and decides on price changes after consultations within the framework of a price committee with the MoIT, the Plock and Gdansk refineries and CPN; and after having received the go-ahead from the Prime Minister. The Council of Ministers is not involved in the decision making process. Ministry of Finance officials fear, probably with good reason, that giving the Council a say would result in endless disagreement and eventually put a stop to the whole tax and price adjustment process.

The Ministry has followed a policy of increasing prices fairly regularly at pre-announced rates. Because of this, and perhaps because of an element of bargaining entering into the balancing of conflicting concerns and interests, the adjustments have not always reflected world market or domestic cost developments very accurately. Wholesalers' and retailers' margins have sometimes fluctuated strongly as a result.

The Economic Committee of the Council of Ministers has adopted a plan to dispose gradually with direct state intervention in motor fuel pricing. Presumably from sometime in 1995, all oil product prices are to be regulated exclusively by means of the excise tax rate system.

Ex-refinery prices paid by CPN and private wholesalers and retailers are not subject to direct state control. Apparently the Ministry of Finance leaves it to the refineries and CPN to divide up the total margins between the maximum motor fuel prices and the costs of supplying the fuels. Ex-refinery prices may thus be affected by domestic market conditions: an abundance of supplies stemming from, say, an overestimation of Poland's need for imported products and a temporary easing of import restrictions could drive the refineries' shares of the margins down while the opposite situation could drive CPN's shares down. However,

the Ministry is clearly aware of the refineries' and CPN's investment needs – such issues are on the Price Committee's agenda – and it seems more likely that the maximum retail prices and the refineries' and CPN's pieces of the cake are decided upon simultaneously by the committee.

Apparently the refineries do not practice price discrimination among their various customers. CPN pays less than the private customers, but the discounts are relatively minor and may be defended on volume grounds.

Wholesale prices charged by CPN to private Polish wholesalers and retailers and foreign companies reflect CPN's market power and the fact that, thanks to its control over logistics, the company faces less competition as a wholesaler than as a retailer. CPN therefore pursues a pricing policy for automotive fuels resulting in large wholesaler and small retailer margins.

Taxes and Duties

The tax shares of oil product prices to end-users dipped considerably during the first year of economic reforms before starting to pick up in 1991-92.

Oil product importers have to pay import duties, currently 15 per cent of the CIF price for gasoline and 35 per cent of the CIF price for diesel fuel. In

Table 9.7
Excise Taxes and VAT on Oil Products
(% of retail prices)

	1989	1990	1991	1992	1993	Q294
Gasoline (regular leaded)	68	41	51	53	59	62
Diesel fuel	58	30	17	27	43	49
LFO (to industry)	0	0	0	0	10	7
HFO (to industry)	0	0	0	0	4	7

Note: VAT is not included in the figures for diesel fuel, LFO and HFO, as companies are refunded for their VAT payments on purchases for commercial purposes.

Sources: CIE, IEA Secretariat

addition they have to pay a so-called border tax, levied on all imports, at 6 per cent of CIF prices. On top of these duties come excise taxes and VAT.

Excise taxes are fixed sums per weight unit of product. They replaced turnover taxes in 1993. These had lagged prices in 1990 and, in the case of diesel fuel, in 1991 as well. By mid-1994 the rates were:

Premium leaded gasoline: Zl 6 400/kg
Unleaded gasoline: Zl 5 700/kg
Diesel fuel: Zl 3 200/kg.

VAT, introduced in 1993, is levied on import or ex-refinery prices plus duties for imports plus excise taxes for all products. Currently the rates are 22 per cent for automotive fuels and 7 per cent for other oil products.

With taxes accounting for 59 per cent of the price of premium leaded gasoline in 1993, Poland had not yet reached western European levels. Excise tax differences were the main reason Polish motorists paid only about half as much for leaded premium gasoline than the average western European motorist (with all prices converted to US dollars at official exchange rates). While Polish drivers in January 1994 paid excise taxes

amounting to US$ 0.22 a litre on gasoline, Germans, for instance, paid US$ 0.62 a litre, implying gasoline excise tax charges in Germany equivalent to 1.33 times the gasoline pump price in Poland.

For diesel fuel, tax as a share of price was higher in Poland than in some western European countries. However, in the bigger OECD Europe countries, tax shares were higher, as a result of much higher excise taxes in absolute terms.

The Government intends to increase excise taxes – and thereby its oil revenues – to the minimum levels found in the European Union, but Ministry of Finance spokesmen emphasise that the rate of increase should not exceed the rate of economic growth significantly. Most excise tax increases will have to be accompanied by oil product price increases; only in periods of falling crude and product import prices may taxes alone be raised, since squeezing the margins accruing to the various links in the oil supply chain would affect investments negatively. However, for fear of inflationary impulses and because it is held that the share of fuel expenses in households' budgets is high enough as it is, Polish authorities feel very constrained in their ability to increase oil product prices.

Figure 9.9
Shares of Taxes in Oil Product Prices, Poland and European IEA Countries, 1993
(%)

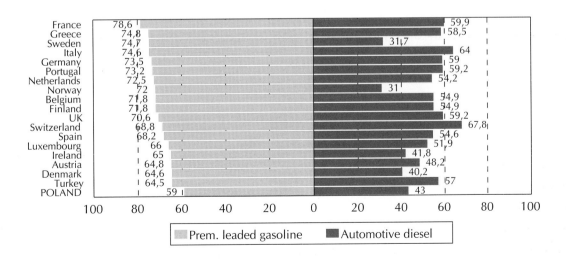

Note: Austrian gasoline price and tax data from 1992.

Source: IEA Secretariat

The Government plans to dispense with maximum prices for automotive fuels, but by late 1994 had not presented a timetable for lifting them. The ceilings are necessitated by – and can hardly be treated in isolation from – the system of import quotas, licences and permits described above, and by the relatively high import duties. Poland is committed in its agreement with the EU to abolish the quantitative restrictions and lower the duties to EU levels over a period of three years.

Terminating the price ceilings without relaxing the motor fuel import regime would probably lead to margin and price increases – there is hardly enough competition among retailers and wholesalers yet to produce any other result, and market leader CPN has an interest in higher margins. Gasoline and diesel price increases resulting if maximum prices were abolished might be arrested by liberalising oil product imports. However, such a move would also bring renewed pressure on the refineries' throughput and profits, as they are not very much better prepared for international competition now than they were four or five years ago.

The Government appears to have concluded that only when inflation has abated sufficiently or the fuel share of the consumer price index has declined sufficiently, or when the refineries are prepared for international competition – whatever happens first – should oil product prices be completely liberalised. MoIT spokesmen, focusing on the latter of these conditions, have stated that the Government's oil industry restructuring plan must be adopted by the Sejm, and core elements of it must be implemented, before prices can be liberalised. The Ministry has also indicated that prices even then will not be allowed to increase to such an extent as to jeopardise the Government's inflation target.

The Plock and Gdansk refineries enjoy certain tax benefits. Not being equipped to produce the most advanced types of gasoline and lubricants on sale in western Europe (for which there is a growing market in Poland), they have to import finished products and components for blending. They are now allowed to deduct the equivalent of the import duties and excise taxes they paid at the border on imported products and components from their payments to the state of excise taxes on sales of blended products. This arrangement reduces the effect on the refineries of competition from imports. Import prices of automotive fuels including duties and taxes have sometimes been higher than ex-refinery prices including taxes.

The system also favours CPN in its competition against private retailers. CPN too imports products and components – the company has its own blending facilities at Bydgoszcz – and may also deduct duties and excise taxes paid on its imports when calculating excise tax payments on its sales. In addition, CPN has been allowed to deduct Zl 1 500/kg of product[4] from its excise tax payments. The Government granted CPN this privilege in October 1993, pointing to the company's special responsibilities and funding needs as maintainer of state oil reserves. With these advantages, CPN can live fairly well with maximum prices that private retailers find very burdensome.

For the time being, discussions within the Polish oil industry on prices and taxes seem to be focusing on the adequacy of the margins left to Poland's wholesalers and retailers, on the Government's timing of excise tax and maximum price adjustments and on the implications of the Government's granting of tax benefits to the state owned companies. Calls for immediate and full liberalisation of automotive fuel prices are not often heard. Companies and observers seem to accept that such a step, if not accompanied by a liberalisation of imports, would have inflationary consequences, and that liberalising imports would hurt refinery sales, profits and investment possibilities.

The Government's interlinked oil product pricing and import policies may be defended as interim solutions. Yet relaxing restrictions faster than planned could have beneficial consequences too. The refineries and other state owned enterprises in the oil sector might be prompted to embark on more aggressive cost cutting strategies. This possibility raises the question of which policies would best underpin the effort to bring the Polish refinery sector up to international standards – if, indeed, there are any circumstances that might do the trick without forcing a more fundamental restructuring of the sector, and possibly inflicting bigger social costs on Polish society, than currently foreseen.

---

4. Reduced to Zl 900/kg product from 1 January 1995.

Allowing the prices of gasoline and diesel fuel to rise towards western European levels more rapidly than planned would also strengthen the incentives for Polish citizens to use public transportation, and might affect Polish motorists' driving habits favourably and focus their attention on vehicle fuel efficiency. Given expected developments in car ownership and driving distances, policies to this effect should be considered in any case.

Discussions of these problems have apparently slowed the reform process. Presumably it is because the authorities suspect that preparing the refineries for international competition may prove more difficult, costly and time consuming than foreseen that they are calling for a two year extension of the EU transition period during which the import restrictions are to be phased out.

RESTRUCTURING AND PRIVATISATION PLANS

The Polish oil industry has undergone considerable structural change since 1990. Crude oil and product imports have been liberalised, Ciech and the major refineries have been turned into joint stock companies and taken steps to transform themselves into internationally competitive corporations and CPN is facing strong competition as a wholesaler and even stronger competition in retailing.

Nevertheless, working out a master plan for the privatisation and restructuring of the oil industry has posed difficulties for successive Polish governments. Consensus has proved elusive concerning such issues as how to secure an adequate share of the industry's aggregate profits for the Polish state while attracting foreign investments, especially in the refinery sector, and how to achieve efficiency in all parts of the industry while avoiding a worsening of unemployment problems in already troubled areas. The authorities have also had to cope with conflicting special interests, inertia and scepticism among managers, Employee Council resistance and instances of rivalry between major players about positions and influence in the future industry structure.

In 1993 the discussion focused on a set of proposals made by Andrzej Olechowsky, then attorney for privatisation of the oil sector and later Poland's Foreign Minister. The Olechowsky plan, which was adopted and recommended by the Council of Ministers in September 1992, is based on the following assumptions:

- The Polish oil market will grow rapidly. The lightening of the barrel that has been going on since the 1980s will continue. Product quality standards will become tighter.

- The outlook for growth in the domestic oil market in general and the motor fuels markets in particular justifies optimism about the Polish oil industry. Refineries, ports, pipelines, other transportation infrastructure, crude and product storage facilities and service station networks may in years to come generate considerable revenue for their owners.

- The oil industry will, however, be facing increased foreign competition. It may be protected for a while, but not indefinitely.

- The industry needs investments to the tune of US$ 2.5-3.5 billion to be able to hold its own in an expanding, increasingly discriminating and ever more competitive market.

- These investments cannot be funded in today's institutional framework. The industry cannot raise US$ 2.5-3.5 billion by increasing prices; such a strategy would necessitate strong protective measures and might fuel inflation and hurt economic growth. The potential for credit financing is limited by the size of the Polish capital market and by foreign lenders' assessments of Polish companies' creditworthiness, including that of state owned companies. Treasury guarantees might enable the industry to obtain loans from abroad, but it would be improper for the Treasury to extend such guarantees. The Polish government – the present owner of the industry – cannot foot the bill through the general budget; the Government is struggling to control the deficit as it is.

Privatising the oil industry is the obvious solution to this dilemma. However, the choice of privatisation procedures and restrictions raises new questions. Letting only the Polish public buy into the industry would probably only go some way towards raising the necessary funds, and might have harmful crowding-out effects. Inviting foreign oil companies to invest in the Polish oil industry would mean a loss of control and a diminishing of future revenue streams to Polish citizens and the Polish state.

Olechowsky suggested:

- commercialising the Polish oil industry – turning the state owned companies forming the bulk of the industry into joint stock companies, initially 100 per cent Treasury owned, operating under commercial law;

- undertaking some restructuring of existing companies, since there are companies with too many tasks to carry out all of them efficiently, as well as instances of "spontaneous" vertical integration stemming from company rivalry and leading to costly duplication of effort;

- creating a holding company, modelled on the international integrated oil companies, to secure continued Polish control of the oil industry and future oil revenue for Polish citizens;

- financing investments by selling shares in this holding company and in the operative companies to the Polish public and to foreign investors.

The restructuring part of the Olechowsky plan included creating an oil trading company from part of Ciech, a loading/unloading, transportation, blending and storage company from PERN, departments of CPN and the enterprise that runs the oil facilities at the Port of Gdansk, and a service station and depot building company and a social services company from other departments of CPN.

The holding company, Polska Kompania Naftowa (PKN), would hold 50 per cent of the shares in the Plock and Gdansk refineries, all the shares in what would be left of CPN, including the service station network, and portions of the shares in the companies created through the restructuring.

The Treasury would at the outset own 100 per cent of the shares in PKN, 50 per cent of the shares in the Plock and Gdansk refineries and 70 per cent of the shares in the new loading/unloading, transportation, blending and storage company. The Treasury would be instructed gradually to dispose of these shares, however; Olechowsky assumed that the state would stop exercising control over the oil industry on the basis of

ownership and instead start influencing strategic decisions made by the companies' new owners on the basis of civil and commercial law.

Shares in PKN would be sold in set proportions to different types of investors, in several steps; 30 per cent would be allocated to Polish strategic investors, i.e. large enterprises and financial institutions, and 40 per cent to Polish small investors. The remaining 30 per cent would be sold over a period of three to five years to international institutions in which the Treasury holds shares, e.g. the European Bank for Reconstruction and Development.

The Treasury would sell its remaining shares in the Plock and Gdansk refineries, preferably to a select number of foreign oil companies. Buyers would have to commit themselves to undertake certain investments in the refinery sector. The Treasury would sell its transportation company shares to the foreign buyers of refinery shares and other operators in the market, and its building company shares to company directors and workers and other domestic and foreign investors.

Realising that foreign oil companies are much more eager to get into retailing than refining in Poland, Olechowsky and his co-authors suggested coupling offers of shares in the refineries with offers of packages of CPN service stations. The Ministry of Ownership Transformation would administer a closed service station tender for holders of refinery shares, and maybe later an open tender for other interested parties, on behalf of PKN. The new integrated oil company would thus after some time include only part – perhaps about 50 per cent – of the present CPN retailing network.

The five small refineries in the south would remain 100 per cent Treasury owned joint stock companies.

Various modifications to the Olechowsky plan have been bandied about. One proposal is to create two integrated Polish oil companies, one built around the Plock refinery, CIECH and the majority of CPN's service stations, the other built around the Gdansk refinery, the envisaged transportation and storage company and the remaining service stations. This structure, it is argued, would be simpler to implement, make the privatisation process more flexible and lead to more competition.

By late 1994, the interministerial working group charged by the Pawlak Government with working out a new plan – which had submitted its proposal the Council of Ministers at the time of publication – was reported to favour a plan whereby:

- the Plock and Gdansk refineries and a holding company to be set up for the five southern refineries take over all the shares in CPN;

- a Treasury owned management company resembling Olechowsky's PKN takes over all the shares in the refineries and gradually sells 20-50 per cent of them off to private, preferably Polish, interests;

- PERN, DEC and the larger fuel depots (spun off from CPN) are maintained as separate, 100 per cent Treasury owned joint stock companies, with PERN obliged to provide third party access to its facilities;

- the private service stations are "encouraged" to conclude long term agreements with the refineries.

Because of the difficulty in reaching any real consensus on oil industry restructuring and privatisation, the Council of Ministers and the Sejm have not yet moved on the issue. The election of a new Parliament in September 1993 and two ensuing changes of government put the process on hold on ministerial level. However, there were delays long before these events complicated matters. Rivalry between companies and a lack of interest in reforms from parts of the oil industry itself may have contributed as much to the difficulties as did the new politicians' need to familiarise themselves with complicated issues and take stands.

The Plock and Gdansk refineries operate near full capacity and are profitable under the present oil import and pricing regimes. Realising that they need foreign investment – the Gdansk refinery management appears open to the idea of a foreign oil company taking over a controlling part of the shares – they may prefer refinery-centred models rather than transferring parts of existing enterprises, including the refineries, to a new holding company. CPN would face an uncertain future under one variation on the Olechowsky plan: its service station network would be split among various domestic and foreign interests. PERN controls big assets and is a very profitable

Figure 9.10
Privatisation of Oil Industry

Today

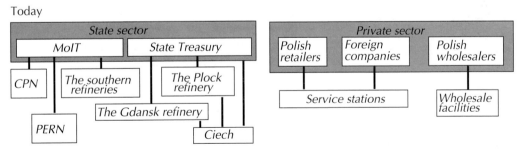

Possible future structure:

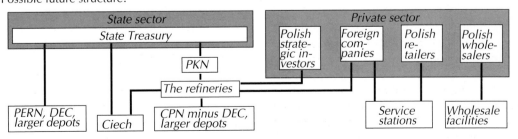

Source: IEA Secretariat

concern, thanks mainly to its crude oil transit business. Its management has no obvious reason to wish PERN to be absorbed into a more broadly based transportation and storage company or turned into a joint stock or private company.

Workers would see their influence and short term job security decline in a privatised oil industry. That their longer term job security would be in danger in an internationally uncompetitive industry may appear a less persuasive argument than the immediate risk of being sacked. Employee Councils have been abolished in parts of the industry, but not everywhere, and unions still exercise considerable influence in the commercialised enterprises. As was noted above, the recent fairly strong performances of the refineries may have galvanised workers into stronger opposition to structural and ownership changes.

Yet the refineries and other centrepieces of the Polish oil industry must transform themselves into modern, market oriented entities very quickly if they are not to become either a drain on the Polish state budget or major bones of contention between the EU and Poland. The industry needs foreign investment to have any chance of becoming internationally competitive. Such investment will not materialise before potential investors see a decision on a privatisation plan and prospects of satisfying, stable operating conditions. Therefore, the Government is in a hurry.

RECOMMENDATIONS

- Polish authorities have made commendable progress in diversifying the country's crude oil and refined product imports. However, the level of Poland's oil stocks is disturbingly low by industrialised country standards. Moreover, the Government does not seem to consider stock building a matter of great urgency – its current target is to have stocks corresponding to about 30 days of net imports at its disposal by 2000. This is not satisfactory from the IEA's point of view. The Government should consider setting a more ambitious target and work out a plan, including evaluation of all possible ways to arrive at a more acceptable

level of stocks earlier (e.g. counting military stocks) and a schedule for stock building.

- The Government's interlinked oil product pricing and import policies may be defended as interim solutions, but relaxing restrictions faster than planned might have beneficial effects, such as prompting the refineries and the other state owned enterprises to embark on more aggressive cost cutting strategies (in the process shedding light on their degree of adaptability and long term viability), stimulating the use of public transportation and prompting Polish motorists to consider their vehicle fuel use and driving habits more closely. The Government should in any case be aware of the dangers inherent in extending transition arrangements, and stay on the liberalisation track agreed with the European Union.

- In the meantime, the setting of maximum prices could be made more transparent and predictable, e.g. more closely linked to product price developments in the Rotterdam market, with prices adjusted more frequently to keep margins from fluctuating too much. It might also make sense for the Government to consider private wholesalers' and retailers' calls for a level playing field – that is, for a re-evaluation of the tax benefits extended to the refineries and to CPN. Supporting the state companies in ways that may weaken the emerging private sector's ability to compete, can easily backfire.

- The Government should decide on and start implementing an industry wide restructuring and privatisation plan as quickly as possible. Sound investments are being delayed and time is being lost because investors do not know what the rules of the game will be. Meanwhile, potentially unsound investments are being made, and resources wasted, as the existing companies try to position themselves to become centrepieces of the new structure. IEA countries provide examples of fully or partly state owned integrated oil companies as well as fully privatised industries. While experience hardly supports the conclusion that one model is to be recommended regardless of circumstances, it does indicate that where governments give privileges to state owned companies or try to shelter them from private competition or support them on anything but a very short term basis, the long term results are invariably that efficiency improvements are slowed down and problems are prolonged. Experience also militates strongly against using the holding company form to keep unprofitable entities in business by means of cross-subsidisation, and against government interference in state owned companies' day-to-day operations; the role of government is to set overall directions, ensure that general industry rules and regulations are respected and collect taxes. The future Polish oil industry may include state owned entities, but these should be forced to compete on equal terms with a strong private sector, including foreign as well as domestic companies.

- The Government should not heed interest group pressure to keep the small, unsophisticated refineries in southern Poland in operation via subsidies or soft loans. This would be a waste of resources and weaken the incentives for the bigger refineries to become more efficient.

CHAPTER 10

NEW AND RENEWABLE ENERGY SOURCE

Renewable energy sources include hydropower, solar thermal energy and photovoltaics, wind energy, biomass, tidal energy and geothermal sources. This chapter does not go into details on hydropower, which is treated in Chapter 7; nor does it focus on tidal energy, as the tides of the Baltic Sea are rather low. It deals mainly with solar and geothermal energy.

Historically, the use of renewables in Poland was considerable, with many small water and wind mills, and much burning of biomass (wood and turf), mostly for space heating. During the 19th and particularly during the 20th century, this use diminished to such an extent that renewable energy sources now account for less than 2 per cent of TPES. One important reason is Poland's limited hydro potential. Relatively small amounts of biomass are still used. Hardly any solar or wind energy projects are in operation.

Renewable supply technology is used on a very modest scale all over central and eastern Europe, accounting in 1990 for 3 per cent of the region's TPES. Hydro power generation represented 98 per cent of total renewables production and 7 per cent of total electricity generation. Some heat production on the basis of renewable supply technology – mainly burning of forest product residues (88 per cent) and use of geothermal sources (11 per cent) – took place. In the European Union, renewable supply technology accounted for 4.3 per cent of total energy production, 10 per cent of total electricity consumption and 3.3 per cent of total heat consumption in 1990.

The technical potential for renewables is much higher than this, both in central and eastern Europe and in the EU countries. The exploitation of this potential will depend on costs of energy production from renewables relative to conventional energy production, primary energy market developments and energy pricing policy. This last factor will in turn depend on, among other things, the extent to which energy policies reflect environmental targets.

Each year the earth receives energy input from the sun estimated at 15 000 times the world's commercial energy consumption, or 100 times the world's proven coal, gas and oil reserves. Yet, solar energy in its various forms – both solar-thermal and photovoltaic technology – along with electricity from wind energy and the use of biomass contributes less than 10 per cent to total energy use world wide. The potential of solar energy, however, is expected to grow as the costs related to pollution abatement, added to the costs of producing conventional fuels from limited deposits, rise while the costs of solar energy applications are reduced through technological improvements.

Unit costs of solar energy production have fallen considerably during the past 15 years. The costs of photovoltaic power production have declined by a factor of ten, and this source is now widely applied in telecommunications, for powering traffic signals and for pumping water in remote areas. The costs of electricity produced by solar-thermal technology can now in some regions of the world match the costs of conventional electricity production. Wind power, because of its cleanliness, is gaining ground in certain regions, albeit still at subsidies that are being applied in recognition of the pollution that the equivalent fuel based generation would produce. The costs of biofuels such as ethanol have also declined considerably since the 1970s with a shift towards cheaper crops and better technology.

SOLAR ENERGY

Solar thermal energy has not yet been used much in Poland because of the limited number of sunny days, added to the relatively high equipment costs. Photovoltaic systems have a brighter future in such typical applications as traffic signalling, telecommunications and remote sites. Nevertheless, the costs of solar energy applications will have to come down much further, and/or the costs of conventional fuel production and use will have to increase considerably, for solar thermal energy and photovoltaics to have a chance of gaining significant shares of the Polish power and heat markets.

Research on alternative solar applications is being conducted at various institutes and universities throughout Poland. The Polish Academy of Sciences in Krakow estimates that, worldwide, each square metre of ground receives up to 2 200 kWh of solar energy annually; the European countries receive 800 to 1 700 kWh per year, with Poland, at around 1 000 kWh, tending towards the lower end of the range. In 1993, the European Renewable Energy Study, which also covers the central and eastern European countries, was completed. In 1994, the Committee for Scientific Research completed a study on possibilities for the use of solar thermal energy in Poland.

Solar energy is generally used in three ways:

1. For low temperature heating of

i) air: directly, for space heating of buildings, greenhouses, storage sheds etc.; or indirectly, in dehydration processes;

ii) liquids: directly, e.g. for swimming pools; or in solar collectors, heating liquids to be consumed or sent through a heat exchanger;

iii) solids, which can be
   a) dehydrated,
   b) heated,
   c) used in heat cumulation (for inner space heating).

2. For high temperature heating of

i) liquid collectors, with liquids sent through a heat exchanger;

ii) fixed substances, e.g. ovens for metallurgy.

3. Solar cells

i) photosynthetic;

ii) photovoltaic.

Low temperature air heating by means of flat solar collectors has been tested in Poland for drying and storage of agricultural goods. The results have been satisfactory, with efficiency of 250-400 watts per square metre achieved. In western Europe, however, better use of materials and more advantageous locations have resulted in efficiency of 500-900 W/m^2. The academy continues to experiment with various types of technology and applications to improve results. There is scope for private enterprises to start commercialising applications.

WIND ENERGY

In the extensive lowlands of Poland and along the Baltic coast, the potential for wind energy production is fairly good. Wind power could supplement conventional power production for the grid and on small, remote farms. The use of wind energy in large installations is only beginning in Poland, but several OECD countries have set up wind farms on a significant scale. Germany and Denmark, for example, have about 2 000 wind power plants each. The advantages of wind energy are its renewability and lack of polluting emissions. The drawbacks include aesthetic objections and risks for birds.

Estimates of the potential share of wind power in total worldwide power supplies – based on the efficiency of today's wind power technology and wind conditions around the world – vary between 5 and 10 per cent. In line with this range, Germany is aiming at supplying 7-10 per cent of northern Germany's electricity needs from wind energy. Poland could achieve a similar market share in the northern half of the country, where wind resources range from 1 000 kW per square metre a year near the coast to less than 400 kW/m²/year closer to the centre.

In most countries where wind energy is used on a significant scale, utilities are obliged by government to pay more for wind power than for conventional power. In Germany, for example, prices paid to independent wind power generators are roughly twice the prices paid to conventional generators, the premium being linked to the capital costs of the wind power producers. As the level of prices for conventional power in Poland is less than half the level for such power in Germany, wind power production in Poland would need heavy subsidisation for the time being. The costs of wind power generation may come down, however, and as the costs of modernising existing plant and abating pollution will eventually have to be reflected in the Polish power prices, the economics of wind power could well improve.

Given the present shortage of capital and the urgency of the need to upgrade existing power stations and improve their environmental performance, the wind option does not seem likely to be high on the short term agenda of the electricity industry or the Government. Nevertheless, the Institute for Buildings, Mechanisation and Electrification of Agriculture in Warsaw estimates that by 2010 installed wind power capacity could be 800 MW and actual wind power production could be 1 200 GWh.

BIOMASS

Wood used as fuel represents about 1 per cent of the heat value of Poland's coal production and accounts for less than 1 per cent of TPES. The use of other types of biomass for energy is extremely limited, though Polish farmers are keen to explore ways of using agricultural products for fuel. Plans to produce diesel from extracts from rapeseed oil have yet to materialise, but a significant ethanol production programme is well on its way. In 1994 about 30 million litres of ethanol was used as a component for producing about 500 000 tonnes of gasoline. The programme thus covered about

12 per cent of total gasoline sales in Poland. The ethanol industry is expected to supply 60 million litres in 1995, and 150 million litres a year when fully developed. The latter volume would suffice to produce 2.5 million tonnes of ethanol blended gasoline, corresponding to 64 per cent of Poland's gasoline consumption in 1993.

GEOTHERMAL ENERGY

Geothermal energy is found in many parts of the world and exploited in about 40 countries. Depending on the temperature of the source, it is most often used in the form of steam for power production or hot water for district heating, industrial use and thermal bathing. It may surface under pressure or have to be pumped up. Its applications rely on conventional technology.

During the past 15 years, substantial sources of enthalpy (low-temperature) geothermal energy have been confirmed in Poland. There are at least three major geothermal water reservoirs: one in the Carpathian sub-basin, between the Tatra Mountains and Pieniny, extending across the Polish-Slovak border; one in the Carpathian foreland; and one in a wide band extending from central Poland to the north-west and continuing into eastern Germany and Denmark. The reservoirs, located at depths of 700 to 3 000 metres, are large; it has been estimated that they could contain over 30 billion tonnes of fuel oil equivalent. Temperatures are reported to range from 30° to 120°C, with averages at test wells around 75° to 85°C. This temperature is well suited for district heating, horticulture and industry. Using pumps, the productivity of wells can reach 200 cubic metres an hour.

Geothermal projects, predominantly for district heating, are under preparation or at the stage of early implementation in the region of Szczecin, near Warsaw and in the Podhale region, focusing on the valleys of Zakopane. The project for the Zakopane area, with an envisaged capacity of about 200 MW, could provide district heating, via heat exchangers, amounting to 2 000 TJ per year for urban agglomerations. Supplemented by natural gas in particularly cold periods, it could allow savings of fossil fuels equivalent to 300 000 tonnes of coal. As a result, emissions of particulate matter, SO_2 and NO_x, as well as CO and CO_2, could almost be eliminated in this region.

As the levels of minerals in the water that would be used are very low, no problems of corrosion or pollution are envisaged. Several of the projects would benefit from sunk costs in the form of existing district heating networks requiring only some modernisation or expansion. Consequently, the return on new investment would be very high. It is important, however, to ensure that appropriate tariffs are charged, to assure the financial viability of the projects and provide funds for further expansion.

CONCLUSIONS

Solar energy and wind energy used for power production or space heating will probably not emerge as interesting options for Polish energy producers and consumers during the next few years. They may become financially attractive only once a number of conditions are met. One important factor is how energy prices develop. Prices of electricity, district heating and gas will probably not reach cost covering levels before 2000. Coal for individual space heating is relatively cheap and there are no regulations concerning small, low stack pollution sources. Given the present shortage of capital, the relatively high investment costs per unit of solar or wind energy produced will be difficult to meet, and the present tightness of budgets means that subsidies for projects in this field are unlikely to be available.

However, solar energy used for drying and storage of agricultural products, wind power generation at small, remote farms and biomass used as supplementary fuel are interesting options with a growth potential now. Geothermal water is an attractive and virtually non-polluting source of space heating that will be used increasingly in areas where its characteristics, in particular its temperature and degree of mineralisation, are suitable.

When energy prices have reached cost covering levels, Poland is likely to see larger scale wind and solar projects as well, particularly if expectations of further technological developments and investment cost reductions prove correct. In the longer term, as environmental issues continue to be addressed and as conventional fuel sources become more scarce and more expensive, the outlook for renewables will improve in Poland and worldwide.

CHAPTER 11

ENERGY AND THE ENVIRONMENT

GENERAL ISSUES

Parts of Poland are known to be among the most polluted areas on earth. Up to the late 1980s, Poland's economy was dominated by industrial production, and industry was dominated by energy-intensive, heavy branches. The Government emphasised autonomy in steel and steel products, heavy chemicals and defence industries, as well as extraction and to some extent exports of natural resources. The share of industry in Poland's economic output, at 44 per cent, was unusually high for a country at its level of development. As a result of subsidisation of energy and lack of attention to efficiency and production costs, the industrial sector was extremely wasteful of energy (see Chapter 5). Environmental performance was not a priority, although increasingly strict standards were in force. During the 1980s the Government introduced fees for the use of the environment and fines for the violation of standards. However, these economic instruments, which normally serve as incentives to reduce pollution, had little effect on Polish polluters, as their levels were extremely low. State enterprises had little incentive anyway to keep costs low: the prime objective was production.

Major shares of Poland's air, water and soil pollution stem from production and consumption of energy. With hard coal and lignite accounting for over 75 per cent of TPES, Poland is among the most coal dependent countries in the world – and coal mining and burning generally cause more environmental damage than production and consumption of other energy carriers, particularly if little investment is undertaken to reduce pollution.

In 1990, when the Mazowiecki Government introduced its economic transformation programme, the country was facing major environmental problems. The most important were:

- Air pollution, predominantly from power, heat and heavy industrial production, but also in dense urban areas from individual coal-fired heating and from traffic. Pollution levels were significant multiples of those observed in OECD countries. The results were major health problems in industrial cities and forestry and agricultural damage in many parts of the country.

- Water pollution, stemming from the coal industry's dumping of saline water into the Vistula and Oder rivers, discharges of in-adequately treated water from refineries and other industries and untreated municipal waste water. A high share of Poland's water resources were unfit even for industrial consumption, and water users downstream of pollution sources suffered major problems.

- Solid waste disposal from coal mines and power plants. The disposal sites were sources of contaminated run-off and harmful dust, causing ground, water and air pollution that affected the health of Polish citizens as well as fauna and flora.

Economic reform introduced policies designed to create or improve on incentives for industry to become more efficient, reduce costs and attend to environmental issues. The Government started moving energy prices towards economic costs,

Figure 11.1
Polish and OECD Air Emission Ratios, 1989

Emissions per Unit of Energy Used
(Kg/toe)

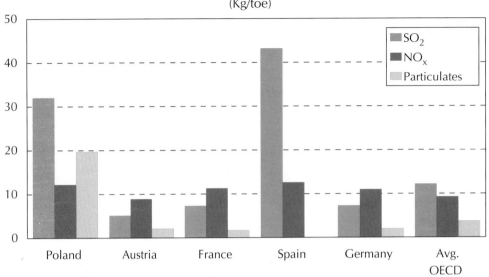

Emissions per Unit of Energy Area
(Kg/km²)

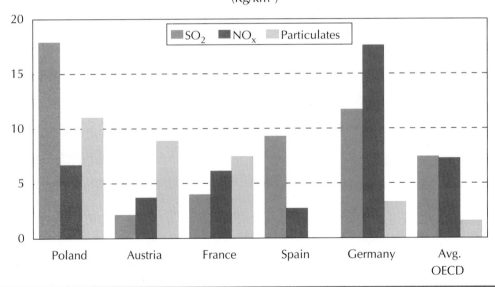

including the costs of pollution abatement, and there were signs of this policy starting to work on energy intensity and resulting in cost savings and reduced pollution. Environmental fees and fines were significantly increased in 1990 and 1991, leading to increased attention to pollution and to measures to reduce it. Policies intended to trigger competition in a context of price and trade liberalisation, hard budget constraints and eventually privatisation were designed to lead to

general efficiency improvements, a focusing on cost structures and savings possibilities, and closure of obsolete facilities.

In the short term, as the transition programme was accompanied by a major contraction of production without a corresponding liquidation of excess capacity, energy intensity rose, as did pollution levels per unit of output. While major reductions in pollution levels have been observed in Poland during the past five years, they have been due largely to economic contraction. Recently, however, structural change, substitution to cleaner fuels and energy saving have made a difference.

In 1993-94, the process of adjusting the real prices of electricity, heat and gas slowed, pollution fees and fines stagnated in real terms and privatisation lost momentum. Moreover, insufficient action on the necessary restructuring of heavy industry, in particular a reluctance to retire obsolete and redundant capacity, has led to continued high levels of pollution from such facilities. Yet there are some striking examples of closure of obsolete, highly polluting facilities having contributed heavily to environmental improvements for the population in the vicinity of the plants. Huta Koscziuszko in Chorzow, which closed its open hearth steel mill and built up downstream metalwork facilities, is a case in point.

Polish policy makers face a number of environmentally related challenges, the biggest of which is to fund the major investments needed to modernise facilities and install pollution abatement equipment. At stake are Poland's environmental performance and the health of its citizens. The power industry alone, including CHP plants and autoproducers, needs investments estimated at US$ 1.9 billion to comply with standards that go into effect in 1998. Considering that Polish ambient air quality standards are to be tightened in 1999 and that the UN-ECE sulphur protocol will pose additional demands, a further US$ 4 billion might be required in the electricity industry before 2000 (see Table 11.13). Similar problems prevail in the area of waste water treatment.

Because of constraints on the central budget, the Government has decided that it will no longer help fund environmental investments. The capital market in Poland is still small and shallow. Funding by international financial institutions is bound to be limited, but could help attract foreign direct investment as well as foreign commercial lending. Yet foreign funding may materialise only if there is a clear indication that energy prices will allow for a sufficient return on investment, i.e. will generate enough cash for investment and servicing of loans. Such price levels would serve as incentives for energy conservation and efficiency.

Poland is therefore at a crucial juncture. The country may move rapidly towards prices reflecting economic costs (including environmental costs), generating the needed funds for modernisation and

environmental investments and providing sufficient incentives to save energy, or the Government may give in to social pressures, producing no new policy initiatives or even backtracking on existing policies, which would trigger a slide towards an even more abysmal environmental situation.

Given the present investment constraints, it will be crucial to develop feasible investment priorities. There is a need to review ambient air standards and some water standards in the light of current time and money constraints, and to phase them in such a way that enterprises will comply with them. Having tough standards but not enforcing them, as in the past, would only lead to lax behaviour and continued high levels of pollution. International agreements on transboundary pollution could not be implemented, and eventually trade restrictions might result, due to unacceptably low expenses for pollution abatement.

In parallel with a redesign of standards and a revised schedule for phasing them in, monitoring procedures should be improved and the institutions charged with monitoring and enforcement strengthened. To achieve all these goals, closer co-operation among ministries, and between central and local government, is needed.

MAIN ENVIRONMENTAL PROBLEMS RELATED TO THE ENERGY SECTOR

Air Pollution

Air pollution in Poland is predominantly caused by the burning of coal in power stations, industrial facilities and both large and small heating facilities; and, more recently, in urban centres, by rapidly growing traffic. Coal use, including lignite and coking processes, accounts for almost 90 per cent of SO_2, 79 per cent of NO_x and over 98 per cent of particulate emissions. Only CO and methane emissions are caused predominantly (over 60 per cent) by transport sector use of gasoline, diesel fuel and kerosene. As most data rely on fuel consumption estimates, there are discrepancies depending on the inputs used, assumptions made and methodologies applied. By and large the database is now more consistent than it was before 1989.

Table 11.1
Air Emission Types by Fuel Source, 1993
(1 000 tonnes, %)

	Hard coal	Brown coal	Heavy fuel oil	Motor fuels	Other fuels	**Total**
SO_2	1 806.4	626.0	119.4	36.0	153.7	**2 741.4**
% of total	66	23	4	1	6	**100**
NO_x	755.0	133.5	20.8	115.9	102.5	**1 127.7**
% of total	67	12	2	10	9	**100**
Particulates	1 350.0	120.0	n.a.	n.a.	n.a.	**1 500.0**
% of total	90	8	–	–	–	**100**
CO	783.4	31.2	1.9	1 924.0	393.8	**3 134.3**
% of total	25	1	0	61	13	**100**
CO_2	246 449.7	58 639.2	8 074.9	29 438.3	54 517.4	**397 119.4**
% of total	62	15	2	7	14	**100**
Methane	453.8	1.4	0.2	8.8	1.9	**466.1**
% of total	97	0.3	0	2	0.4	**100**

Sources: CIE, State Inspectorate for Environmental Protection, GUS

Table 11.2
Air Emission Types by Economic Sector, 1993
(1000 tonnes, %)

	Transformation	Industry	Transport	Energy	Other sectors	**Total**
SO_2	2 066.3	187.0	34.6	22.3	431.3	**2 741.4**
% of total	75	7	1	1	16	**100**
NO_x	715.4	83.8	100.9	11.0	216.7	**1 127.7**
% of total	63	7	9	1	19	**100**
Particulates	1 350.0	120.0	n.a.	n.a.	n.a.	**1 500.0**
% of total	90	8	–	–	–	**100**
CO	348.1	147.3	1 938.0	3.8	697.2	**3 134.3**
% of total	11	5	62	0	22	**100**
CO_2	249 902.3	35 209.0	23 854.9	5 620.7	82 532.6	**397 119.4**
% of total	63	9	6	1	21	**100**
Methane	2.7	0.5	9.1	451.6	2.1	**466.1**
% of total	1	0.1	2	97	0.5	**100**

Source: CIE

Air pollution from stationary sources is highly concentrated, with two voivodships (Katowice and Piotrkow) accounting for about 30 per cent of SO_2 and NO_x emissions, and 12 voivodships accounting for about two-thirds. The pollution comes essentially from industrial concentrations and major industrialised cities. The level of concentration of emissions can also be shown in terms of major power plants: In 1993, the eight biggest plants accounted for two-thirds of SO_2 emissions and just over half of NO_x emissions in the power sector. The biggest lignite-fired power plant, Belchatow, with capacity of over 4 000 MW, accounts for as much SO_2 as Denmark, Norway and Sweden together.

The combination of airborne particulate matter with SO_2 and other pollutants accounts for the most serious health problems resulting from air pollution. In an environmental study carried out by Polish and foreign researchers with World Bank support, a strong link was established between the high levels of air emissions in certain regions and the health and mortality patterns in these regions.

Associated health costs appear to dominate the costs resulting from environmental problems. This has important implications for environmental policy making and priority setting.

The economic reform programme called for major increases of gas, electricity and district heating prices in order to foster energy savings and investments in modernisation and pollution abatement. Significant progress was made until about 1992. Since then, heat prices have increased marginally, gas and electricity prices to households have remained on their 1992 level and prices to industry have declined in real terms. Power companies' cash flows have allowed them to improve the efficiency of existing electrostatic precipitators or install new ones, but not to modernise entire plants or install expensive FGD equipment. The increase in environmental fees and fines has made the management of power and industrial plants more aware of the need to install abatement equipment or change processes to achieve compliance levels. Fees now represent about 3 per cent of total generation costs; the percentage of fines in total costs is not known since they are taken out of profits. Most companies have prepared plans to modernise/retrofit plants and install needed environmental equipment. The bottleneck for the power industry is the lack of

Table 11.3
Emissions of Key Pollutants, by Voivodship, 1988-93
(1 000 tonnes/year)

	SO₂		NO₂		Particulates		CO	
	1988	1993	1988	1993	1988	1993	1988	1993
Warsaw	143	57	72		166	18	72	4
Jelenia Gora	233	177	22		116	48	22	10
Katowice	856	334	264		473	115	264	155
Konin	178	134	25		93	45	25	9
Krakow	124	50	61		134	24	61	142
Piotrkow	382	329	86		61	29	86	15
Radom	144	51	36		54	13	36	4
Tarnobrzeg	202	76	51		67	15	51	3
Others	1 789	576	605			292	605	191
Total	**4 052**	**1 784**	**1 221**	**1 310**	**2 585**	**599**	**1 221**	**533**
Rate of change		-56%		+7%		-77%		-56%

Sources: GUS (1993), World Bank Environmental Strategy Report, 1992

Table 11.4
Emissions from Power Generation, by Plant, 1988 and 1993
(1 000 tonnes/year)

	SO₂		NO₂		Particulates		CO	
	1988	1993	1988	1993	1988	1993	1988	1993
Belchatow	342	323	61	38	34	24	27 216	38 622
Turow	205	173	13	22	90	44	15 726	10 246
Kozienice	116	47	35	26	30	9	10 004	6 609
Dolna Odra	78	55	23	24	35	12	7 571	6 300
Rybnik	97	46	29	26	22	8	9 939	7 788
Patnow	84	85	10	15	18	17	8 280	6 442
Jaworzno III	142	69	12	22	11	6	6 498	4 371
Laziska	78	38	39	18	17	7	5 230	n.a.
Others	778	447	226	181	521	167	75 212	40
Total	**1 920**	**1 283**	**447**	**373**	**778**	**295**	**160 446**	**134 394**
Rate of change		-33%		-17%		-62%		-16%

Sources: GUS, World Bank Environmental Strategy Report, 1992, CIE (1993)

funding and inadequate cash flows resulting from low tariffs. In some heavy industry branches, depressed prices due to overcapacity and an inadequate exit policy render cash flows insufficient for modernisation.

Emission standards and ambient air quality standards were updated with a February 1990 ordinance on protection of the air against pollution. Emission standards are stipulated only for SO_2, NO_x and particulates. The standards distinguish among combustion technologies and fuels, and between existing and new plants, the latter being defined as those starting up after 31 December 1994. Existing plants face tighter standards from 1998 – in part identical to, in part slightly less tough than, those for new plants. A Voivodship Department of Environmental Protection may decide on a lower limit on emissions from a given facility than that stipulated by the Ministry of Environmental Protection in the ordinance.

The ambient standards distinguish between general areas and specially protected areas, being much tougher for the latter. As of this writing, 44 substances have been categorised under the

ambient standards, and the list will grow. The standards distinguish between annual average concentrations of these substances, 24 hour concentrations and peak concentrations within any 30 minute period.

The existing Polish air emission standards for combustion plants over 0.2 MW are similar to the EU standards for SO_2 and NO_x emissions. For particulate matter they are considerably more liberal than the EU standards. The deadline of 1 January 1998 for compliance with tighter standards for existing plants should be reviewed in the light of financial constraints and the sheer time needed for modernisation and environmental investments.

The Polish ambient air quality standards are extremely ambitious. Although not easily comparable, they are considered much stricter in many substance categories than the EU or even the Swiss standards. Though they cover 44 substances, monitoring facilities are available in only a few regions even for the most common substances, such as SO_2, NO_x and particulates. Given the limited resources and analytical techniques available for measurement and

Table 11.5
Air Emission Standards
(g/GJ)

Permitted emissions for combustion processes

Fuel	Furnace	Category A			Category B			Category C		
		SO_2	NO_x	Part.	SO_2	NO_x	Part.	SO_2	NO_x	Part.
Hard coal	Fixed grate	990	35	1 850	720	35	1 370	650	35	1 370
	Mech. grate	990	160	800	640	95	600	200	95	600
	Pulv. coal 1	1 240	495	170	870	170	90	200	170	90
	Pulv. coal 2	1 240	330	260	870	170	130	200	170	130
Lignite	Pulv. coal 1	1 540	225	140	1 070	150	70	200	150	95
	Pulv. coal 2	1 540	225	195	1 070	150	95	200	150	70
Coke	Fixed grate	720	35	1370	410	45	235	410	45	235
	Mech. grate	240	95	600	250	145	235	250	110	235
Oil	Boilers < 50 MW	1 720	120	–	1 250	120	–	125	90	–
	Boilers > 50 MW	1 720	160	–	170	160	–	170	120	–
Natural gas	Boilers < 50 MW	–	60	–	–	35	–	–	35	–
	Boilers > 50 MW	–	145	–	–	85	–	–	85	–
Wood	Grate	–	50	–	–	50	–	–	50	–

Notes:
Category A = Standards applicable to existing plants until 1998.
Category B = Standards applicable to existing plants from 1998.
Category C = Standards applicable to new plants.
NO_x signifies the sum of NO and NO_2 converted into NO_2.
Pulverised coal 1 = pulverised with dry slag removal.
Pulverised coal 2 = pulverised with wet slag removal.

Sources: PAN, CIE

continuous monitoring, it will be difficult if not impossible to establish meaningful monitoring and enforcement programmes for all listed substances. The Government should consider adopting the EU standards, which are designed to lead to a process with a planning horizon to assure continued compliance of polluters, in line with available resources and time needs.

Emissions of most pollutants declined significantly from 1988 to 1993 thanks to i) industrial contraction due to declining domestic and foreign demand and industrial obsolescence; ii) energy savings due to increasing prices; iii) use of cleaner fuels; iv) better management, including improved operation and maintenance procedures; and v) investment in modern facilities and abatement equipment. It is not possible to quantify exactly the impact of each of these forces. Emissions related to industrial production have probably fallen mainly because of declines in production; there are few cases of quick responses to energy price increases on the part of heavy industry, and investments in more efficient and cleaner processes have been limited by funding constraints.

Improvements in the quality of the hard coal sold domestically – the backbone of the Polish energy sector – have contributed significantly to the declines in emissions. As demand for hard coal started to fall, and as increasing fees and fines made consumers more concerned about air pollution, low quality coal became more difficult to sell. As a result, coal washing became more widespread. Figure 11.2 illustrates how the quality of hard coal produced in Poland has improved. Table 11.6 focuses on the same aspects of the coal and lignite consumed in the power sector.

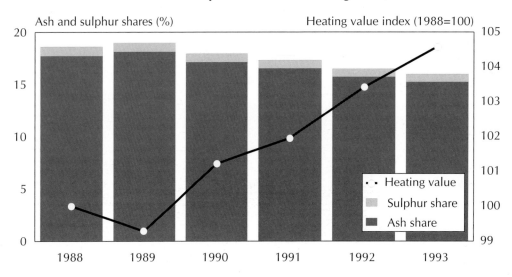

Figure 11.2
Hard Coal: Ash and Sulphur Shares and Heating Value, 1988-93

Table 11.6
Quality Evolution of Hard Coal and Lignite for the Power Industry, 1988-93

HARD COAL

Year	Consumption (Mt)	Ash content (%)	Sulphur content (%)	Heating value (kJ/kg)
1988	58	28.4	1.15	18 217
1989	60	28.5	1.13	18 308
1990	49	25.6	0.97	19 600
1991	47	24.0	0.93	20 373
1992	42	22.3	0.86	20 920
1993	40	21.5	0.83	21 331

LIGNITE

Year	Consumption (Mt)	Ash content (%)	Sulphur content (%)	Heating value (kJ/kg)
1988	70	13.6	0.62	7 933
1989	70	12.5	0.66	8 103
1990	66	11.6	0.59	8 292
1991	67	11.2	0.59	8 332
1992	65	10.9	0.59	8 418
1993	66	11.3	0.60	8 295

Sources: State Hard Coal Agency, CIE

The **power industry**, including CHP units, accounted in 1993 for more than half of all SO_2 emissions, more than one-third of all NO_x emissions and more than 15 per cent of all particulate emissions. Existing data show a decrease in power production of only 10 per cent between 1988 and 1993, but a weighted average decline in hard coal and lignite consumption of about 20 per cent, as average coal quality went up by 11 per cent and as there were some efficiency improvements in addition to the slight decline in power production. This decline in the use of hard coal and lignite, and a simultaneous decline of about 16 per cent in the sulphur content of the coal and lignite used, account for the entire 35.5 per cent drop in SO_2 emissions from the power sector between 1988 and 1993: no FGD facility went on-stream in the electricity industry during these years. A decline of about 50 per cent in particulate emissions reflects mainly a 20 per cent drop in the ash content of the coal used, as well as the 20 per cent drop in coal consumption; about 5 per cent of the decline is due to better use of filters and installation of new filters.

Large power and CHP plants have been equipped with high stacks and electrostatic precipitators, or at least bag filters, enabling them to capture increasing amounts of particulates and disperse the remaining exhaust over a wide area. Because of this and the use of lower sulphur coal – driven by fees and fines and a heightened environmental awareness – these plants' environmental performance has improved considerably. However, they are still far from meeting the standards that are scheduled to be in force from the beginning of 1998. Moreover, projected electricity tariff increases will hardly generate sufficient cash for required upgrading and environmental installations, especially since coal prices have been increasing in real terms since late 1993 and are now fairly close to import parity levels. Unless the power industry is permitted to pass coal price increases on to final consumers and increase its tariffs in real terms, the needed funding for modernisation and environmental improvement may not become available and the tighter standards of 1998 may not be met.

Smaller heat-only boilers and individual coal-fired residential heating units represent a special problem. At present they are not subject to any controls, fees or fines. They create major pollution problems in urban areas with old housing stock and small boilers for new blocks. In some cities, these **low stack sources** account for more than 50 per cent of overall air pollution during the winter. As coal prices have increased, households have increasingly switched to low quality coal with high ash and sulphur contents, aggravating the situation. It is important for municipalities to develop policies to deal with this problem. One model is the UK smog clean-up programme, which relied on incentives for conversion to gas and electricity, combined with a ban on coal burning in the future. Krakow has similar plans – small boilers are to be eliminated and replaced by CHP generated district heat, or converted to gas. The World Bank and the Global Environment Facility are assisting in this programme.

Upper Silesian **steelworks**, another key source of air emissions, represent over 85 per cent of total Polish steel production. Major sources of pollution are sinter plants, coke ovens, blast furnaces and basic oxygen furnace shops. The closure of most open hearth furnaces brought about considerable environmental progress. Moreover, output reductions by almost 50 per cent led to major pollution level declines between 1988 and 1992. Nevertheless, most of the plants require major environmental investments. It is estimated that the industry will need to invest US$ 300-500 million by 2000 to comply fully with environmental standards.

Coal quality and the need for coal preparation also play a vital role, as the major source of air pollution in Poland is the predominant use of coal for heat and power generation. The Polish standards for power plants will not only require rehabilitation of existing installations, but also lead coal customers to request cleaner coal. The average ash content of run-of-mine coal has already gone down, from 17.7 per cent in 1992 to 15.2 per cent in 1993, and the sulphur content dropped from about 1 per cent to 0.75 per cent, thanks to better mining techniques and changes in demand patterns. Power producers have also invested increasingly in coal washing equipment, a trend that is likely to continue. Rising washing costs are offset to a large extent by higher prices for coal of improved quality. The resulting increased need for fines disposal will have to be satisfied by increasing underground stowage.

Coal deposits contain significant amounts of **methane**, which is released as the coal is fractured. Apart from the danger of explosions, methane released to the atmosphere contributes to the greenhouse effect. (On the other hand, coal-bed methane may represent an important addition to Poland's natural gas resources; see Chapter 8.)

Table 11.7
Emissions and Capture of Methane from Hard Coal Mines, 1990-92
(million cubic metres)

EMISSIONS			
	1990	1991	1992
Through ventilating shafts	727.70	649.10	598.14
From degassing systems	66.82	60.09	60.65
Total	**794.52**	**709.19**	**658.79**
CAPTURE			
	1990	1991	1992
From the regions of coal mine exploitation	255.44	246.63	228.58
By wells from surface	6.06	4.78	4.20
Total	**261.50**	**251.41**	**232.78**
AMOUNT OF CAPTURED METHANE USED	194.68	191.33	172.14

Source: Mineral & Energy Economy Research Centre, Krakow

The impact of **road transportation** is being felt acutely in the cities, as the passenger car fleet in Poland has almost doubled during the past eight years. CO emissions related to road transport rose from 1.5 to 2 Mt between 1988 and 1993, and the road transport share in total CO emissions increased from 47 to 60 per cent. These data are estimates and are likely to be on the low side. Methane emissions from transport have risen from 8 600 tonnes to 9 500 tonnes, i.e. from 55 to 66 per cent of total non-mining methane emissions.

The share of leaded gasoline in total gasoline consumption is still as high as 90 per cent. However, the specifications for leaded gasoline have improved. Until 1985, up to 1.1 gram of lead per litre was allowed; then the limit was set at 0.56 g/litre and since 1992 it has been 0.15 g/litre. The Government has also imposed stricter limits on the sulphur content of diesel fuel. These improvements in specifications, and the introduction of unleaded gasoline, have had beneficial impacts – but these are largely being offset by the growth in the number of cars.

Polish **refineries** are sources of pollution, mainly in the form of gases. Their emissions of volatile organic compounds (VOCs) are large and constitute a major health problem in the vicinity of the plants, as they take place near ground level. The refining industry needs to institute vapour recovery in process and storage facilities, process improvements (tail gas treatment, waste gas recovery, etc.) and power plant modernisation, particularly at the Plock and Gdansk plants. On the demand side, the refineries must improve their products quickly to keep up with consumers' requests for higher quality products, particularly low lead and unleaded gasoline, and low sulphur diesel fuel and fuel oil. None of the refineries had to pay fines for gaseous emissions in 1991. It is estimated that the industry would need US$ 140 million for supply side investments. The demand side issues require even greater investments as they would have to be combined with plant modernisation (Gdansk and Plock) and expansion (Gdansk).

Complete data on **transboundary air pollution** are difficult to obtain. The European Monitoring Environmental Programme records transboundary SO_2 and the data for 1991-93 substantiate two important messages: i) overall imports and exports of SO_2 are declining and ii) Poland is a net exporter of SO_2, but on a declining trend. With further drops in SO_2 emissions due to FGD units now being built, this trend can probably be maintained. The key polluters to the west and south, Germany and the Czech and Slovak Republics, are also cleaning up

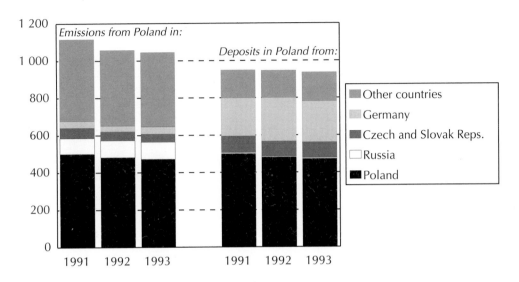

Figure 11.3
Transboundary Air Pollution, 1991-93
(Tonnes of pure sulphur equivalent)

Source: EMEP

their SO_2 emissions, which will improve the overall air quality picture in the region but at the same time make it harder for Poland to keep its net exports down.

Water Pollution

Annual available water flow per capita is only about a third of the European average – comparable with the level in Egypt. Rainfall is limited (about 550 mm in 1993), as are surface water resources; and groundwater resources, if heavily exploited, are not easily replenished. Yet water quality issues received little attention during the central planning period. The quality of Polish rivers continued to deteriorate into the late 1980s and is only now slowly recovering.

As a result of the high levels of pollution, the Polish water law of 1974 distinguishes among three classes of water quality and includes a fourth category that is so poor as to be beyond classification. Table 11.8 shows how the proportions of good quality water and poorer quality water have changed.

Water availability is a problem, especially for areas surrounding open pit mines. Because this

technique, used for lignite mining in central Poland, involves lowering the groundwater table, these areas lose their access to water from shallow wells, and agricultural yields may decline considerably. Compensation of farmers and water users in nearby villages has been limited but could increase in the future if quality of life issues come more to the fore.

Total water consumption in Poland declined from well over 15 bcm in 1985 to over 12 bcm – more than 300 cubic metres per capita – in 1992. Industry takes about two-thirds of this total, and the energy sector accounts for about 80 per cent of industry's share. Power and CHP plants use water for cooling and the refineries need process water. Whereas total industrial use of groundwater was about 600 million cubic metres, only a small fraction of the water consumed by the energy sector – about 60 million cubic metres – was pumped from underground. The energy sector is thus not a heavy exploiter of Poland's most precious water resources. Overall industrial water use declined by 7 per cent a year from 1989 to 1992. The use of water in industry should be reviewed carefully, and closed circuit cooling and recirculating of process water should be used wherever feasible.

Table 11.8
Water Quality in Polish Rivers, 1967-92

| Year | Length of monitored rives (km) | % of monitored length | | | | | | | |
| | | Physico chemical criteria | | | | Biological criteria | | | |
		Water class I	Water class II	Water class III	Beyond class	Water class I	Water class II	Water class III	Beyond class
1967	11 493	33.0	28.7	15.5	22.8	–	–	–	–
1970	17 764	25.0	32.0	20.0	23.0	–	–	–	–
1973	"	24.0	34.0	18.0	24.0	–	–	–	–
1977	"	10.0	32.0	28.0	31.0	–	–	–	–
1983	16 238	6.0	25.0	31.0	38.0	–	–	–	–
1989	n.a.	3.4	28.3	27.6	40.7	0.5	3.9	17.9	77.7
1990	8 621	6.0	27.9	30.3	35.8	0.0	3.0	16.8	80.2
1991	9 122	2.3	32.7	30.0	35.0	0.0	3.7	18.4	77.9
1992	7 006	2.4	12.8	24.8	60.0	-	1.6	10.4	88.0

Sources: Industry and Energy Operation Division, State Inspectorate for Environmental Protection; GUS

Table 11.9
Industrial and Municipal Sewage and Waste Water
(million cubic metres)

	1985	1990	1992	1993	Share of total, 1993
Discharged to surface water from industrial plants	10 485	9 055	7 973	7 757	80%
of which: cooling water	8 279	7 254	6 587	6 587	66%
Discharged to surface water from municipal sewage networks	2 419	2 314	2 075	1 981	21%
Total	**12 903**	**11 368**	**10 048**	**9 739**	**100%**
Sewage requiring treatment	4 624	4 115	3 461	3 151	34%
Sewage treated	2 624	2 772	2 466	2 308	25%
Mechanically	1 506	1 459	1 173	1 039	12%
Chemically	228	218	168	144	2%
Biologically	890	1 096	1 126	1 124	11%
Sewage untreated	2 000	1 343	995	844	10%

Sources: IEA, Energy Policies Poland: 1990 Survey; GUS

Energy sector activities give rise to three key water pollution problems: i) saline water disposal from coal mines, ii) VOC pollution from the downstream oil industry and iii) water use and often inadequate treatment of waste water at coal mines, power plants and refineries. Exploration for natural gas, coal-bed methane and oil may in time cause new pollution sources to emerge.

Table 11.9 shows total waste water and sewage quantities by major categories from 1980 to 1993. Cooling water stems almost exclusively from power and CHP plants. Refinery waste water, amounting to about 38 million cubic metres in 1991, is included in industrial sewage.

Poland's two major rivers, the Oder and the Vistula, are heavily polluted by large volumes of saline water from Upper Silesian coal mines. The water of both rivers is unfit even for industrial use for much of their length, as the highly saline water is extremely corrosive. In 1992 a total of 200 million cubic metres of water was disposed of by the hard coal mining industry in Upper Silesia. Of this, about 90 per cent had a salinity level putting it into the third water category, and 8 per cent was in the unclassified category (above 42 000 mg/litre). This water comes from five mines. Salinity ranges from 0.1 to 59.4 g/litre of chlorides, with three mines exceeding 50 g/litre, and from 0.1 to 2.6 g/litre of sulphides. Disposal is either directly into rivers, or via a settling pond that reduces salinity and serves as intermediate storage pending high river levels to achieve maximum dilution.

Damage caused by saline river water costs Polish society an estimated US$ 200 million per year. The discharges lead to corrosion in pipes and equipment of downstream users, they necessitate investments in water treatment facilities and they hurt river flora and fauna. This problem needs to be addressed immediately.

Studies on saline water disposal have called for a combination of disposal techniques to minimise the impact on the rivers: a) better mining management to help stem the amounts produced, b) deep well injection into porous rock at least 2 000 metres below ground and c) desalination.

Improved management, including selective mining, sealing of inflow points and reinjection from underground will have a limited impact, since the most offending mines have the best quality coal deposits in the salt bearing strata. Nevertheless this

is an important first step, already being taken. Shallow injection is risky because of potential contamination of groundwater reservoirs. Deep well injection has been used successfully in the United States, but costly test wells would have to be drilled to establish its feasibility in Poland. The GEF is considering whether to help fund test wells in the context of a coal-bed methane exploration programme under foreign oil/gas company sponsorship and with International Finance Corporation support.

Desalination plants are seen as the most promising solution to the problem, particularly for the most offending mines, and is considered feasible. One small plant has been operating since 1987 and a bigger one was commissioned in 1994. A plant treating a major portion of the saline water from the three most offending mines would produce about 1 Mt of high quality salt per year, for which a market would have to be found. This would significantly affect the regional salt mining industry. Much will depend on the restructuring of the hard coal sector to bring costs down and prices up to economic levels. A feasibility study of a major desalination plant for the Nadwislanska Coal Mining Company is being made, with PHARE funding, but financing such a project will most likely become possible only as prospects for the entire sector improve.

Little is known about spillage in the oil product distribution system, which leads to VOCs finding their way into the groundwater flow. There are almost 4 000 gasoline stations in Poland, and more than half have no adequate soil protection devices. The refinery sector also contributes to VOC pollution of water. Poland's seven refineries discharged about 38 million cubic metres in 1991, though the larger ones meet all Polish standards (few meet the much tougher German standards).

Most power plants, CHP plants and large heating plants have water treatment facilities to deal with sewage and treat cooling water before release. Many of these facilities are reported to work less than optimally and need to be improved. The system of monitoring and fines has helped with this issue during the past few years, and overall waste water quantities also have come down as water is increasingly recirculated and used more sparingly since water costs have risen.

The water law of 1974 and a considerable number of subsequent executive acts contain rules and regulations on abstracting water from surface water bodies and groundwater reservoirs, treating and using water and disposing of waste water. They also define surface water quality classes and purposes, set limits for the pollution contents of each class and provide limits on the pollution contents of waste water to be discharged to water bodies and the soil.

Solid Waste Disposal

In 1992, the total amount of solid waste accumulated in Poland was about 1.8 billion tonnes. The coal industry accounted for 42 per cent of this, including some 45 Mt a year of rock waste and fines from coal mining – i.e. 0.4 tonnes per tonne of hard coal – and about 250 Mt from lignite mining (3.5 tonnes per tonne of lignite). The power industry, with over 20 Mt of ash per year, accounted for 15 per cent of the total. Lignite waste is typically replaced in the pit from which it came, but some central Polish lignite mines have built up huge waste heaps nearby. For the hard coal sector, underground storage of waste

is difficult and costly. The mines prefer open air storage.

Disposal of solid waste from hard coal mining is a triple issue. First, solid waste generated by mining amounts to over 200 000 tonnes per day (1993 data). Second, that amount includes 7 500 tonnes a day of solid fines – containing significant amounts of pyrites (sulphur) – generated by coal preparation and washing plants. This quantity is likely to increase as more washing plants are established (though reducing the ash contents of coal by washing will cut transport costs and reduce buyers' need for ash disposal). Third, accumulated solid waste from the past often represents a major liability, leaking minerals into surface and groundwater and typically not reclaimed for any economic use. This past liability should not receive a high priority, however, as long as mining continues producing new problems.

Solid waste from refineries comprises acid tar, oily sludge, special waste (e.g. spent bleaching soil) and slag or ash. Acid tar is becoming a problem of the past, and special clean-up technology is being used on the tar pits.

Table 11.10
Waste Generated by Hard Coal Mines, 1993
(Mt)

Name of company	Coal production	Run of mine reject:		Share of production
		Large & medium fraction	Fine fraction	
Katowice Holding	23.62	4.31		18%
Bytomska	14.62	2.61	0.06	18%
Nadwislanska	24.16	4.03		17%
Jastrzebska	15.21	9.52	9.92	69%
Rybnicka	15.33	5.84	0.28	40%
Rudzka	12.75	4.58		36%
Gliwicka	17.21	9.62	0.34	58%
Other mines (under liquidation)	7.30	1.79	0.20	27%
Subtotal	130.20	42.29	1.80	34%
Total	**130.20**	**44.09**		**34%**

Source: Institute of Waste Management, Katowice

Rules and regulations for handling and disposing of solid waste are established in a 1980 environmental protection law and a Decree of the Council of Ministers on protection of the environment against waste and pollutants. The regulations call for waste to be recycled to the extent possible. Only waste that cannot be used, either directly or after treatment, can be stored. Storage is permitted only in locations designated in land use plans for that purpose, and must be based on decisions of local authorities. Those decisions define technical specifications, management methods, obligations regarding routine measurements, etc. Stored waste is divided into four types, with fees calculated on the basis of this classification. There are not yet any specific regulations concerning hazardous waste. The Environmental Protection Department of the voivodship of Katowice, where most coal mines are located, has decided that as from 2000, further disposal of solid waste above ground will be illegal. All solid mining waste would have to be stowed underground, at rather high cost, in abandoned mines or behind advancing longwalls to prevent subsidence. Alternatives are to fill up nearby open pit mines or to follow the German example of filling construction gravel pits with mine waste, which would increase the costs of coal mining only marginally.

Other Environmental Issues

Subsidence often occurs where mines have caved in after supports are removed. The resulting ground movements can damage buildings and infrastructure and sometimes affect farming as groundwater levels may change. When densely populated areas are affected, damage may be severe. The mines pay 1-2 per cent of their total costs into annual accounts to pay for such damage. For the future, a more systematic programme, including a reserve to cover damage, should be envisaged. Increased use of stowage behind advancing longwalls, and selective mining leaving safety pillars under endangered structures, would help reduce subsidence but also increase operating costs marginally.

Communist Poland had a system of obligatory **used oil recovery**, enforced by CPN and its distribution network. From 1980 to 1988, between 85 000 and 100 000 tonnes of used oil were recovered and reprocessed annually. The system started to disintegrate in the late 1980s, however, and by 1992 only about 36 000 tonnes, i.e. the equivalent of 10 per cent of all new lubricating oil sales, were recovered. The system now covers only major industrial oil users; there is no systematic collecting of spent lubricating oil at service stations. With appropriate incentives and privatisation of collection, a much higher degree of recovery would be possible.

COSTS AND FUNDING CONSTRAINTS

Cost of Needed Environmental Improvements

The investments required to deal with the major environmental problems in Poland are enormous. Below are estimates of the investments that will have to be made by the major fuel and energy producer and consumer groups, given existing and decreed environmental standards. Some of these estimates are crude and need to be refined further, while others are based on careful industry studies and are fairly reliable.

Air pollution abatement

The electricity industry (public power, CHP and autoproducers) alone will have to undertake investments of the order of US$ 6 billion to comply with tightened air emission standards in 1998, ambient standards and the UN-ECE sulphur protocol – assuming that the cheapest methods of desulphurisation are used. This figure also assumes that a number of plants will be modernised on the basis of fluidised bed combustion technology and will therefore not need any special FGD installations.

Industries chiefly using coal may have to invest an estimated US$ 3.50/GJ for environmental improvements. Given the level of coal consumption in industry, an investment level of US$ 2 billion would be required – not counting the steel industry, which alone is expected to require US$ 450 million for air emission improvements.

Refineries are estimated to need US$ 140 million to reduce emissions from their power/steam plants and to deal with VOC emissions. In addition, the oil product distribution sector will require some US$ 1.5 billion to comply with VOC standards. In urban areas, traffic related pollution points to a need for better diesel engines and for catalytic converters on gasoline engines; such investments are not counted here. Addressing low stack pollution would require investments of almost US$ 2 billion to switch to gas or district heating.

Water pollution abatement

It will take investment of over US$ 800 million to bring water quality levels up to present standards through desalination of about 60 per cent of coal mine saline water discharges, injection of the rest into deep wells and installation of waste water treatment plants at mines. Improving waste water treatment plants at refineries would cost an estimated US$ 55 million. The costs of preventing leaks at service stations of gasoline into groundwater could amount to well over US$ 1 billion. Improving water treatment plants – or building new plants, as needed – in the power industry, would cost about US$ 60 million.

Solid waste disposal

Major past liabilities include tar pits at the southern refineries and polluted lagoons near the bottom of waste piles from coal mining. US$ 200 million is allocated for tar pit clean-up.

Conclusions

Table 11.11 summarises expected levels of investments needed by 2000 to mitigate the most important ongoing pollution problems.

In terms of priorities, investments to reduce emissions to air from power and CHP plants and low stack sources should be on top of the list. Investments to lower VOC emissions to air and water are also urgent. Bringing these problems under control would improve living and health conditions significantly. In addition, given the large costs posed by saline water pollution, investments in this area are also important from an economic point of view. The sum of these priority investments would be the order of US$ 5 billion.

POTENTIAL FINANCING SOURCES AND FUNDING CONSTRAINTS

The application of the polluter pays principle, which is an integral part of Poland's environmental policies, requires companies responsible for pollution to finance the necessary abatement measures. In sectors where market forces are already at work and free prices prevail, companies need to develop strategies and business plans emphasising four principles: i) maximise energy savings to the extent economical, ii) where there is more than one feasible alternative, use the cleanest energy source, iii) emphasise maintenance to achieve high levels of efficiency and minimise pollution, iv) accumulate cash to fund investments required to meet standards.

In the energy sector, controlled prices are still the rule rather than the exceptions. Point iv) depends critically on prices being raised to meet economic costs, as planned. In the power sector, for instance, it is estimated that prices will have to rise by something like 3 per cent annually in real terms in the years ahead for the industry to be able just to maintain its equipment in its present state. If cash flows sufficient for environmental improvements and modernisation are to be generated, power prices will have to increase by about 8 per cent annually in real terms until 2000.

There are many potential financing sources, but their capacities are limited. The Polish capital market is still very shallow. Therefore, domestic private equity investments are likely to be very scarce for many years to come. At the same time the Government has announced that it wants to withdraw from the energy sector, selling its stakes rather than place new equity. Foreign investors show strong interest in Poland, but are increasingly discouraged by legal and bureaucratic hurdles, continued governmental scepticism on privatisation and, in the case of the grid-based energy forms, low revenue. Commercial lending from domestic banks will be limited by the small size of the banks, their preference for short term funding, their unfamiliarity with appraising large projects and assessing risk, high demands for securities and collateral, and high interest rates and the crowding out effects of the Government's funding needs. Foreign banks will require government guarantees or very sound projects with strong sponsors and good cash flow projections. As long

Table 11.11

Estimated Modernisation and Environmental Investment
(US$ million)

Industry	Total investment programme to 2000	Of which : Environmental investment programme		Air pollution investment to 1997
Coal (70 mines, 11 other facilities)	4 200 [a]	Air Water Solid waste	150 800 –	150 – –
Refineries (7 refineries, 5 other facilities)	2 000	Air Water Solid waste	140 55 200	140 – –
Oil product distribution	2 500	Air Water Solid waste	1 500 1 000 –	1 500 – –
Public power (22 plants)	5 000	Air Water Solid waste [b]	3 200 30 –	1 100 – –
Public CHPs (33 companies)	2 500	Air Water Solid waste	1 800 30 –	500 – –
Autoproducers (193 plants)	1 500	Air Water Solid waste	900 – –	400 – –
Other heat-only boilers (est. 6 500 plants)	1 950 [c]	Air Water Solid waste	1 950 – –	600 – –
Subtotals		Air Water Solid waste	9 640 1 915 200	4 390 – –
Total	**19 650**		**11 755**	**4 390**

a) Includes about US$ 100 million for past environmental liabilities.
b) For public power, CHP, autoproducers and other heat-only boilers, expenses related to solid waste are included in operating costs.
c) Calculated as an estimated average investment of US$ 300 000 each to a) shut down and connect to district heating, b) switch from coal to gas, c) install fluidised bed combustion unit, d) switch to gas boiler or gas heater.

Sources: PPGC, World Bank

as tariffs for grid-based energy are too low, foreign banks will show little interest in investments in those subsectors. The same is true for the large international financial institutions.

Major environmental investments could be funded to a certain extent by fees and fines from polluters collected by the national and voivodship environmental funds. Theoretically, these institutions should have annual incomes of US$ 500 million per year. Since a number of polluters do not pay their fees and fines, however, a more realistic figure is about US$ 270 million per year. Another local source is the Ecofund, which manages the resources generated from a debt-for-environment swap of up to 10 per cent of Poland's official debt under a Paris Club agreement. So far, only the United States and Switzerland have pledged the full level of 10 per cent of their debts, however; France has pledged

1 per cent, preferring to manage the use the remaining 9 per cent itself. In addition there are multilateral and bilateral grant funds such as the GEF, PHARE and programmes of the Netherlands, Scandinavian countries, Switzerland and the United States, which help pay for environmental studies and investment. In 1993, the total of their contributions to Poland for environmental purposes amounted to about US$ 30 million.

Thus, funding constraints are substantial. During 1993-94, Poland spent US$ 600 million a year, or close to 1 per cent of GDP, on environmentally related investments. Only about 5 per cent of these funds came from abroad. The share of the energy and fuel sector in the total was about two-thirds. It is expected that during the next few years, investments with environmental purposes may reach about US$ 1 billion. Assuming that the energy sector share stays roughly the same, these investments would amount to about US$ 700 million per year – far short of the US$ 1.5 billion a year or so that is needed.

EXISTING RESOURCES

Policy and Institutional Framework

Poland's Constitution gives "citizens ... the right to benefit from the values of the environment and the duty to protect it". The Government's objectives with respect to environmental protection can be summarised as follows:

- elimination of serious public health hazards;

- reduction of the economic costs of environmental damage;

- conservation of living natural resources, in particular to avoid irreversible damage.

Policy is spelled out in a comprehensive document of 1990, "The National Environmental Policy". Key elements include:

- harnessing market forces to achieve economic efficiency and minimise total costs of policy implementation;

- setting clear limits to the use of the environment;

- decentralising and regionalising environmental activities;

- following the polluter pays principle;

- ensuring that all development options to be considered for implementation are environmentally sound and "sustainable", in the sense used by the Brundtland Commission.

The Government pursues a strategy of decentralisation of decision making on environmental issues. The polluter pays principle helps generate funds in the regions: in the past few years 60 per cent of fees and fines have been collected by the voivodship environmental funds and 40 per cent by the National Fund for Environmental Protection and Water Management. More recently, municipalities have become entitled to the first 10 per cent of such payments. These funds are to be used exclusively for the improvement of the environment. The system works through incentives to reduce pollution (fees and fines – the "stick"), and through incentives to invest in cleaner production facilities (low cost funding from national and regional funds – the "carrot"). Polluters are responsible for monitoring themselves, but there is an agency charged with monitoring companies' performance and enforcing legislation. A system of regularly renewable permits and licences provides additional checking and reinforcement of polluters' responsibility to adhere to standards and norms. Through international agreements the Government assures and encourages exchanges of ideas, transfers of know-how and international co-operation to solve common and transboundary problems.

Institutional framework and responsibilities

The Minister of Environmental Protection, Natural Resources and Forestry is the chief executor of state administration for environmental protection. The National Council of Environmental Protection, the National Council for Protection of Nature and the Geology Council co-operate with the Minster as advisory bodies. The Minister is responsible for the Government's environmental policy and is an appeal instance with authority to repeal Voivodship decisions concerning environmental protection, geology and forestry. The State Inspectorate for Environmental

Protection controls economic units affecting the environment and is subordinated to the Minister. The State Inspectorate has a very broad range of responsibilities – it may impose fines for violation of environmental protection regulations, and even order an activity hazardous to the environment to be stopped until the cause of the hazard is removed. Within the Ministry are five commissions with authority to co-ordinate and voice opinions to the Ministry: the Commissions for Geological Licences, Hydro-geological Documentation, Mined Mineral Resources, Geological Engineering Documentation and Evaluation of Geological Research Project Drafts. There is also a Commission for Environmental Impact Assessment, an advisory body.

The Minister supervises six state research institutions, all based in Warsaw:

- the Institute of Environmental Protection;

- the Institute of Meteorology and Water Management;

- the National Institute of Geology;

- the Research Institute of Forestry;

- the Research and Development Centre of Geological Technique;

- the Institute of Ecology in Industrial Terrains.

Voivods, who administer voivodships in the name of the Government, are in charge of matters concerning the state and use of the environment within their territories. Among their duties are: issuing permits, collecting fees and imposing punishments, issuing administrative orders and interdictions, carrying out measurement and control activity, and record keeping.

In Poland much practical action in the field of environmental protection is initiated by non-governmental organisations (NGOs) and foundations for environmental protection.

Legal and regulatory framework

Poland has a large body of laws, decrees and regulations, most dating from the 1970s and 1980s. The framework pieces of legislation are the environmental protection law of 1980, the water law of 1974, the 1991 law on the State Inspectorate for Environmental Protection, the geology and mining law of 1993, which combines the mining law of 1953 and the geological law of 1960, and some others that are of less importance for the energy sector. According to the Institute for Environmental Protection, environmental regulation is aimed primarily at disciplining economic units in how their activities affect the environment by defining standards such as permissible concentrations of harmful substances and intensity of environmentally harmful effects – which are being adjusted to European requirements – and by creating effective legal, economic and administrative instruments to exert pressure on enterprises. Those instruments include, or will include:

- material liability and criminal responsibility of persons harming the environment;

- high fees for engaging in activities affecting the environment and fines for violating provisions of environmental laws;

- environmental duties on certain goods, to finance environmental protection;

- licences for some types of economic activity, especially mining;

- rationalisation of inspection through creation of a national monitoring system;

- preventive measures such as requirements for environmental impact assessment.

Priority tasks within this framework are to reduce SO_2 and NO_x emissions substantially, mainly by modernising the power and coal industries and transport sector; reduce the levels of surface water pollution due to saline mine water, hazardous industrial waste water (from the chemical, metallurgical, paper and food industries) and municipal waste water discharges; and increase the recycling of industrial and municipal waste, eliminate illegal waste dumps and improve the operation of legal waste disposal sites.

International co-operation

Poland is a member of many international organisations dealing with problems of environment, health and occupational safety and hygiene. The country carries out programmes and implements recommendations of these organisations in accordance with statutory requirements and agreements. Poland is a party to over 40 international conventions and protocols in the above areas. Important for the energy sector are, in particular, the UN-ECE Convention on Long Range Transboundary Air Pollution (Geneva, 1979) and related protocols: i) the Geneva Protocol of 1984 on long term financing of the co-operative programme for monitoring and evaluating long range transmission of air pollutants in Europe, ii) the Sofia Protocol of 1988 on reducing emissions of NO_x or their transboundary fluxes, and iii) the Oslo Protocol of 1994 on reduction of sulphur emissions; the Convention on Protection of the Ozone Layer (Vienna, 1985) and the related Montreal Protocol on ozone depleting substances (1987); and the Convention on Environmental Impact Assessment in the Transboundary Context (Espoo, 1991). The most expensive agreement to implement will probably be the Oslo Protocol on sulphur emissions, under which Poland commits itself to reduce its sulphur emissions by 37 per cent by 2000, 47 per cent by 2005 and 66 per by 2010, from the 1980 level.

Plans for policy, strategy and institutional changes

As a result of the reformulation of objectives and redirection of policies that took place in 1990, Poland is amending its body of laws and regulations as well as the institutional framework for protecting the environment. As a general rule, the changes adopted and considered serve to tighten environmental requirements. In particular it is expected that:

- the standards concerning emissions will gradually be sharpened;

- the list of substances controlled by standards will be expanded;

- the requirements concerning the environmental impact of manufactured products will be tightened;

- the standards will be adjusted gradually to EU requirements;

- the polluter pays principle will be more commonly used.

Draft laws under preparation concerning the overall environment and water management include a water law that would provide the legal underpinning for the River Basin Authorities. The Ministry of Environmental Protection, Natural Resources and Forestry is being reorganised, and regional bodies such as the environmental departments in voivodships and municipalities, regional inspectorate offices and the River Basin Authorities are being strengthened through training, increased resources and support from academia and scientific foundations.

Economic Instruments

Reductions in emissions related to energy production and consumption can be achieved in many ways, most of which can be classified as command and control measures or economic instruments. The latter are preferable from a cost-efficiency point of view. They include cost based energy prices, taxes on emissions and markets in emission permits. Economic instruments not only help reduce pollution levels, they also facilitate the development of least cost energy supply strategies.

The forces of economic restructuring and energy price reform can have a tremendous effect on pollution levels. The substantial real increases in domestic energy prices since the beginning of 1990 have probably contributed more to the declines in pollution levels than any environmental policy based action. Energy price increases provide strong incentives for energy conservation in all sectors of the economy, leading to substantial reductions in emissions. Further measures to speed up the responsiveness of energy demand to higher energy prices will bring large environmental benefits in addition to their general economic merits. The process of capital replacement and upgrading in Poland in response to higher energy prices will lead to significant reductions in emissions on top of the gains due to improvements in energy efficiency. It is estimated that energy price reform could bring down the level of particulate matter in the air by almost 80 per cent by the end of the century. SO_2, NO_x and CO_2 levels could be reduced significantly as well.

Emission taxes, or fees/fines and charges, also provide major economic incentives. Emission taxes are well established in Poland, levied directly on monitored sources and indirectly on motor fuels. The system for monitoring compliance with standards also allows monitoring of tax payments. Enforcement has been less strict than could be wished, particularly recently, when there were substantial dislocations in the economy and taxes rose sharply. It serves no purposes to raise tax levels if there are frequent waivers or if tax payments are subsidised from public budgets. Tax levels have been increased sharply since the beginning of 1990; their real level is higher than at any time during the 1980s. Even so, in view of the damage caused by the emissions of the main air pollutants, and the level and enforcement of water pollution charges (especially for saline discharges), the general level of fees is too low. Moreover, the pattern of fees is poorly matched to the severity of the problems associated with the various pollutants, and the regional differentiation in fee levels may be too low. In 1992-94, fees hardly rose in real terms.

Emission trading, a concept developed in the United States under the Clean Air Act, may take the form of "netting," "offsets" or "bubbles". Netting allows a firm creating a new source of emissions to avoid stringent new performance standards if it reduces emissions from other sources. Netting always refers to internal trade within a company. Offsets allow new sources to enter non-attainment areas if they reduce existing source emissions by an even greater amount; offsets can involve internal and external trade. Bubbles are aggregated pollution levels covering all sources in a particular plant or area; only the aggregate is controlled, rather than individual source emissions. Bubbles can involve internal or external trade. Although emission trading has been carried out in Poland on a small scale, its legal status is not clear. Air pollution legislation currently under consideration is understood to include a clarification of how individual polluting entities might trade off controls on their own contiguous sources (e.g. controls on multiple sources within the same power or steel plant).

A recent World Bank study suggests a dynamic and mixed strategy for economic instruments in Poland. Starting from a situation with command and control measures, emission fees could be increased to encourage some additional abatement and technical innovation and to provide added revenue for clean-up of environmental damage. It is unlikely, however, that fees can be increased to the level necessary to meet current emission standards. To accomplish this goal cost-effectively, an evolutionary movement towards emission trading should be considered. Trading could start

with informal bilateral transactions and become more extensive as circumstances and the interests of polluters warrant. However, even limited emission trading would require clearer legal and regulatory authority, as well as continued progress in economic restructuring. In the longer term, the combined effects of higher energy prices and an effective system of environmental charges will push up the relative prices of goods produced by energy-intensive and polluting industries, creating a price-driven structural change that will further reduce the level of emissions.

ACHIEVEMENTS TO DATE

To the credit of decision makers, along with pressure from Polish NGOs and the public at large, Poland has embarked on a process of environmental improvement that seems irreversible. In 1990, a very strong policy statement was issued that has served as a model for several other central and eastern European countries. Tight standards have been supplemented by stiff fees and fines, which force an increasingly market oriented business community to stay environmentally aware. Training and technical assistance have built a core of qualified and motivated government officials. Different ministries have started to co-operate in interministerial working groups to hammer out compromises in the interest of environmental improvements. Polish commercial banks have started taking the environment seriously – a recent survey showed that more than 60 per cent of the banks now routinely ask for permits and no-objection statements from environmental authorities with respect to investment projects, and the share is growing. Energy price adjustments, while recently slowing down due to public resistance, are moving in the right direction. And levels of pollution have come down considerably as a result of declines in heavy industrial production as well as clean-up efforts.

The progress on air emissions has been due mainly to the contraction of heavy industry following the introduction of economic reforms, to the production of cleaner coal and to installation of abatement equipment. Even though the FGD projects now under way at ten plants (including Belchatow, Skawina, Jaworzno and Opole) had not yet been started, between 1988 and 1992 sulphur emissions came down by an impressive 34 per cent, almost reaching the levels stipulated under the recently signed Oslo Protocol. During the same period NO_x emissions fell by almost 24 per cent, again mostly because of contraction, as expensive burner improvements have not yet been carried out on a large scale. The most impressive results have been achieved with respect to particulate emissions, which declined by over 40 per cent between 1988 and 1992 thanks to a combination of heavy industry contraction, cleaner coal, better efficiency of existing filters and installation of new filters. This progress is very important, as particulates create more health problems than other emissions. Regarding low stack emissions, little progress has been made, but policy decisions in Krakow and Zakopane are pointing the way – within the central parts of these cities, the use of dirty coal has been forbidden, and switching to high quality coal, coke, gas or district heating is under way or envisaged. In Krakow, the pilot operation of a GEF funded coal to gas conversion project will start soon. Zakopane is promoting a geothermal project that, in addition to reducing SO_2, NO_x and particulate emissions, would bring down CO_2 emissions. In the steel sector all but a few open hearth furnaces have been shut down. On the other hand, air pollution from mobile sources – in particular CO and lead emissions – has grown significantly and is still growing.

For water pollution, progress has been less pronounced. Saline water remains a big problem for the Vistula, though a second desalination plant at the Debiensko mine will significantly reduce saline water pollution of the Oder. Studies have established that the Nadwislanska Mining Company, owner of the three most heavily polluting mines discharging into the Vistula, could undertake investments that would ameliorate the situation if not solve the problem completely (i.e. affect 50 per cent of the discharged water). These investments would be feasible provided that the exit policy announced by the MoIT is implemented, and unprofitable overcapacity closed. Test wells will be drilled in the context of coal-bed methane exploration to examine the feasibility of deep well injection as a disposal method. VOC pollution from refineries has been reduced to meet the most important Polish standards, but further progress is desirable in the interests of improved water quality for downstream users.

Solid waste disposal in the hard coal sector has declined significantly. A contraction in coal production between 1988 and 1993 of almost 33 per cent was accompanied by waste reduction of 34 per cent. A better underground performance, including more careful coal production practices bringing up less waste, was to some extent offset by more intense coal preparation aimed at improving coal quality. Lignite waste developments are not known, but presumably waste quantities have remained more or less level, as production has not changed much recently. Old spoil heaps with significant coal content are being reworked to extract the coal. Unfortunately, little attention is being paid to the opportunity to landscape waste piles in more environmentally friendly and aesthetic ways. Some of the contents of old tar pits at the southern refineries are being reprocessed to turn them into harmless or even useful substances.

Mining communities in Upper Silesia are pushing for better compensation programmes to meet costs resulting from subsidence damage. These claims are supported by the public at large and are expected to lead to a more systematic funding mechanism that would build reserves to cover likely future damage. Indiscriminate exploitation of old supporting pillars in mines is being discontinued.

CONCLUSIONS

Strategy Review

Although decision makers realise that, in view of the high costs of needed investments and the present funding constraints, priorities need to be set, this has not yet been done systematically. The lack of readily available funds means reviews of overall investment needs for environmental improvements are required. Based on these estimates and cost-benefit analyses, priorities must be established, taking account of the scarcity of funds and concentrating on the most important issues and most beneficial solutions. This holds true at the national level (where a sector focus should be sought, particularly with regard to the setting of standards and economic instruments to meet them), at the regional level and for individual enterprises.

A systematic process of setting priorities would have to start at the level of policy making. It has become clear that funding constraints, energy price adjustment constraints (which no one expected in 1990) and sheer time constraints will prevent Poland's power industry from meeting the ambient standard levels that the country has set for itself. Rather than permitting industry to simply ignore these standards, the Government may want to reconsider its own statements in favour of harmonising its norms and standards with those of the EU, and opt to phase in such standards over a more realistic period. This phase-in period could be accompanied by incentives to help enterprises take advantage of available financial support and technical assistance to make the needed investments for environmental improvements.

As this chapter has noted, it is important to give decision makers in enterprises the motivation to reduce pollution. Fees and fines, as now applied, are powerful negative incentives. Positive incentives, motivating people to behave in environmentally benign ways because they recognise the value of doing so, might be even more effective. Emission trading has become a powerful tool in the US power industry, and it has been demonstrated through a pilot project in Chorzow that this tool would work in Poland. With respect to energy, the most powerful economic tool aimed at energy conservation, and thereby pollution reduction, is energy pricing. All possible avenues should be explored to move energy prices towards cost covering levels as quickly as possible.

Recommendations

- **Environmental policy making institutions, implementation agencies and environmental departments in voivodships, municipalities and companies should be strengthened.**

- **There is a need for closer co-operation among individual ministers within the Central Government and among central decision**

makers, voivodship authorities, local government and industry to devise practical plans for environmental improvements.

- **Public relations campaigns should be carried out to explain the need for costly pollution abatement, rapid energy price adjustments and energy savings.**

- **Energy prices should be adjusted quickly to cover energy supply costs including the costs of pollution abatement.**

- **The energy sector restructuring programmes should be continued so as to achieve efficiency and competitiveness in the supply of fuels of energy suppliers. Implementing exit policies for the coal industry is particularly important in order to assure the remaining part of this sector a chance to become profitable.**

- **Foreign private participation in the restructuring of the energy sector should be promoted in order to attract foreign capital, foreign commercial loan funding and transfer of know-how.**

- **The estimated costs and benefits of the most urgently needed environmental improvements should be reviewed. Priorities should be set at central government level, local government level and company level.**

- **The existing system of environmental taxes should be refined. Tax levels should be maintained in real terms or adjusted upwards. Cancellation of fees and fines should be avoided. Tax incentives for installation of emission abatement equipment, and new economic instruments to drive down pollution, such as emission trading, should be adopted.**

- **A review of ambient air quality standards, in light of cost-benefit analysis and time and funding constraints, should be carried out. EU standards may not be appropriate for Poland at this stage. Revised standards and phase-in schedules should be worked out. Companies should be made to conform to these standards.**

- **International co-operation on environmental matters should receive high priority.**

Table 11.12
Emissions of Sulphur Dioxide, 1980-93

Specification	1980 1000 t	Share of total	1988 1000 t	Share of total	1989 1000 t	Share of total	1990 1000 t	Share of total	1991 1000 t	Share of total	1992 1000 t	Share of total	1993 1000 t	Share of total
TRANSFORMATION SECTOR	n.a.	n.a.	3 079.9	75%	3 034.4	76%	2 482.4	80%	2 312.9	79%	2 105.1	77%	2 066.3	75%
Coke Ovens	n.a.	n.a.	427.2	10%	414.7	10%	344.1	11%	288.8	10%	283.2	10%	260.9	10%
Autoprod. of Electr.	n.a.	n.a.	217.5	5%	262.7	7%	241.1	8%	227.0	8%	217.0	8%	223.8	8%
Public Plants and CHP	n.a.	n.a.	2 019.1	49%	2 008.4	50%	1 564.3	50%	1 469.0	50%	1 311.2	48%	1 283.0	47%
Heating Plants	n.a.	n.a.	347.3	8%	285.3	7%	272.8	9%	283.3	10%	255.5	9%	263.1	10%
Others	n.a.	n.a.	68.8	2%	63.3	2%	60.2	2%	44.8	2%	38.2	1%	35.6	1%
ENERGY SECTOR	n.a.	n.a.	30.5	1%	27.4	1%	22.1	1%	19.8	1%	20.5	1%	22.3	1%
Coal mines	n.a.	n.a.	4.1	0%	3.5	0%	2.8	0%	3.7	0%	2.6	0%	3.3	0%
Coke Ovens	n.a.	n.a.	20.9	1%	19.4	0%	14.8	0%	14.0	0%	15.8	1%	0.0	0%
Others Non-Specified	n.a.	n.a.	5.5	0%	4.4	0%	4.5	0%	2.1	0%	2.0	0%	18.9	1%
INDUSTRY SECTOR	n.a.	n.a.	294.3	7%	278.4	7%	225.0	7%	197.4	7%	185.1	7%	187.0	7%
Iron & Steel	n.a.	n.a.	107.0	3%	94.6	2%	83.5	3%	63.4	2%	61.9	2%	63.6	2%
Chemical	n.a.	n.a.	12.3	0%	13.8	0%	10.2	0%	8.3	0%	6.7	0%	6.6	0%
Non-metalic Minerals	n.a.	n.a.	87.4	2%	86.1	2%	62.0	2%	57.7	2%	56.7	2%	57.0	2%
Machinery	n.a.	n.a.	19.2	0%	17.4	0%	13.3	0%	11.5	0%	9.5	0%	9.1	0%
Food & Tobacco	n.a.	n.a.	21.7	1%	25.3	1%	25.3	1%	27.4	1%	24.7	1%	24.4	1%
Others	n.a.	n.a.	46.9	1%	41.2	1%	30.7	1%	29.1	1%	25.7	1%	26.3	1%
TRANSPORTATION SECTOR	n.a.	n.a.	67.1	2%	64.0	2%	52.5	2%	54.3	2%	53.2	2%	34.6	1%
Road Transportation	n.a.	n.a.	41.8	1%	42.1	1%	36.6	1%	37.4	1%	41.4	2%	23.0	1%
Railways	n.a.	n.a.	19.3	0%	15.2	0%	11.1	0%	11.6	0%	7.5	0%	6.2	0%
Others	n.a.	n.a.	6.0	0%	6.7	0%	4.8	0%	5.3	0%	4.3	0%	5.3	0%
OTHER SECTORS	n.a.	n.a.	661.7	16%	581.7	15%	318.3	10%	359.9	12%	368.9	13%	431.3	16%
Agriculture	n.a.	n.a.	30.9	1%	31.1	1%	29.3	1%	25.8	1%	19.0	1%	8.9	0%
Residential	n.a.	n.a.	418.2	10%	1.0	0%	n.a.	n.a.	n.a.	n.a.	n.a.	n.a.	n.a.	n.a.
Others Non-Specified	n.a.	n.a.	212.7	5%	549.5	14%	289.0	9%	334.1	11%	349.9	13%	422.4	15%
TOTAL	**4 100.0**	**100%**	**4 133.6**	**100%**	**3 985.8**	**100%**	**3 100.3**	**100%**	**2 944.2**	**100%**	**2 732.8**	**100%**	**2 741.4**	**100**

Table 11.13

Emissions of Nitrogen Oxides, 1980-93

Specification	1980 1000 t	1980 Share of total	1988 1000 t	1988 Share of total	1989 1000 t	1989 Share of total	1990 1000 t	1990 Share of total	1991 1000 t	1991 Share of total	1992 1000 t	1992 Share of total	1993 1000 t	1993 Share of total
TRANSFORMATION SECTOR	n.a.	n.a.	878.9	60%	862.0	62%	787.2	67%	753.1	66%	720.9	65%	715.4	63%
Coke Ovens	n.a.	n.a.	166.8	11%	162.0	12%	134.4	11%	112.9	10%	110.8	10%	102.1	9%
Autoprod. of Electr.	n.a.	n.a.	106.0	7%	109.7	8%	102.1	9%	96.2	8%	92.3	8%	93.3	8%
Public Plants and CHP	n.a.	n.a.	433.5	30%	431.8	31%	402.0	34%	397.1	35%	386.1	35%	383.9	34%
Heating Plants	n.a.	n.a.	145.3	10%	133.3	10%	127.1	11%	130.6	11%	117.8	11%	120.9	11%
Others	n.a.	n.a.	27.4	2%	25.2	2%	21.6	2%	16.2	1%	13.9	1%	15.1	1%
ENERGY SECTOR	n.a.	n.a.	17.7	1%	17.6	1%	12.8	1%	10.6	1%	10.9	1%	11.0	1%
Coal mines	n.a.	n.a.	1.7	0%	1.5	0%	1.1	0%	1.5	0%	1.1	0%	1.7	0%
Coke Ovens	n.a.	n.a.	6.0	0%	5.9	0%	5.1	0%	4.3	0%	4.3	0%	4.2	0%
Oil Refineries	n.a.	n.a.	6.7	0%	7.1	1%	3.8	0%	2.9	0%	3.3	0%	3.3	0%
Others Non-Specified	n.a.	n.a.	3.2	0%	3.1	0%	2.8	0%	1.8	0%	2.2	0%	1.8	0%
INDUSTRY SECTOR	n.a.	n.a.	130.6	9%	122.5	9%	103.9	9%	91.0	8%	83.2	7%	83.8	7%
Iron & Steel	n.a.	n.a.	51.5	4%	46.0	3%	40.6	3%	31.6	3%	30.7	3%	30.2	3%
Non-metalic Minerals	n.a.	n.a.	36.1	2%	35.2	3%	26.0	2%	24.6	2%	23.7	2%	23.6	2%
Machinery	n.a.	n.a.	9.3	1%	8.5	1%	6.5	1%	5.4	0%	4.4	0%	4.4	0%
Food & Tobacco	n.a.	n.a.	8.1	1%	9.5	1%	9.5	1%	10.4	1%	9.4	1%	9.5	1%
Others	n.a.	n.a.	25.5	2%	23.3	2%	21.2	2%	19.0	2%	15.0	1%	16.1	1%
TRANSPORTATION SECTOR	463	n.a.	134.0	9%	130.7	9%	107.6	9%	105.3	9%	104.1	9%	100.9	9%
Road Transportation	n.a.	n.a.	78.8	5%	79.6	6%	68.5	6%	69.3	6%	76.0	7%	70.7	6%
Railways	n.a.	n.a.	47.9	3%	42.6	3%	34.2	3%	27.4	2%	20.6	2%	20.4	2%
Others	n.a.	n.a.	7.2	0%	8.5	1%	5.0	0%	8.6	1%	7.5	1%	9.8	1%
OTHER SECTORS	n.a.	n.a.	305.5	21%	268.8	19%	158.7	14%	180.0	16%	197.1	18%	216.7	19%
Agriculture	n.a.	n.a.	25.6	2%	26.4	2%	25.8	2%	24.1	2%	24.2	2%	24.2	2%
Residential	n.a.	n.a.	193.2	13%	8.2	1%	n.a.	n.a.	n.a.	n.a.	n.a.	n.a.	8.2	n.a.
Others Non-Specified	n.a.	n.a.	86.7	6%	234.2	17%	132.9	11%	155.9	14%	173.0	15%	184.3	16%
TOTAL	**n.a.**	**n.a.**	**1 466.7**	**100%**	**1 401.6**	**100%**	**1 170.2**	**100%**	**1 140.0**	**100%**	**1 116.2**	**100%**	**1 127.7**	**100%**

Table 11.14
Emissions of Carbon Monoxide, 1980-93

Specification	Year 1980 1000 t	Share of total	1988 1000 t	Share of total	1989 1000 t	Share of total	1990 1000 t	Share of total	1991 1000 t	Share of total	1992 1000 t	Share of total	1993 1000 t	Share of total
TRANSFORMATION SECTOR	n.a.	n.a.	404.7	13%	368.4	11%	361.1	13%	357.6	12%	353.8	11%	348.1	11%
Coke Ovens	n.a.	n.a.	146.1	5%	141.8	4%	117.7	4%	98.8	3%	96.9	3%	89.3	3%
Autoprod. of Electr.	n.a.	n.a.	43.0	1%	44.2	1%	107.9	4%	125.4	4%	125.4	4%	130.5	4%
Public Plants and CHP	n.a.	n.a.	78.1	2%	77.9	2%	73.4	3%	80.4	3%	76.7	2%	72.4	2%
Heating Plants	n.a.	n.a.	119.0	4%	87.0	3%	47.3	2%	42.0	1%	45.4	1%	46.9	1%
Others	n.a.	n.a.	18.5	1%	17.4	1%	14.7	1%	11.0	0%	9.4	0%	9.1	0%
ENERGY SECTOR	n.a.	n.a.	103.6	3%	122.1	4%	35.5	1%	3.5	0%	8.1	0%	3.8	0%
Coal mines	n.a.	n.a.	0.5	0%	0.5	0%	0.4	0%	0.5	0%	0.4	0%	2.3	0%
Coke Ovens	n.a.	n.a.	1.2	0%	1.6	0%	0.8	0%	0.7	0%	0.7	0%	0.7	0%
Oil Refineries	n.a.	n.a.	100.8	3%	119.2	4%	31.6	1%	1.9	0%	6.6	0%	0.4	0%
Others Non-Specified	n.a.	n.a.	1.0	0%	0.9	0%	2.8	0%	0.5	0%	0.5	0%	0.4	0%
INDUSTRY SECTOR	n.a.	n.a.	164.2	5%	155.2	5%	252.6	9%	211.4	7%	152.3	5%	147.3	5%
Iron & Steel	n.a.	n.a.	48.0	1%	46.1	1%	24.1	1%	58.9	2%	57.8	2%	44.7	1%
Chemical	n.a.	n.a.	21.8	1%	19.8	1%	86.3	3%	55.3	2%	42.8	1%	49.1	2%
incl. Petrochemical	n.a.	n.a.	0.0	0%	0.0	0%	79.9	3%	41.1	1%	28.5	1%	35.7	1%
Non-metalic Minerals	n.a.	n.a.	25.2	1%	26.2	1%	15.9	1%	11.4	0%	9.9	0%	9.7	0%
Wood & Wood Products	n.a.	n.a.	39.2	1%	36.2	1%	31.6	1%	29.7	1%	28.9	1%	29.4	1%
Others	n.a.	n.a.	30.1	1%	26.9	1%	94.7	4%	56.1	2%	12.8	0%	14.4	0%
TRANSPORTATION SECTOR	1 457.0	43%	1 570.6	49%	1 729.9	53%	1 568.6	58%	1 864.0	61%	2 111.2	64%	1 938.0	62%
Road Transportation	n.a.	n.a.	1 525.2	47%	1 672.0	51%	1 530.0	57%	1 680.5	55%	2 004.8	60%	1 798.1	57%
Others	n.a.	n.a.	45.3	1%	57.9	2%	38.6	1%	183.5	6%	106.3	3%	139.8	4%
OTHER SECTORS	n.a.	n.a.	992.7	31%	877.8	27%	477.9	18%	622.6	20%	690.7	21%	697.2	22%
Agriculture	n.a.	n.a.	34.1	1%	32.8	1%	29.5	1%	26.6	1%	18.5	1%	14.7	0%
Residential	n.a.	n.a.	635.2	20%	1.5	0%	n.a.	n.a.	0.0	0%	n.a.	n.a.	1.6	n.a.
Others Non-Specified	n.a.	n.a.	323.4	10%	843.5	26%	448.4	17%	596.0	19%	672.2	20%	680.9	22%
TOTAL	3 403.0	100%	3 235.7	100%	3 253.4	100%	2 695.7	100%	3 059.2	100%	3 316.0	100%	3 134.3	100%

Table 11.15
Emissions of Carbon Dioxide, 1980-93

Specification	Year 1980 1000 t	Share of total	1988 1000 t	Share of total	1989 1000 t	Share of total	1990 1000 t	Share of total	1991 1000 t	Share of total	1992 1000 t	Share of total	1993 1000 t	Share of total
TRANSFORMATION SECTOR	n.a.	n.a.	304 539	59%	298 907	60%	273 174	66%	261 286	65%	250 837	64%	249 902	63%
Coke Ovens	n.a.	n.a.	60 793	12%	59 094	12%	49 030	12%	41 204	10%	40 436	10%	37 291	9%
Autoprod. of Electr.	n.a.	n.a.	33 381	6%	35 115	7%	32 821	8%	31 000	8%	29 756	8%	30 093	8%
Public Plants and CHP	n.a.	n.a.	153 153	30%	152 855	31%	142 863	34%	141 574	35%	137 696	35%	137 110	35%
Heating Plants	n.a.	n.a.	46 765	9%	42 287	9%	40 217	10%	41 319	10%	37 303	9%	38 317	10%
Others	n.a.	n.a.	10 448	2%	9 554	2%	8 243	2%	6 189	2%	5 647	1%	7 091	2%
ENERGY SECTOR	n.a.	n.a.	17 918	3%	17 930	4%	13 186	3%	11 044	3%	5 591	1%	5 621	1%
Coal mines	n.a.	n.a.	742	0%	636	0%	507	0%	660	0%	503	0%	798	0%
Coke Ovens	n.a.	n.a.	3 451	1%	3 397	1%	2 900	1%	2 476	1%	248	0%	2 327	1%
Oil Refineries	n.a.	n.a.	3 114	1%	3 296	1%	1 755	0%	1 312	0%	1 481	0%	1 510	0%
Others Non-Specified	n.a.	n.a.	10 612	2%	10 601	2%	8 024	2%	6 595	2%	3 360	1%	985	0%
INDUSTRY SECTOR	n.a.	n.a.	55 886	11%	52 206	11%	44 409	11%	38 460	10%	34 886	9%	35 209	9%
Iron & Steel	n.a.	n.a.	22 872	4%	20 432	4%	17 822	4%	13 832	3%	13 180	3%	12 901	3%
Chemical	n.a.	n.a.	2 364	0%	2 362	0%	2 727	1%	2 244	1%	1 984	1%	2 393	1%
Non-metalic Minerals	n.a.	n.a.	14 510	3%	14 143	3%	10 538	3%	9 926	2%	9 560	2%	9 501	2%
Machinery	n.a.	n.a.	3 968	1%	3 594	1%	2 755	1%	2 234	1%	1 808	0%	1 854	0%
Food & Tobacco	n.a.	n.a.	3 244	1%	3 745	1%	3 724	1%	4 033	1%	3 663	1%	3 731	1%
Others	n.a.	n.a.	8 928	2%	7 930	2%	6 843	2%	6 192	2%	4 691	1%	4 830	1%
TRANSPORTATION SECTOR	n.a.	n.a.	27 151	5%	27 193	5%	22 625	5%	23 760	6%	24 999	6%	23 855	6%
Road Transportation	n.a.	n.a.	21 570	4%	22 013	4%	19 140	5%	19 637	5%	21 873	6%	20 195	5%
Others	n.a.	n.a.	5 581	1%	5 181	1%	3 484	1%	4 123	1%	3 126	1%	3 660	1%
OTHER SECTORS	n.a.	n.a.	113 115	22%	100 932	20%	61 375	15%	68 732	17%	76 801	20%	82 532	21%
Agriculture	n.a.	n.a.	7 147	1%	7 177	1%	7 043	2%	6 524	2%	6 213	2%	6 089	2%
Residential	n.a.	n.a.	70 134	14%	8 279	2%	n.a.	n.a.	n.a.	n.a.	n.a.	n.a.	9 214	2%
Others Non-Specified	n.a.	n.a.	35 834	7%	85 477	17%	54 333	13%	62 208	15%	70 588	18%	67 230	17%
TOTAL	410 000	100%	518 610	100%	497 168	100%	414 768	100%	403 283	100%	393 114	100%	397 119	100%

Table 11.16
Emissions of Methane, 1980-93

Specification	Year 1980 1000 t	1980 Share of total	1988 1000 t	1988 Share of total	1989 1000 t	1989 Share of total	1990 1000 t	1990 Share of total	1991 1000 t	1991 Share of total	1992 1000 t	1992 Share of total	1993 1000 t	1993 Share of total
TRANSFORMATION SECTOR	n.a.	n.a.	2.5	17%	2.4	16%	2.2	0%	2.1	0%	2.0	0%	2.7	1%
Coke Ovens	n.a.	n.a.	0.7	4%	0.6	4%	0.5	0%	0.4	0%	0.4	0%	0.4	0%
Autoprod. of Electr.	n.a.	n.a.	0.4	2%	0.4	2%	0.3	0%	0.3	0%	0.3	0%	0.3	0%
Public Plants and CHP	n.a.	n.a.	1.0	7%	1.0	6%	0.9	0%	0.9	0%	0.9	0%	1.4	0%
Heating Plants	n.a.	n.a.	0.5	3%	0.4	3%	0.4	0%	0.4	0%	0.4	0%	0.4	0%
Others	n.a.	n.a.	0.0	0%	0.0	0%	0.0	0%	0.0	0%	0.1	0%	0.2	0%
ENERGY SECTOR	n.a.	n.a.	n.a.	n.a.	n.a.	n.a.	533.3	98%	476.0	97%	442.2	97%	451.6	97%
Coal mines	n.a.	n.a.	n.a.	n.a.	n.a.	n.a.	533.2	98%	475.9	97%	442.1	97%	451.4	97%
Coke Ovens	n.a.	n.a.	0.1	0%	0.1	0%	0.1	0%	0.0	0%	0.0	0%	0.0	0%
Oil Refineries	n.a.	n.a.	0.1	0%	0.1	0%	0.1	0%	0.1	0%	0.1	0%	0.1	0%
Others Non-Specified	n.a.	n.a.	0.0	0%	0.0	0%	0.0	0%	0.0	0%	0.0	0%	0.0	0%
INDUSTRY SECTOR	n.a.	n.a.	0.9	6%	0.8	5%	0.7	0%	0.6	0%	0.5	0%	0.5	0%
Iron & Steel	n.a.	n.a.	0.3	2%	0.3	2%	0.3	0%	0.2	0%	0.2	0%	0.2	0%
Non-metalic Minerals	n.a.	n.a.	0.2	1%	0.2	1%	0.1	0%	0.1	0%	0.1	0%	0.1	0%
Machinery	n.a.	n.a.	0.1	0%	0.1	0%	0.0	0%	0.0	0%	0.0	0%	0.0	0%
Construction	n.a.	n.a.	0.1	1%	0.1	1%	0.1	0%	0.1	0%	0.0	0%	0.0	0%
Others	n.a.	n.a.	0.2	2%	0.2	1%	0.2	0%	0.2	0%	0.2	0%	0.2	0%
TRANSPORTATION SECTOR	n.a.	n.a.	8.6	57%	9.4	61%	7.7	1%	8.6	2%	9.5	2%	9.1	2%
Air Transportation	n.a.	n.a.	1.0	7%	1.4	9%	0.6	0%	1.1	0%	0.9	0%	1.3	0%
Road Transportation	n.a.	n.a.	7.1	47%	7.6	49%	6.8	1%	7.2	1%	8.3	2%	7.6	2%
Others	n.a.	n.a.	0.5	3%	0.4	3%	0.4	0%	0.3	0%	0.2	0%	0.2	0%
OTHER SECTORS	n.a.	n.a.	2.8	19%	2.6	17%	1.7	0%	1.9	0%	2.1	0%	2.1	0%
Residential	n.a.	n.a.	1.4	9%	0.2	1%	n.a.	n.a.	n.a.	n.a	n.a.	n.a.	1.7	0%
Others Non-Specified	n.a.	n.a.	1.4	9%	2.4	16%	1.7	0%	2	0%	2	0%	0.4	n.a.
TOTAL	**n.a.**	**n.a.**	**15.1**	**100%**	**15.5**	**100%**	**545.6**	**100%**	**489.2**	**100%**	**456.5**	**100%**	**466.0**	**100%**

Note: for the years 1988 and 1989 figures show emissions from combustion processes only.

Table 11.17
Air Emissions by Fuel Source

1992

		Hard Coal	Brown Coal	Coke	Gas	Heavy Fuel Oil	Motor Fuels	Other Fuels	TOTAL
SO_2	1 000 t	1 816.5	612.5	155.5	0.4	122.7	53.3	3.3	2 764.2
	% of total	66%	22%	6%	0%	4%	2%	0%	100%
NO_x	1 000 t	743.4	132.0	49.4	29.4	18.2	118.0	25.8	1 116.2
	% of total	67%	12%	4%	3%	2%	11%	2%	100%
Particulate	1 000 t	1 400.0	130.0	n.a.	n.a.	n.a.	n.a.	n.a.	1 600.0
	% of total	88%	8%	–	–	–	–	–	100%
CO	1 000 t	721.6	28.4	42.2	4.8	1.7	2 099.8	417.5	3 316.0
	% of total	22%	1%	1%	0%	0%	63%	13%	100%
CO_2	1 000 t	243 030.6	57 983.0	22 775.9	20 929.9	7 056.2	29 081.8	12 257.0	393 114.4
	% of total	62%	15%	6%	5%	2%	7%	3%	100%
Methane	1 000 t	3.1	–	0.2	0.4	0.2	9.3	1.2	14.4
	% of total	22%	n.a.	1%	3%	1%	65%	8%	100%

1993

		Hard Coal	Brown Coal	Coke	Natural & other Gas	Heavy Fuel Oil	Gasoline Diesel	Other Fuels	TOTAL
SO_2	1 000 t	1 806.4	626.0	150.7	0.7	119.4	36.0	2.3	2 741.4
	% of total	66%	23%	5%	0%	4%	1%	0%	100%
NO_x	1 000 t	755.0	133.5	48.5	29.5	20.8	115.8	24.6	1 127.7
	% of total	67%	12%	4%	3%	2%	10%	2%	100%
Particulate	1 000 t	1 350.0	120.0	n.a.	n.a.	n.a.	n.a.	n.a.	1 500.0
	% of total	90%	8%	–	–	–	–	–	100%
CO	1 000 t	783.4	31.2	41.3	4.9	1.9	1 923.9	356.8	3 143.3
	% of total	25%	1%	1%	0%	0%	61%	11%	100%
CO_2	1 000 t	246 449.7	58 639.2	22 076.2	21 137.5	8 074.9	29 438.2	11 303.8	397 119.4
	% of total	62%	15%	6%	5%	2%	7%	3%	100%
Methane	1 000 t	453.8	1.4	0.2	0.2	0.2	8.8	1.5	466.1
	% of total	97%	n.a.	0%	0%	0%	2%	0%	100%

Source: CIE

Table 11.18
Emission standards according to the Decree of 12 February 1992

Admissible emissions of sulphur dioxides, nitrogen dioxide and dust from coal burning in power plants, gGJ

Fuel	Furnace	Installations								
		Type A			Type B			Type C		
		SO_2	NO_2	Dust	SO_2	NO_2	Dust	SO_2	NO_2	Dust
Pit coal	Fixed grate	990	35	1 850	720	35	1 370	650	35	1370
	Automatic grate	990	160	800	640	95	600	200	95	600
	Pulverized coal with wet deslaging	1 240	495	170	870	175	90	200	170	90
	Pulverized coal with dry deslaging	1 240	330	260	870	170	130	200	170	130
Brown coal/lignite	Pulverized coal with wet deslaging	1 540	225	140	1 070	150	70	200	150	70
	Pulverized coal with dry deslaging	1 540	225	195	1 070	150	95	200	150	95
Coke	Fixed grate	410	45	720	410	45	235	410	45	235
	Automatic grate	500	145	310	250	145	235	250	110	235
Heating oil	Boilers < 50 MW	1 720	120	–	1 250	120	–	1 250	90	–
	Boilers > 50 MW	1 720	160	–	170	160	–	170	120	–
Natural gas	Boilers < 50 MW	–	60	–	–	35	–	–	35	–
	Boilers > 50 MW	–	50	–	–	50	–	–	50	–
Wood	grate	–	50	–	–	50	–	–	–	50

NO_2: Total nitrogen oxides, expressed as nitrogen dioxide

Note: Installations in operation before 28 March 1990 must comply with the requirements for Type A until 31 December 1997, and after that with the requirements for Type B. Installations under construction on 28 March 1990 and in operation before 31 December 1994 have to comply with the requirements for Type B until 31 December 1997 and after that with the requirements for Type C. Installations under construction on 28 March 1990 and in operation after 31 December 1994 and installations whose construction began after 28 March 1990 have to fulfil the requirements for Type C. The requirements are considered met when the installations are in compliance with overall emissions.

Table 11.19
Ambient Air Standards in the Ordinance of 12 February 1990

	Limiting values in μg/m³ for :		
	30 minutes	24 hours	Annual average
Dust	250	120	50
SO_2	600	200	32
NO_x	500	150	50
CO	5 000	1 000	120
Heavy metals:			
Cd	–	0.22	0.01
Cr	–	2	0.4
Cu	20	5	0.6
Mn	–	4	1
Ni	–	100	25
Pb	–	1	0.2
Benzo-a-pyrene	0.02	0.005	0.001

Note: The Ordinance of 12 February 1990 on the Protection of the Air against Pollution regulates the permissible levels of a large number of pollutants in ambient air. Permissible concentration levels of these pollutants are regulated over periods of 30 minutes, one day or as an annual average. Different concentration levels apply in specially protected areas and in other areas.

Table 11.20
Selected EU, German and Polish Standards for Emissions from New Combustion Plants (mg/m³)

Fuel type	Type of installation/ thermal capacity	EU			Germany			Poland		
		SO_2	NO_x	Dust	SO_2	NO_x	Dust	SO_2	NO_x	Dust
Solid fuels	50-500 MW	–	650	100						
	> 500 MW	–	650	50						
	100-300 MW				2000	800	50			
	> 300 MW				400	800	50			
Hard coal	Moving bed							480	410	1450
	Pulverized bed							480	410	215
Fuel oil	50-300 MW	1700	450	50	1700	300	50	570	400	–
	300-500 MW		450	50	400	150	50	570	400	–
	> 500 MW	400	450	50	400	150	50	570	400	–

Notes: The Polish standards have been calculated from g/GJ to mg/m³ assuming a heating value of 4.1 MJ/kg oil and 21 MJ/kg coal, and 3 % O_2/6 % O_2 respectively, in dry flue gas

Table 11.21
Surface Water Quality Classes and their Prescribed Purposes

Class	Purpose
I	Drinking water supply, supply for production units requiring water of drinking water quality, and natural existence of fish of the family Salmonidae
II	Natural existence of fish other than the family Salmonidae , breeding and raising of farm animals, recreation, water sports, and bathing places
III	Water supply for units other than those requiring water of high quality, agricultural and horticultural irrigation, and irrigation of greenhouses, etc.

Discharges of waste water to surface water as well as to sewerage systems and coastal water are regulated by:
- the 26 December 1986 Regulation of the Council of Ministers on water supply and sewerage installations management and fees for abstracting water and discharging waste waters – Dz. U. 1986, no. 47, item 234, changes: 1989, no. 4, item 25, 1990, no. 22, item 14 and no. 89, item 520;
- the 25 June 1990 Regulation of the Council of Ministers on fines for breaching rules on discharging waste water to water bodies or to soil – Dz. U. 1990, no. 42, item 244 and no. 88, item 514;
- the 5 November 1991 Regulation of the Minister of Environmental Protection, Natural Resources and Forestry on classes of water quality and regulations on discharging waste waters to water bodies or to soil;
- the 5 November 1991 Regulation of the Minister of Environmental Protection, Natural Resources and Forestry on establishing protective zones around water sources and water abstraction points;
- the 21 December 1991 Regulation of the Council of Ministers on fees for special use of water and water installations – Dz. U. 1991, no.125.

Table 11.22
Pollution Limits for Inland Surface Water, by Water Quality Class

Index	Unit	Water quality class		
		I	II	III
Dissolved Oxygen	mg O$_2$/l	≥ 6	≥ 5	≥ 4
5 Day Biochemical Oxygen Demand (BOD$_5$)	mg O$_2$/l	≤ 4	≤ 8	≤ 12
Chlorides:	mg Cl/l	≤ 250	≤ 300	≤ 400
– Sulphates	mg SO$_4$/l	≤ 150	≤ 200	≤ 250
– Ammonia Nitrogen	mg N$_{NH4}$/l	≤ 1.0	≤ 3.0	≤ 6.0
– Nitrate Nitrogen	mg N$_{NO3}$/l	≤ 1.5	≤ 7.0	≤ 15.0
– Total Iron	mg Fe/l	≤ 1.0	≤ 1.5	≤ 2.0
– Volatile Phenols	mg/l	≤ 0.005	≤ 0.02	≤ 0.05
Detergents	mg/l	≤ 1.0	≤ 2.0	≤ 3.0
Mercury	mg Hg/l	≤ 0.001	≤ 0.005	≤ 0.01

Table 11.23
Pollution Limits for Waste Water Discharged to Water Bodies or Soil

Index	Unit	Value
Temperature	Dgr C	35.0
BOD$_5$	mg O$_2$/l	30.0
Chemical Oxygen Demand dichromium method (COD$_{Cr}$)	mg O$_2$/l	150.0
Concentration of		
– Volatile Phenols	mg/l	0.5
– Lead	mg Pb/l	0.5
– Cadmium	mg Cd/l	0.1
– Sulphides	mg S/l	0.2
– Ammonia Nitrogen	mg N$_{NH4}$/l	6.0
– Total Phosphate	mg P/l	5.0
– Total Iron	mg Fe/l	10.0
– Chlorides	mg Cl/l	1 000.0
– Suspended Solids	mg/l	50.0

Table 11.24
Polish and German Effluent Standards

	Poland	Germany[1]
Oil (mg/l)	50.0	2.0
Phenols (mg/l)	0.5	0.15
SS (mg/l)	50.0	30.0
COD mg/l)	150.0	100.0
BOD$_5$ (mg/l)	30.0	25.0
Sulphides (mg/l)	0.2	0.6
pH	6.5-9.0	–

1. The German standards are specific for refineries. The Polish standards are common for all industry, and more stringent requirements are specified in permits.

Table 11.25
Solid Waste Disposal by Hard Coal Industry, 1988-93

Year	Amont of waste (1 000 tonnes)			Change (%)
	Run-of-Mine Reject	Preparation Reject	Total	
1988	63 061.6	17 429.5	80 491.2	n.a.
1989	57 607.8	15 324.8	72 932.6	-9
1990	46 270.0	16 936.0	63 206.0	-13
1991	46 913.9	8 798.5	55 712.5	-12
1992	44 972.6	7 505.1	52 477.7	-6
1993	45 368.8	7 712.6	53 081.4	1

Source: Institute of Waste Management, Katowice

Table 11.26
Environment Fees and Fines, 1989-1993
(Zl million)

Year	Type of Pollution	Fees		Fines		Total
		Assessed	Collected	Assessed	Collected	Collected
1989	Water Pollution of this:	39 196	36 567	24 698	9 818	46 385
	saline water	10 463	8 617	1	1	8 618
	Air Pollution of this:	56 997	58 392	1 868	1 846	60 238
	NO_x	1 622	1 520	7	4	1 524
	SO_4	14 580	12 956	105	75	13 031
	Solid Wastes	22 060	24 221	244	475	24 696
1990	Water Pollution of this:	58 859	63 771	18 739	11 905	75 676
	saline water	16 167	19 188	791	791	19 979
	Air Pollution of this:	125 764	121 605	3 449	3 613	125 218
	NO_x	6 808	6 411	19	19	6 430
	SO_4	67 381	66 987	323	319	67 306
	Solid Wastes	33 854	36 373	3 390	1 841	38 214
1991	Water Pollution of this:	1 646 648	1 132 874	28 638	72 834	1 205 708
	saline water	653 788	404 963	20 629	25 199	430 162
	Air Pollution of this:	2 626 745	2 143 716	82 612	19 025	2 162 741
	NO_x	400 957	340 346	3 389	291	340 637
	SO_4	1 490 311	1 283 796	37 214	6 166	1 289 962
	Solid Wastes	718 359	455 868	8 468	1 050	456 918
1992	Water Pollution of this:	2 829 424	1 423 445	305 652	84 873	1 508 318
	saline water	1 196 824	70 696	13 474	1 807	72 503
	Air Pollution of this:	3 527 719	2 955 055	288 527	44 182	2 999 237
	NO_x	566 713	453 484	4 581	2 501	455 985
	SO_4	1 770 136	1 519 413	69 077	22 226	1 541 639
	Solid Wastes	890 539	761 498	29 551	4 525	766 023
1993	Water Pollution of this:	2 460 641	1 357 630	523 804	149 847	1 507 477
	saline water	790 394	37 192	93 704	10 695	47 887
	Air Pollution of this:	4 703 426	3 798 481	434 604	55 307	3 853 788
	NO_x	760 501	648 418	65 478	4 599	653 017
	SO_4	2 224 481	3 376 827	120 761	24 114	3 400 941
	Solid Wastes	1 675 030	1 141 767	382 012	2 279	1 144 046

Source : National Fund for Environmental Protection

Table 11.27
Conventions signed by Poland, under coordination by the Ministry of Environmental Protection, Natural Resources and Forestry:

No.	Convention/Protocol	Date of signature	Date of ratification or entry into force
1.	Convention on Wetlands of International Importance Especially as a Waterfowl Habitat, Ramsar	2.2.1971	22.3.1978
1.1	Protocol to Amend the Ramsar Convention, Paris	3.12.1982	8.2.1984
2.	Convention on International Trade in Endangered Species of Wild Fauna and Flora, Washington	3.3.1973	12.3.1990
3.	Convention on Long-range Transboundary Air Pollution, Geneva	13.11.1979	17.10.1985
3.1	Protocol to the Convention on Long-range Transboundary Air Pollution, on Long-term Financing of the Co-operative Programme for Monitoring and Evaluation of the Long-range Transmission of Air Pollutants in Europe, Geneva	28.9.1984	13.12.1988
3.2	Protocol Concerning the Control of Emissions of Nitrogen or their Transboundary Fluxes, Sofia	1.11.1988	
4.	Convention for the Protection of the Ozone Layer, Vienna	22.3.1985	11.10.1990
4.1	Protocol on Substances that Deplete the Ozone Layer, Montreal	16.9.1987	11.10.1990
5.	Convention on the Protection of the Marine Environment of the Baltic Sea Area, Helsinki	22.3.1974 9.4.1992	3.5.1980
6.	Convention on the Control of Transboundary Movement of Hazardous Wastes and Their Disposal, Basel	22.3.1989	10.1.1992
7.	Convention on Environmental Impact Assessment in a Transboundary Context, Espoo	25.2.1991	
8.	Convention on the Transboundary Effects of Industrial Accidents, Helsinki	18.3.1992	
9.	Conv. on Protection and Use of Transboundary Watercourses and International Lakes, Helsinki	17.3.1992	
10.	Framework Convention on Climate Change, Rio de Janeiro	5.6.1992	
11.	Convention on Biological Diversity, Rio de Janeiro	5.6.1992	

Convention signed by Poland, under co-ordination by other ministries:

No.	Convention/Protocol	Date of signature	Date of ratification or entry into force
1.	Convention Concerning the Use of White Lead in Painting, Geneva	25.10.1921	21.6.1924
2.	Convention for the Establishment of the European and Mediterranean Plant Protection Organisation, Paris	8.4.1951	5.9.1958
3.	International Convention for the Prevention of Pollution of the Sea by Oil, London	12.5.1954	28.5.1961 with reservation/ declaration
4.	Convention on the Continental Shelf, Geneva	29.4.1958	10.6.1964
5.	Convention on the High Seas, Geneva	29.4.1958	30.9.1962
6.	North-East Atlantic Fisheries Convention, London	24.1.1959	27.6.1963, with drawal 29.4.1984

7.	Convention Concerning the Protection of Workers Against Ionizing Radiations, Geneva	22.6.1960	23.12.1965
8.	Convention for the International Council for the Exploration of the Sea, Copenhagen	12.9.1964	22.7.1968
9.	Convention on the Conservation of the Living Resources of the South-East Atlantic, Rome	23.10.1969	1.4.1972
10.	International Convention on Civil Liability for Oil Pollution Damage, Brussels	29.11.1969	16.6.1976
11.	International Convention Relating to Intervention on the High Seas in Cases of Oil Pollution Casualities, Brussels	29.11.1969	30.3.1983
12.	International Convention on the Establishment of an International Fund for Compensation for Oil Pollution Damage, Brussels	18.12.1971	15.12.1985
13.	Convention for the Conservation of Antarctic Seals, London	1.6.1972	14.9.1980
14.	Convention on the Prohibition of the Development, Production and Stockpiling of Bacteriological (Biological) and Toxic Weapons, and on Their Destruction, London, Moscow, Washington	10.4.1972	26.3.1975
15.	Convention Concerning the Protection of the World Cultural and Natural Heritage, Paris	23.11.1972	29.9.1976
16.	Convention on the Prevention of Marine Pollution by Dumping of Wastes and Other Matter, London, Mexico City, Moscow, Washington	29.12.1972	22.2.1979
17.	Convention on Fishing and Conservation of the Living Resources in the Baltic Sea, Gdansk	13.9.1973	28.7.1974
18.	Protocol of 1978 Relating to the International Convention for the Prevention of Pollution from Ships, London	17.2.1978	1.7.1986
19.	Convention on the Prohibition of Military or Any Other Hostile Use of Environmental Modification Techniques, Geneva	18.5.1977	5.10.1978
20.	Convention on Future Multilateral Cooperation in the Northwest Atlantic Fisheries, Ottawa	24.10.1978	6.11.1979
21.	Convention on the Physical Protection of Nuclear Material, Vienna, New York	3.3.1980	8.2.1987
22.	Convention on the Conservation of Antarctic Marine Living Resources, Canberra	20.5.1980	27.4.1984
23.	Convention on Future Multilateral Cooperation in North-east Atlantic Fisheries, London	8.11.1980	2.11.1984
24.	Convention on the Law of the Sea, Montego Bay		10.12.1982
25.	Convention on Early Notification of a Nuclear Accident, Vienna	26.9.1986	24.4.1988 with reservation/ declaration
26.	Convention on Assistance in the Case of a Nuclear Accident or Radiological Emergency, Vienna	26.9.1986	24.4.1988 with reservation/ declaration
27.	Joint Protocol Relating to the Application of the Vienna Convention and the Paris Convention, Vienna	21.9.1988	23.1.1990
28.	International Convention on Salvage, London	12.6.1990	

ENERGY BALANCES, KEY STATISTICAL TABLES

Poland Primary Energy Balances

1988

Thousand toe

	Coal	Crude Oil	Petroleum Products	Gas	Nuclear	Hydro	Elec- tricity	Heat	Total
Indigenous Production	120278	176	.	3702	.	361	.	.	124517
Import	761	15077	3127	5958	.	.	1071	.	25993
Export	-21270	.	-617	.	.	.	-686	.	-22573
Intl. Marine Bunkers	.	.	-1467	.	.	.	.	.	-1467
Stock Changes	-1372	-157	39	-56	.	.	.	.	-1546
TPES	98396	15096	1082	9603	.	361	385	.	124924

1989

Thousand toe

	Coal	Crude Oil	Petroleum Products	Gas	Nuclear	Hydro	Elec- tricity	Heat	Total
Indigenous Production	111137	178	.	3428	.	323	.	.	115067
Import	656	14854	3275	6299	.	.	1037	.	26121
Export	-19435	.	-1013	-1	.	.	-883	.	-21332
Intl. Marine Bunkers	.	.	-1405	.	.	.	.	.	-1405
Stock Changes	964	339	-100	-300	.	.	.	.	903
TPES	93322	15372	757	9427	.	323	154	.	119354

1990

Thousand toe

	Coal	Crude Oil	Petroleum Products	Gas	Nuclear	Hydro	Elec- tricity	Heat	Total
Indigenous Production	94459	175	.	2353	.	285	.	.	97273
Import	393	13122	2886	6708	.	.	898	.	24007
Export	-19302	.	-1484	-1	.	.	-987	.	-21774
Intl. Marine Bunkers	.	.	-427	.	.	.	.	.	-427
Stock Changes	-176	-434	-385	-211	.	.	.	.	-1205
TPES	75374	12863	591	8850	.	285	-90	.	97874

Poland 1991

Thousand toe

	Coal	Crude Oil	Petroleum Products	Gas	Nuclear	Hydro	Electricity	Heat	Total
Indigenous Production	90703	173	.	2631	.	293	.	.	93800
Import	38	11547	2702	5267	.	.	577	.	20131
Export	-14324	.	-1395	.	.	.	-802	.	-16521
Intl. Marine Bunkers	.	.	-181	.	.	.	.	.	-181
Stock Changes	-1245	115	275	-33	.	.	.	.	-888
TPES	**75173**	**11835**	**1401**	**7864**	.	**293**	**-225**	.	**96341**
Returns and Transfers	42	.	.	-41	.	.	.	.	.
Statistical Differences	403	-1	153	-1	.	.	1	.	553
Public Electricity	.	.	.	.	.	-293	293	.	.
Autoproducers of Electr.	-7438	.	-949	-49	.	.	675	.	-7761
CHP Plants	-34382	.	-179	-6	.	.	10617	4271	-19679
Autoproducer CHP	.	.	.	.	.	.	.	6382	6382
District Heating	-9675	.	-381	-334	.	.	.	7701	-2688
Gas Works	-244	.	-11	61	.	.	.	.	-194
Petroleum Refineries	-1	-11834	11231	-36	.	.	-32	-290	-962
Coal Transformation	-1025	.	.	.	.	.	.	.	-1025
Liquefaction	.	.	.	.	.	.	.	.	.
Other Transformation	.	.	.	-39	.	.	.	.	-39
Own Use	-1186	.	-54	-242	.	.	-2438	-1737	-5656
Distribution Losses	-57	.	-9	-370	.	.	-1203	.	-1639
TFC	**21610**	.	**11202**	**6807**	.	.	**7688**	**16327**	**63633**
INDUSTRY SECTOR	**7640**	.	**792**	**1960**	.	.	**3244**	**8936**	**22572**
Iron and Steel	3125	.	190	798	.	.	547	947	5607
Chemical	217	.	145	107	.	.	752	2749	3971
(of which:Feedstocks)	.	.	86	.	.	.	.	.	86
Non-ferrous Metals	137	.	20	109	.	.	184	96	547
Non-metallic Minerals	2041	.	87	611	.	.	257	271	3267
Transport Equip. & Mach.	130	.	21	42	.	.	123	369	685
Machinery	455	.	20	169	.	.	366	761	1771
Mining and Quarrying	91	.	42	64	.	.	272	818	1286
Food and Tobacco	929	.	60	47	.	.	258	1119	2414
Paper, Pulp and Printing	49	.	31	2	.	.	170	748	999
Wood and Wood Products	139	.	29	5	.	.	84	228	485
Construction	145	.	134	3	.	.	85	260	627
Textile and Leather	168	.	5	4	.	.	136	552	865
Non-specified Industry	15	.	6	1	.	.	9	17	48
TRANSPORT SECTOR	**429**	.	**7358**	**4**	.	.	**503**	**158**	**8452**
Air	.	.	263	.	.	.	.	.	263
Road	66	.	6710	1	.	.	75	85	6937
Rail	361	.	327	3	.	.	422	61	1175
Internal Navigation	2	.	58	.	.	.	6	11	77
Non-specified Transport	.	.	.	.	.	.	.	.	.
OTHER SECTORS	**13417**	.	**1319**	**3337**	.	.	**3940**	**7230**	**29243**
Agriculture	675	.	1294	6	.	.	716	222	2913
Public/Commerce	.	.	.	.	.	.	.	.	.
Residential	.	.	.	.	.	.	1738	7008	8746
Non-specified Other	12742	.	25	3330	.	.	1487	.	17583
Non-Energy Use	124	.	1713	1506	.	.	.	.	3343
MEMO ITEMS:									
Electricity Generated (GWh)	*127620*	.	*3534*	*151*	.	*3410*	.	.	*134715*
Public	.	.	.	.	.	*3410*	.	.	*3410*
Autoproducers	.	.	.	.	.	.	.	.	.
Public CHP	*122887*	.	*555*	*12*	.	.	.	.	*123454*
Autoproducers CHP	*4733*	.	*2979*	*139*	.	.	.	.	*7851*

Source: CIE

Poland 1992

Thousand toe

	Coal	Crude Oil	Petroleum Products	Gas	Nuclear	Hydro	Electricity	Heat	Total
Indigenous Production	89225	216	.	2559	.	307	.	.	92306
Import	91	13233	1636	5336	.	.	433	.	20729
Export	-14882	.	-915	-2	.	.	-780	.	-16579
Intl. Marine Bunkers	.	.	-287	.	.	.	.	.	-287
Stock Changes	-608	-106	67	-128	.	.	.	.	-774
TPES	73826	13343	502	7764	.	307	-347	.	95395
Returns and Transfers	18	96	-1	-18	.	.	.	.	95
Statistical Differences	-43	-282	309	3	.	.	.	-1	-14
Public Electricity	.	.	.	.	.	-307	307	.	.
Autoproducers of Electr.	-7153	.	-929	-39	.	.	671	.	-7449
CHP Plants	-33212	.	-152	-6	.	.	10438	4191	-18741
Autoproducer CHP	.	.	.	.	.	.	.	6259	6259
District Heating	-8817	.	-306	-187	.	.	.	6860	-2450
Gas Works	-185	.	-10	32	.	.	.	.	-163
Petroleum Refineries	-1	-13157	12229	-36	.	.	-34	-285	-1284
Coal Transformation	-1043	.	.	.	.	.	.	.	-1043
Liquefaction	.	.	.	.	.	.	.	.	.
Other Transformation	.	.	.	-49	.	.	.	.	-49
Own Use	-1144	.	-56	-322	.	.	-2377	-1577	-5476
Distribution Losses	-33	.	-18	-367	.	.	-1299	.	-1717
TFC	22213	.	11568	6775	.	.	7359	15447	63363
INDUSTRY SECTOR	7297	.	800	1639	.	.	3055	8028	20819
Iron and Steel	3186	.	130	543	.	.	480	896	5235
Chemical	240	.	203	108	.	.	724	2669	3945
(of which:Feedstocks)	.	.	4	.	.	.	.	.	4
Non-ferrous Metals	76	.	3	28	.	.	168	57	333
Non-metallic Minerals	1933	.	104	590	.	.	251	238	3115
Transport Equip. & Mach.	85	.	17	41	.	.	111	326	581
Machinery	374	.	24	131	.	.	342	661	1532
Mining and Quarrying	146	.	71	129	.	.	288	592	1225
Food and Tobacco	845	.	57	55	.	.	238	980	2175
Paper, Pulp and Printing	39	.	35	1	.	.	168	690	932
Wood and Wood Products	132	.	34	6	.	.	86	229	487
Construction	96	.	116	3	.	.	66	179	461
Textile and Leather	135	.	5	5	.	.	128	503	776
Non-specified Industry	11	.	1	.	.	.	4	6	23
TRANSPORT SECTOR	311	.	7408	4	.	.	451	148	8322
Air	.	.	438	.	.	.	.	.	438
Road	68	.	6659	1	.	.	68	70	6866
Rail	241	.	262	3	.	.	377	68	952
Internal Navigation	2	.	49	.	.	.	6	10	67
Non-specified Transport	.	.	.	.	.	.	.	.	.
OTHER SECTORS	14513	.	1524	3766	.	.	3853	7269	30926
Agriculture	472	.	1479	1	.	.	685	150	2787
Public/Commerce	.	.	.	.	.	.	.	.	.
Residential	276	.	.	18	.	.	1629	7119	9042
Non-specified Other	13766	.	45	3748	.	.	1538	.	19097
Non-Energy Use	92	.	1836	1365	.	.	.	.	3293
MEMO ITEMS:									
Electricity Generated (GWh)	125575	.	3488	117	.	3571	.	.	132751
Public	.	.	.	.	.	3571	.	.	3571
Autoproducers	.	.	.	.	.	.	.	.	.
Public CHP	120815	.	548	12	.	.	.	.	121375
Autoproducers CHP	4760	.	2940	105	.	.	.	.	7805

Source: CIE

Poland 1993

Thousand toe

	Coal	Crude Oil	Petroleum Products	Gas	Nuclear	Hydro	Electricity	Heat	Total
Indigenous Production	89179	255	.	3270	.	307	.	.	93011
Import	92	14189	1356	4686	.	.	482	.	20804
Export	-16602	.	-1026	-13	.	.	-689	.	-18330
Intl. Marine Bunkers	.	.	-126	.	.	.	.	.	-126
Stock Changes	1918	-494	-31	212	.	.	.	.	1606
TPES	**74587**	**13950**	**173**	**8155**	**.**	**307**	**-207**	**.**	**96965**
Returns and Transfers	9	63	13	-9	.	.	.	.	76
Statistical Differences	-269	-102	335	3	.	.	1	-1	-32
Public Electricity	.	.	.	.	.	-307	314	.	6
Autoproducers of Electr.	-6722	.	.	-49	.	.	685	.	-6085
CHP Plants	-33070	.	-168	-5	.	.	10512	4042	-18689
Autoproducer CHP	-451	.	-962	.	.	.	.	6036	4623
District Heating	-9040	.	-367	-167	.	.	.	7545	-2030
Gas Works	-118	.	-8	46	.	.	.	.	-80
Petroleum Refineries	-1	-13911	13016	-36	.	.	-37	-295	-1264
Coal Transformation	-917	.	.	.	.	.	.	.	-917
Liquefaction	.	.	.	.	.	.	.	.	.
Other Transformation	.	.	.	-60	.	.	.	.	-60
Own Use	-1074	.	-129	-1120	.	.	-2397	-1745	-6465
Distribution Losses	-19	.	-14	-610	.	.	-1456	.	-2099
TFC	**22915**	**.**	**11889**	**6148**	**.**	**.**	**7415**	**15582**	**63949**
INDUSTRY SECTOR	**7204**	**.**	**752**	**1818**	**.**	**.**	**3203**	**7888**	**20864**
Iron and Steel	3137	.	94	551	.	.	528	860	5169
Chemical	188	.	170	252	.	.	742	2659	4011
(of which:Feedstocks)	.	.	104	.	.	.	.	.	104
Non-ferrous Metals	78	.	3	35	.	.	173	54	342
Non-metallic Minerals	1956	.	102	574	.	.	259	218	3108
Transport Equip. & Mach.	78	.	21	34	.	.	108	303	545
Machinery	355	.	34	161	.	.	371	684	1606
Mining and Quarrying	160	.	66	129	.	.	289	394	1038
Food and Tobacco	825	.	79	63	.	.	267	1102	2336
Paper, Pulp and Printing	39	.	42	1	.	.	169	718	969
Wood and Wood Products	115	.	39	4	.	.	91	242	491
Construction	125	.	97	7	.	.	64	150	443
Textile and Leather	138	.	5	6	.	.	136	499	785
Non-specified Industry	10	.	.	1	.	.	5	6	21
TRANSPORT SECTOR	**307**	**.**	**7676**	**4**	**.**	**.**	**460**	**161**	**8608**
Air	.	.	610	.	.	.	.	.	610
Road	65	.	6754	1	.	.	68	67	6955
Rail	240	.	260	2	.	.	385	86	974
Internal Navigation	2	.	52	.	.	.	7	8	69
Non-specified Transport	.	.	.	.	.	.	.	.	.
OTHER SECTORS	**15281**	**.**	**1627**	**3068**	**.**	**.**	**3752**	**7531**	**31259**
Agriculture	376	.	1550	3	.	.	574	141	2644
Public/Commerce	.	.	.	.	.	.	.	.	.
Residential	.	.	.	.	.	.	1567	7389	8956
Non-specified Other	14905	.	77	3065	.	.	1611	.	19658
Non-Energy Use	123	.	1834	1258	.	.	.	.	3215
MEMO ITEMS:									
Electricity Generated (GWh)	126553	.	3605	113	.	3572	.	.	133843
Public	.	.	.	.	.	3572	.	.	3572
Autoproducers	.	.	.	.	.	.	.	.	.
Public CHP	121681	.	605	15	.	.	.	.	122301
Autoproducers CHP	4872	.	3000	98	.	.	.	.	7970

Source: CIE

POLAND 1993

SUPPLY AND CONSUMPTION	1000 metric tons					(TJ)				GWh	(TJ)
	Hard Coal	Brown Coal	Coking Coal	Patent Fuel	BKB	Natural Gas	Gas Works	Coke Ovens	Blast Furnaces	Electricity	Heat
Production	130047	68105	10282	-	102	144775	3640	84170	38158	133843	737957
From Other Sources	432	-	-	-	-	7389	355	1309	-	-	-
Imports	129	1	3	1	-	217865	183	-	-	5600	-
Exports	-22968	-909	-1892	-9	-	-602	-	-	-	-8011	-
Intl. Marine Bunkers	-	-	-	-	-	-	-	-	-	-	-
Stock Changes	2944	24	143	19	-96	9885	-	-	-	-	-
DOMESTIC SUPPLY	**110584**	**67221**	**8536**	**11**	**6**	**379312**	**4178**	**85479**	**38158**	**131432**	**737957**
Returns to Supply	-	-	-	-	-	-	-	-	-	-	-
Transfers	-	-	-	-	-	-616	186	425	-	-	-
TOTAL REQUIREMENTS	110584	67221	8536	11	6	378696	4364	85904	38158	131432	737957
Statistical Differences	3	-2	-5	-	-	-	105	-	-	22	-
TRANSFORMATION	**82480**	**66747**	**1744**	**11**	**2**	**14653**	**263**	**10292**	**11928**	**-**	**-**
Transfer to Solids	13742	205	55	-	-	2779	-	-	271	-	-
Transfer to Gases	171	21	1325	-	-	1855	-	-	-	-	-
Petroleum Refineries	-	-	-	-	-	-	-	-	-	-	-
Public Electricity + CHP	39224	66178	-	-	-	222	-	-	-	-	-
Autoproducer Electricity + CHP	12279	115	-	-	-	2289	-	8572	10099	-	-
District Heating Plants	17064	228	364	11	2	7508	263	1720	1558	-	-
Other Transformation Sector	-	-	-	-	-	-	-	-	-	-	-
ENERGY SECTOR	**326**	**11**	**9**	**-**	**-**	**53790**	**-**	**37551**	**1853**	**28299**	**85452**
Coal Mines	189	10	6	-	-	546	-	-	-	8484	20033
Oil and Gas Extraction	-	-	-	-	-	2354	-	-	-	85	37
Petroleum Refineries	1	-	-	-	-	1684	-	-	-	429	12358
Electric Plants	-	-	-	-	-	-	-	-	-	9107	4360
Pumped Storage (Elec.)	-	-	-	-	-	-	-	-	-	2879	-
Other Energy Sector	136	1	3	-	-	49206	-	37551	1853	7315	48664
Distribution Losses	-	-	-	-	-	28375	-	898	-	16929	-
FINAL CONSUMPTION	**27781**	**461**	**6778**	**-**	**4**	**281878**	**4206**	**37163**	**24377**	**86226**	**652505**
INDUSTRY SECTOR	**6073**	**46**	**4101**	**-**	**2**	**81118**	**3466**	**27442**	**24377**	**37241**	**330306**
Iron and Steel	75	-	3062	-	-	25057	570	23336	24274	6143	36006
Chemical and Petrochemical	192	5	63	-	-	11579	140	1873	11	8623	111347
of which: Feedstocks	-	-	-	-	-	-	-	-	-	-	-
Non-Ferrous Metals	30	-	92	-	-	1615	-	47	-	2013	2244
Non-Metallic Minerals	3062	10	374	-	-	24090	2620	1371	92	3007	9126
Transport Equipment	123	-	16	-	-	1603	-	10	-	1260	12685
Machinery	423	1	165	-	-	7376	131	669	-	4315	28653
Mining and Quarrying	104	-	155	-	2	6010	-	9	-	3361	16511
Food and Tobacco	1368	19	107	-	-	2922	1	113	-	3103	46149
Paper, Pulp and Print	60	-	9	-	-	67	-	3	-	1969	30056
Wood and Wood Products	201	4	7	-	-	171	-	2	-	1058	10122
Construction	192	1	30	-	-	303	3	4	-	747	6266
Textiles and Leather	228	6	18	-	-	299	1	4	-	1587	20892
Non Specified	15	-	3	-	-	26	-	1	-	55	249
TRANSPORT SECTOR	**354**	**2**	**126**	**-**	**1**	**160**	**8**	**6**	**-**	**5360**	**6844**
Air	-	-	-	-	-	-	-	-	-	10	106
Road	82	2	20	-	-	48	3	4	-	786	2803
Rail	270	-	105	-	1	111	5	2	-	4479	3604
Internal Navigation	2	-	1	-	-	1	-	-	-	85	331
Non Specified	-	-	-	-	-	-	-	-	-	-	-
OTHER SECTORS	**21329**	**412**	**2385**	**-**	**1**	**142052**	**732**	**9715**	**-**	**43625**	**315355**
Agriculture	564	67	13	-	-	146	1	1	-	6671	5918
Commerce and Publ. Serv.	-	-	-	-	-	-	-	-	-	-	-
Residential	-	-	-	-	-	-	-	-	-	18219	309437
Non Specified	20765	345	2372	-	1	141906	731	9714	-	18735	-
NON-ENERGY USE	**25**	**1**	**166**	**-**	**-**	**58548**	**-**	**-**	**-**	**-**	**-**
in Industry	18	1	166	-	-	58548	-	-	-	-	-
in Transport	-	-	-	-	-	-	-	-	-	-	-
in Other Sectors	-	-	-	-	-	-	-	-	-	-	-

Sources: AEEF, MOL, sectetariat estimates

POLAND 1993

											1000 metric tons		
Crude Oil	NGL	Feedstocks /Additives	Refinery Gas	LPG + Ethane	Motor Gasoline	Aviation Gasoline	Jet Fuel	Kerosene	Gas/ Diesel	Residual Fuel Oil	Naphtha	Petrol. Coke	Other Prod.
257	-	-	293	170	3172	-	229	12	4955	3341	850	-	880
-	-	-	-	-	-	-	-	-	-	-	-	-	-
13647	-	459	1	2	643	8	119	-	455		-	-	61
-	-	-	-	-	-	-	-14	-	-3	-1005	-	-	-45
-	-	-	-	-	-	-	-	-	-47	-81	-	-	-
-496	-	-	-	-	-39	-2	1	-	3	-4	-	-	13
13408	-	**459**	**294**	**172**	**3776**	**6**	**335**	**12**	**5363**	**2251**	**850**	**-**	**909**
-	-	59	-	-	-	-	-	-	-	-	-	-	-
-	-	-	-	1	132	-2	-8	-	-6	-	-	-	-117
13408	-	**518**	**294**	**173**	**3908**	**4**	**327**	**12**	**5357**	**2251**	**850**	**-**	**792**
-	-	-	-	-	-	-	-	-	-	348	-	-	-
13408	-	**518**	**17**	**8**	-	-	-	-	**468**	**1523**	-	-	-
-	-	-	-	-	-	-	-	-	-	-	-	-	-
-	-	-	-	7	-	-	-	-	-	-	-	-	-
13408	-	518	-	1	-	-	-	-	453	-	-	-	-
-	-	-	17	-	-	-	-	-	3	151	-	-	-
-	-	-	-	-	-	-	-	-	2	1000	-	-	-
-	-	-	-	-	-	-	-	-	10	372	-	-	-
-	-	-	**187**	**1**	**2**	-	-	-	**102**	**617**	-	-	-
-	-	-	-	-	1	-	-	-	63	19	-	-	-
-	-	-	-	1	-	-	-	-	3	-	-	-	-
-	-	-	187	1	-	-	-	-	-	595	-	-	-
-	-	-	-	-	-	-	-	-	-	-	-	-	-
-	-	-	-	-	-	-	-	-	-	-	-	-	-
-	-	-	-	-	1	-	-	-	36	3	-	-	-
-	-	-	-	-	10	-	-	-	2	-	-	-	1
-	**-**	**-**	**90**	**164**	**3896**	**4**	**327**	**12**	**4785**	**459**	**850**	**-**	**791**
-	-	-	**90**	**6**	**29**	-	-	-	**223**	**396**	-	-	-
-	-	-	-	-	-	-	-	-	7	90	-	-	-
-	-	-	90	1	7	-	-	-	16	43	-	-	-
-	-	-	*90*	-	-	-	-	-	-	-	-	-	-
-	-	-	-	-	-	-	-	-	2	1	-	-	-
-	-	-	-	1	-	-	-	-	17	88	-	-	-
-	-	-	-	1	5	-	-	-	15	5	-	-	-
-	-	-	-	1	5	-	-	-	15	13	-	-	-
-	-	-	-	-	-	-	-	-	36	23	-	-	-
-	-	-	-	-	-	-	-	-	27	53	-	-	-
-	-	-	-	1	3	-	-	-	1	38	-	-	-
-	-	-	-	1	1	-	-	-	4	34	-	-	-
-	-	-	-	-	8	-	-	-	81	5	-	-	-
-	-	-	-	-	-	-	-	-	2	3	-	-	-
-	-	-	-	-	-	-	-	-	-	-	-	-	-
-	-	-	-	-	**3849**	**4**	**327**	-	**3069**	**30**	-	-	-
-	-	-	-	-	240	4	327	-	1	-	-	-	-
-	-	-	-	-	3601	-	-	-	2801	2	-	-	-
-	-	-	-	-	8	-	-	-	243	-	-	-	-
-	-	-	-	-	-	-	-	-	24	28	-	-	-
-	-	-	-	-	-	-	-	-	-	-	-	-	-
-	-	-	-	**68**	-	-	-	-	**1490**	**8**	-	-	-
-	-	-	-	-	-	-	-	-	1490	8	-	-	-
-	-	-	-	-	-	-	-	-	-	-	-	-	-
-	-	-	-	68	-	-	-	-	-	-	-	-	-
-	-	-	-	**90**	**18**	-	-	**12**	**3**	**25**	**850**	-	**791**
-	-	-	-	-	18	-	-	12	2	-	850	-	791
-	-	-	-	-	-	-	-	-	-	-	-	-	-
-	-	-	-	-	-	-	-	-	-	-	-	-	-

Source: AEEF, MOL, sectretariat estimates

Energy Indicators

	1985	1986	1987	1988	1989	1990	1991	1992	1993
Poland[1]									
TPES (Mtoe)[2]	126.45	128.50	132.87	124.92	119.35	97.87	96.34	95.40	96.96
Oil requirements (Mtoe)	16.35	16.83	16.49	16.18	16.13	13.45	13.24	13.84	14.12
Electricity consumption (TWh)	135.60	140.37	147.49	148.85	147.26	135.27	132.10	128.72	131.43
Population (Millions)	37.20	37.46	37.66	37.86	37.96	38.12	38.00	38.00	38.00
GDP (Billion 1987 $US)	60.06	62.59	63.90	66.49	66.67	58.60	54.16	55.12	57.33
TPES/GDP (Toe per 000 $US)	2.11	2.05	2.08	1.88	1.79	1.67	1.78	1.73	1.69
TPES/Pop. (Toe per capita)	3.40	3.43	3.53	3.30	3.14	2.57	2.54	2.51	2.55
Oil Req./GDP (Toe per 000 $US)	0.27	0.27	0.26	0.24	0.24	0.23	0.24	0.25	0.25
Oil Req./Pop. (Toe per capita)	0.44	0.45	0.44	0.43	0.42	0.35	0.35	0.36	0.37
Elec. con./GDP (kWh per $US)	2.26	2.24	2.31	2.24	2.21	2.31	2.44	2.34	2.29
Elec. con./Pop. (kWh per capita)	3645	3748	3916	3931	3879	3549	3476	3387	3459
OECD Europe									
TPES (Mtoe)[2]	1198.38	1154.65	1232.13	1233.02	1273.37	1331.02	1290.10	1253.90	1222.96
Oil requirements (Mtoe)	685.75	644.04	691.63	678.65	704.87	718.83	668.49	614.39	584.74
Electricity consumption (TWh)	1503.91	1503.41	1615.87	1657.31	1735.26	1826.69	1847.95	1867.66	1873.68
Population (Millions)	420.64	422.62	424.78	427.12	429.71	432.68	435.79	438.76	440.50
GDP (Billion 1987 $US)	4112.40	4228.40	4344.90	4512.90	4659.90	4794.90	4853.20	4901.60	4883.30
TPES/GDP (Toe per 000 $US)	0.29	0.27	0.28	0.27	0.27	0.28	0.27	0.26	0.25
TPES/Pop. (Toe per capita)	2.85	2.73	2.90	2.89	2.96	3.08	2.96	2.86	2.78
Oil Req./GDP (Toe per 000 $US)	0.17	0.15	0.16	0.15	0.15	0.15	0.14	0.13	0.12
Oil Req./Pop. (Toe per capita)	1.63	1.52	1.63	1.59	1.64	1.66	1.53	1.40	1.33
Elec. con./GDP (kWh per $US)	0.37	0.36	0.37	0.37	0.37	0.38	0.38	0.38	0.38
Elec. con./Pop. (kWh per capita)	3575	3557	3804	3880	4038	4222	4240	4257	4254

(1) Source of GDP and population data: The World Bank, *World Tables 1992, OECD Economic Outlook June 1994.*
(2) Total Primary Energy Supply

Poland

Total Primary Energy Supply (Mtoe)*

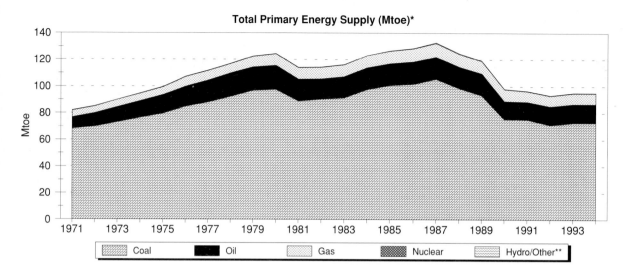

Legend: Coal, Oil, Gas, Nuclear, Hydro/Other**

Oil Product Consumption
(Million Metric Tons)

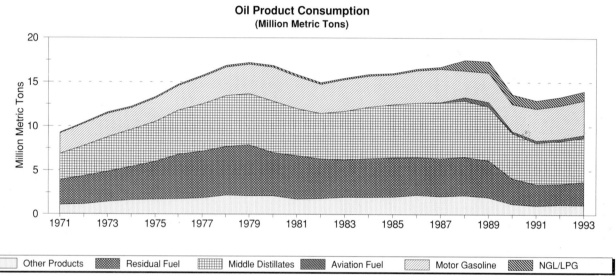

Legend: Other Products, Residual Fuel, Middle Distillates, Aviation Fuel, Motor Gasoline, NGL/LPG

Electricity Production by Fuel (TWh)

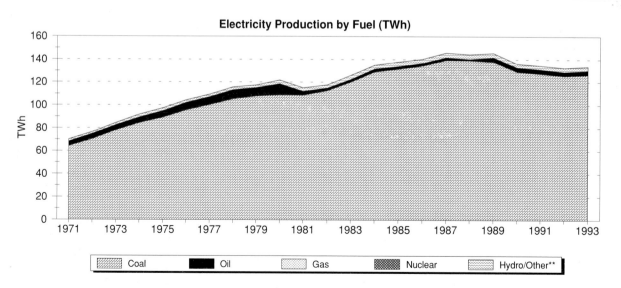

Legend: Coal, Oil, Gas, Nuclear, Hydro/Other**

* Excluding electricity trade. ** Includes electricity generated by traditional fuels and geothermal.

TPES/GDP
Toe per 000 $US

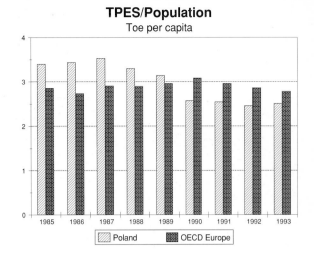

TPES/Population
Toe per capita

Oil Requirements/GDP
Toe per 000 $US

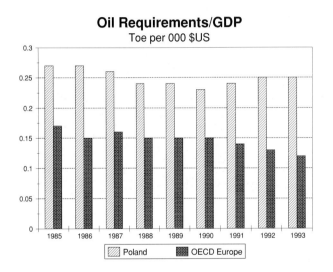

Oil Requirements/Population
Toe per capita

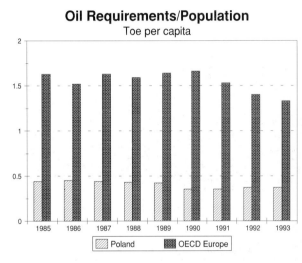

Electricity Consumed/GDP
kWh per $US

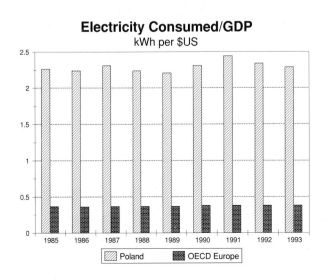

Electricity Consumed/Population
kWh per capita

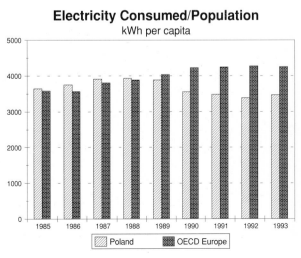

GLOSSARY

bcm	Billion cubic metres	IEA	International Energy Agency
CENTREL	Central European Power Association	IMF	International Monetary Fund
CHP	Combined heat and power, or co-generation	KBN	Komitet Badan Naukowych, State Committee for Scientific Research
CIE	Centrum Informatyki Energetyki, the Energy Information Centre	kg	Kilogram
CIF	Cost, insurance and freight	kJ	Kilojoule
CMEA	Council for Mutual Economic Assistance, also known as Comecon	km	Kilometre
		kV	Kilovolt
CO	Carbon monoxide	kW	Kilowatt
CO_2	Carbon dioxide	kWh	Kilowatt-hour
CPN	Centrala Produktow Naftowych, state oil product wholesaling and retailing enterprise	LFO	Light fuel oil
		LPG	Liquefied petroleum gas
		MJ	Megajoule, 10^6 joules
CZW	now Weglosbyt, joint stock company in charge of domestic coal sales to industry and retailers	MoIT	Ministry of Industry and Trade
		Mt	Million tonnes (metric tons)
		MTBE	Methyl-tertiary-butyl ether
DEC	CPN owned rail tanker rental company	Mtoe	Million tonnes (metric tons) of oil equivalent
DSM	Demand side management	MVA	Million volt amperes
dwt	Deadweight ton(nage)	MW	Megawatt, 10^6 watt
EFTA	European Free Trade Association	n.a.	Not available
EMEP	European Monitoring Environmental Programme	NGL	Natural gas liquids
		NGO	Non-governmental organisation
ERA	Energy Regulatory Authority	NO	Nitrogen monoxide
EU	European Union	NO_2	Nitrogen dioxide
FEWE	Fundacja na rzecz Efektywnego Wykorzystania Energii, the Polish Foundation for Energy Efficiency	NO_x	Nitrogen oxides
		OECD	Organisation for Economic Co-operation and Development
FCC	Fluidal catalytic cracking	PAN	Polish Academy of Sciences
FGD	Flue gas desulphurisation	PERN	Przedsiebiorstwo Eksploatacji Rurociagow Naftowych, state enterprise in charge of crude oil and refined product pipeline transportation and storage
FOB	Free on board		
GATT	General Agreement on Tariffs and Trade		
GDP	Gross domestic product		
GEF	Global Environment Facility		
GJ	Gigajoule, 10^9 joule	PKN	Polska Kompania Naftova, proposed oil holding company
GUS	Glowny Urzad Statystyczny, the Central Statistical Office		
		PKP	Polish railway company
GW	Gigawatt, 10^9 W or 10^6 kW	PJ	Petajoule, 10^{15} joules
HFO	Heavy fuel oil	POGC	Polish Oil and Gas Company

PPGC	Polish Power Grid Company	UCPTE	Union for the Co-ordination of Production and Transmission of Electricity
R&D	Research and development		
SO2	Sulphur dioxide		
tce	Tonnes (metric tons) of coal equivalent	UN-ECE	United Nations Economic Commission for Europe
TFC	Total final consumption of energy	USAID	US Agency for International Development
TJ	Terrajoule, 10^{12} joules	VAT	Value added tax
toe	Tonnes (metric tons) of oil equivalent	VOCs	Volatile organic compounds
		WSE	Warsaw Stock Exchange
TPES	Total primary energy supply	WTO	World Trade Organisation
TWh	Terawatt-hour	Zl	Polish zloty

THE IEA REGISTER

The IEA Register is an on-line database on energy assistance to the Former Soviet Union (FSU) and the Central and Eastern European Countries (CEEC). It contains information on energy assistance projects and serves as a reference point for users wishing to inform themselves about the range of governmental and non-governmental activities in the energy field. It also reduces the possibility of duplication of energy-related assistance to the FSU and CEEC. Finally, by providing information to the Register, donors make their areas of competence known to other members of the private sector and the economies in transition. If you are interested in obtaining access to the Register please contact: Ms. Siobhán Cantwell, tel: (+33 1) 4524 9469 or fax: (+33 1) 4524 1744. Use of the Register is free of charge.

MAIN SALES OUTLETS OF OECD PUBLICATIONS
PRINCIPAUX POINTS DE VENTE DES PUBLICATIONS DE L'OCDE

ARGENTINA – ARGENTINE
Carlos Hirsch S.R.L.
Galería Güemes, Florida 165, 4° Piso
1333 Buenos Aires   Tel. (1) 331.1787 y 331.2391
Telefax: (1) 331.1787

AUSTRALIA – AUSTRALIE
D.A. Information Services
648 Whitehorse Road, P.O.B 163
Mitcham, Victoria 3132   Tel. (03) 873.4411
Telefax: (03) 873.5679

AUSTRIA – AUTRICHE
Gerold & Co.
Graben 31
Wien I   Tel. (0222) 533.50.14

BELGIUM – BELGIQUE
Jean De Lannoy
Avenue du Roi 202
B-1060 Bruxelles   Tel. (02) 538.51.69/538.08.41
Telefax: (02) 538.08.41

CANADA
Renouf Publishing Company Ltd.
1294 Algoma Road
Ottawa, ON K1B 3W8   Tel. (613) 741.4333
Telefax: (613) 741.5439
Stores:
61 Sparks Street
Ottawa, ON K1P 5R1   Tel. (613) 238.8985
211 Yonge Street
Toronto, ON M5B 1M4   Tel. (416) 363.3171
Telefax: (416)363.59.63

Les Éditions La Liberté Inc.
3020 Chemin Sainte-Foy
Sainte-Foy, PQ G1X 3V6   Tel. (418) 658.3763
Telefax: (418) 658.3763

Federal Publications Inc.
165 University Avenue, Suite 701
Toronto, ON M5H 3B8   Tel. (416) 860.1611
Telefax: (416) 860.1608

Les Publications Fédérales
1185 Université
Montréal, QC H3B 3A7   Tel. (514) 954.1633
Telefax : (514) 954.1635

CHINA – CHINE
China National Publications Import
Export Corporation (CNPIEC)
16 Gongti E. Road, Chaoyang District
P.O. Box 88 or 50
Beijing 100704 PR   Tel. (01) 506.6688
Telefax: (01) 506.3101

DENMARK – DANEMARK
Munksgaard Book and Subscription Service
35, Nørre Søgade, P.O. Box 2148
DK-1016 København K   Tel. (33) 12.85.70
Telefax: (33) 12.93.87

FINLAND – FINLANDE
Akateeminen Kirjakauppa
Keskuskatu 1, P.O. Box 128
00100 Helsinki

Subscription Services/Agence d'abonnements :
P.O. Box 23
00371 Helsinki   Tel. (358 0) 12141
Telefax: (358 0) 121.4450

FRANCE
OECD/OCDE
Mail Orders/Commandes par correspondance:
2, rue André-Pascal
75775 Paris Cedex 16   Tel. (33-1) 45.24.82.00
Telefax: (33-1) 49.10.42.76
Telex: 640048 OCDE
Orders via Minitel, France only/
Commandes par Minitel, France exclusivement :
36 15 OCDE

OECD Bookshop/Librairie de l'OCDE :
33, rue Octave-Feuillet
75016 Paris   Tel. (33-1) 45.24.81.67
(33-1) 45.24.81.81

Documentation Française
29, quai Voltaire
75007 Paris   Tel. 40.15.70.00
Gibert Jeune (Droit-Économie)
6, place Saint-Michel
75006 Paris   Tel. 43.25.91.19
Librairie du Commerce International
10, avenue d'Iéna
75016 Paris   Tel. 40.73.34.60
Librairie Dunod
Université Paris-Dauphine
Place du Maréchal de Lattre de Tassigny
75016 Paris   Tel. (1) 44.05.40.13
Librairie Lavoisier
11, rue Lavoisier
75008 Paris   Tel. 42.65.39.95
Librairie L.G.D.J. - Montchrestien
20, rue Soufflot
75005 Paris   Tel. 46.33.89.85
Librairie des Sciences Politiques
30, rue Saint-Guillaume
75007 Paris   Tel. 45.48.36.02
P.U.F.
49, boulevard Saint-Michel
75005 Paris   Tel. 43.25.83.40
Librairie de l'Université
12a, rue Nazareth
13100 Aix-en-Provence   Tel. (16) 42.26.18.08
Documentation Française
165, rue Garibaldi
69003 Lyon   Tel. (16) 78.63.32.23
Librairie Decitre
29, place Bellecour
69002 Lyon   Tel. (16) 72.40.54.54

GERMANY – ALLEMAGNE
OECD Publications and Information Centre
August-Bebel-Allee 6
D-53175 Bonn   Tel. (0228) 959.120
Telefax: (0228) 959.12.17

GREECE – GRÈCE
Librairie Kauffmann
Mavrokordatou 9
106 78 Athens   Tel. (01) 32.55.321
Telefax: (01) 36.33.967

HONG-KONG
Swindon Book Co. Ltd.
13–15 Lock Road
Kowloon, Hong Kong   Tel. 366.80.31
Telefax: 739.49.75

HUNGARY – HONGRIE
Euro Info Service
Margitsziget, Európa Ház
1138 Budapest   Tel. (1) 111.62.16
Telefax : (1) 111.60.61

ICELAND – ISLANDE
Mál Mog Menning
Laugavegi 18, Pósthólf 392
121 Reykjavik   Tel. 162.35.23

INDIA – INDE
Oxford Book and Stationery Co.
Scindia House
New Delhi 110001   Tel.(11) 331.5896/5308
Telefax: (11) 332.5993
17 Park Street
Calcutta 700016   Tel. 240832

INDONESIA – INDONÉSIE
Pdii-Lipi
P.O. Box 269/JKSMG/88
Jakarta 12790   Tel. 583467
Telex: 62 875

ISRAEL
Praedicta
5 Shatner Street
P.O. Box 34030
Jerusalem 91430   Tel. (2) 52.84.90/1/2
Telefax: (2) 52.84.93
R.O.Y.
P.O. Box 13056
Tel Aviv 61130   Tél. (3) 49.61.08
Telefax (3) 544.60.39

ITALY – ITALIE
Libreria Commissionaria Sansoni
Via Duca di Calabria 1/1
50125 Firenze   Tel. (055) 64.54.15
Telefax: (055) 64.12.57
Via Bartolini 29
20155 Milano   Tel. (02) 36.50.83
Editrice e Libreria Herder
Piazza Montecitorio 120
00186 Roma   Tel. 679.46.28
Telefax: 678.47.51
Libreria Hoepli
Via Hoepli 5
20121 Milano   Tel. (02) 86.54.46
Telefax: (02) 805.28.86
Libreria Scientifica
Dott. Lucio de Biasio 'Aeiou'
Via Coronelli, 6
20146 Milano   Tel. (02) 48.95.45.52
Telefax: (02) 48.95.45.48

JAPAN – JAPON
OECD Publications and Information Centre
Landic Akasaka Building
2-3-4 Akasaka, Minato-ku
Tokyo 107   Tel. (81.3) 3586.2016
Telefax: (81.3) 3584.7929

KOREA – CORÉE
Kyobo Book Centre Co. Ltd.
P.O. Box 1658, Kwang Hwa Moon
Seoul   Tel. 730.78.91
Telefax: 735.00.30

MALAYSIA – MALAISIE
Co-operative Bookshop Ltd.
University of Malaya
P.O. Box 1127, Jalan Pantai Baru
59700 Kuala Lumpur
Malaysia   Tel. 756.5000/756.5425
Telefax: 757.3661

MEXICO – MEXIQUE
Revistas y Periodicos Internacionales S.A. de C.V.
Florencia 57 - 1004
Mexico, D.F. 06600   Tel. 207.81.00
Telefax : 208.39.79

NETHERLANDS – PAYS-BAS
SDU Uitgeverij Plantijnstraat
Externe Fondsen
Postbus 20014
2500 EA's-Gravenhage   Tel. (070) 37.89.880
Voor bestellingen: Telefax: (070) 34.75.778

**NEW ZEALAND
NOUVELLE-ZÉLANDE**
Legislation Services
P.O. Box 12418
Thorndon, Wellington   Tel. (04) 496.5652
                              Telefax: (04) 496.5698

NORWAY – NORVÈGE
Narvesen Info Center – NIC
Bertrand Narvesens vei 2
P.O. Box 6125 Etterstad
0602 Oslo 6   Tel. (022) 57.33.00
                             Telefax: (022) 68.19.01

PAKISTAN
Mirza Book Agency
65 Shahrah Quaid-E-Azam
Lahore 54000   Tel. (42) 353.601
                             Telefax: (42) 231.730

PHILIPPINE – PHILIPPINES
International Book Center
5th Floor, Filipinas Life Bldg.
Ayala Avenue
Metro Manila   Tel. 81.96.76
                          Telex 23312 RHP PH

PORTUGAL
Livraria Portugal
Rua do Carmo 70-74
Apart. 2681
1200 Lisboa   Tel.: (01) 347.49.82/5
                          Telefax: (01) 347.02.64

SINGAPORE – SINGAPOUR
Gower Asia Pacific Pte Ltd.
Golden Wheel Building
41, Kallang Pudding Road, No. 04-03
Singapore 1334   Tel. 741.5166
                             Telefax: 742.9356

SPAIN – ESPAGNE
Mundi-Prensa Libros S.A.
Castelló 37, Apartado 1223
Madrid 28001   Tel. (91) 431.33.99
                             Telefax: (91) 575.39.98

Libreria Internacional AEDOS
Consejo de Ciento 391
08009 – Barcelona   Tel. (93) 488.30.09
                             Telefax: (93) 487.76.59
Llibreria de la Generalitat
Palau Moja
Rambla dels Estudis, 118
08002 – Barcelona
              (Subscripcions) Tel. (93) 318.80.12
              (Publicacions) Tel. (93) 302.67.23
                             Telefax: (93) 412.18.54

SRI LANKA
Centre for Policy Research
c/o Colombo Agencies Ltd.
No. 300-304, Galle Road
Colombo 3   Tel. (1) 574240, 573551-2
                  Telefax: (1) 575394, 510711

SWEDEN – SUÈDE
Fritzes Information Center
Box 16356
Regeringsgatan 12
106 47 Stockholm   Tel. (08) 690.90.90
                             Telefax: (08) 20.50.21

Subscription Agency/Agence d'abonnements :
Wennergren-Williams Info AB
P.O. Box 1305
171 25 Solna   Tel. (08) 705.97.50
                             Téléfax : (08) 27.00.71

SWITZERLAND – SUISSE
Maditec S.A. (Books and Periodicals - Livres
et périodiques)
Chemin des Palettes 4
Case postale 266
1020 Renens   Tel. (021) 635.08.65
                             Telefax: (021) 635.07.80

Librairie Payot S.A.
4, place Pépinet
CP 3212
1002 Lausanne   Tel. (021) 341.33.48
                             Telefax: (021) 341.33.45

Librairie Unilivres
6, rue de Candolle
1205 Genève   Tel. (022) 320.26.23
                             Telefax: (022) 329.73.18

Subscription Agency/Agence d'abonnements :
Dynapresse Marketing S.A.
38 avenue Vibert
1227 Carouge   Tel.: (022) 308.07.89
                             Telefax : (022) 308.07.99

See also – Voir aussi :
OECD Publications and Information Centre
August-Bebel-Allee 6
D-53175 Bonn (Germany)   Tel. (0228) 959.120
                             Telefax: (0228) 959.12.17

TAIWAN – FORMOSE
Good Faith Worldwide Int'l. Co. Ltd.
9th Floor, No. 118, Sec. 2
Chung Hsiao E. Road
Taipei   Tel. (02) 391.7396/391.7397
                   Telefax: (02) 394.9176

THAILAND – THAÏLANDE
Suksit Siam Co. Ltd.
113, 115 Fuang Nakhon Rd.
Opp. Wat Rajbopith
Bangkok 10200   Tel. (662) 225.9531/2
                             Telefax: (662) 222.5188

TURKEY – TURQUIE
Kültür Yayinlari Is-Türk Ltd. Sti.
Atatürk Bulvari No. 191/Kat 13
Kavaklidere/Ankara   Tel. 428.11.40 Ext. 2458
Dolmabahce Cad. No. 29
Besiktas/Istanbul   Tel. 260.71.88
                             Telex: 43482B

UNITED KINGDOM – ROYAUME-UNI
HMSO
Gen. enquiries   Tel. (071) 873 0011
Postal orders only:
P.O. Box 276, London SW8 5DT
Personal Callers HMSO Bookshop
49 High Holborn, London WC1V 6HB
                             Telefax: (071) 873 8200
Branches at: Belfast, Birmingham, Bristol, Edin-
burgh, Manchester

UNITED STATES – ÉTATS-UNIS
OECD Publications and Information Centre
2001 L Street N.W., Suite 700
Washington, D.C. 20036-4910 Tel. (202) 785.6323
                             Telefax: (202) 785.0350

VENEZUELA
Libreria del Este
Avda F. Miranda 52, Aptdo. 60337
Edificio Galipán
Caracas 106   Tel. 951.1705/951.2307/951.1297
                        Telegram: Libreste Caracas

Subscription to OECD periodicals may also be
placed through main subscription agencies.

Les abonnements aux publications périodiques de
l'OCDE peuvent être souscrits auprès des
principales agences d'abonnement.

Orders and inquiries from countries where Distributors have not yet been appointed should be sent to:
OECD Publications Service, 2 rue André-Pascal,
75775 Paris Cedex 16, France.

Les commandes provenant de pays où l'OCDE n'a
pas encore désigné de distributeur peuvent être
adressées à : OCDE, Service des Publications,
2, rue André-Pascal, 75775 Paris Cedex 16, France.

11-1994

OECD PUBLICATIONS, 2, rue André-Pascal, 75775 PARIS Cedex 16
PRINTED IN FRANCE
(61 95 12 1) ISBN 92-64-14410-2 – No. 47844 1995